I AM MY BIGGEST STRANGER

MIKE DEE

Table of Contents

Dedication:

To my son, Mikey—I'm so proud of the man you're becoming. Every day I see more of myself reflected in you, yet you're growing into something even greater. A father's hope is always that his son will become a better man than he is. Keep striving, keep believing, and never forget how deeply you're loved.

—Dad

ISBN: 979-8-218-86180-3 (Paperback)
Book
Library of Congress Control Number: 2025923706
Ebook:
Edited by Elizabeth Sain
Front cover image and book design by Mike Dee

Published in the United States of America
First print edition 2026

Foreword

There are rare moments in life when you watch a young person grow up before your eyes and you just know God's hand is on this one.

Mike was one of those young men.

As his youth director, I saw firsthand the spark of leadership, the hunger for God, and the quiet strength that set Mike apart from his peers. Long before he ever wrote a book, Mike was a young man who loved Jesus Christ deeply. That love shaped his decisions, guided his steps, and anchored his character even when life pulled him in different directions. He carried an unusual mix of ambition and humility, confidence and compassion, and he continually pointed his life back toward the heart of Christ. Today, as a devoted father and a man of integrity, that same love is still evident, and it breathes through every page of this book.

I Am My Biggest Stranger is more than a collection of reflections: it is a journey. A journey into the parts of ourselves we often avoid, overlook, or only meet in moments of crisis. Mike writes with the honesty of someone who has wrestled with his fears, confronted his pain, and chosen transformation over stagnation. And he writes as a man whose healing and identity are rooted not in self-help clichés but in the grace, presence, and guidance of Jesus.

The themes woven throughout these pages—legacy, forgiveness, alignment, resilience, healing, rest, boldness, discipline, spiritual grounding—reflect the shaping work of Christ in Mike's life. He invites you into a process of becoming, not through polished perfection, but through courageous self-discovery and surrender. Mike understands that true growth is rarely instant and never accidental. It is formed through daily choices, intentional reflection, small acts of faith, and a willingness to allow God to confront and transform the "stranger" within.

He reminds you that the greatest battles are not always fought in public but in the private corners of our hearts, where the Holy Spirit gently reveals what needs to be healed, corrected, or strengthened. And he demonstrates that when you confront your fears, doubts, pride, and wounds through the lens of Christ's love, you reclaim your peace, your clarity, and your God-given purpose.

What I love most is that Mike does not write as an expert standing above you but as a brother in Christ walking beside you. His words carry pastoral tenderness, a fatherly weight, and the humility of someone who knows he is still being shaped by God's hand. This book is a companion for anyone longing to live more awake, more aligned, and more anchored in Christ.

If you are willing to lean in, you will find wisdom.

If you are willing to search, you will find grace.

If you are willing to be honest, you may discover that the "stranger" within you is not an obstacle to avoid but a doorway God uses to bring you into deeper transformation.

I am proud of the man Mike has become, and I am

honored to stand with him as he releases this powerful work. My prayer is that, as you read, you will encounter courage, clarity, conviction, and the restoring presence of Jesus Christ.

May this book challenge you.

May it comfort you.

May it call you higher.

And may it lead you closer to the One who knows you better than anyone else, Jesus Christ.

Pastor Alfred D. Watts

Preface

In 2022, I hit one of the hardest seasons of my life. I'm the type of person who finds peace in simple things—prayer, nature, quiet moments with God—so people rarely notice when something's weighing on me. But that year, loss hit my life in waves. I lost someone I cared deeply for, and at the same time everything else around me seemed to unravel—business, relationships, direction, purpose.

I'm sure you know what those seasons feel like: when one thing after another falls apart, and you can't catch a break. I've lived through many storms, but that particular year broke something open in me. It forced me to face myself in ways I had avoided for a long time.

I stepped back from everything. I disappeared. And somewhere in that silence, *I Am My Biggest Stranger* was born.

Originally, this book wasn't supposed to be a journey through the soul. It was going to be called *Just Disappear*, a simple reflection on stepping away from noise and rediscovering who you really are. I had no idea it would grow into something deeper, something spiritual, something that mirrored Dante's *Divine Comedy* in ways I never expected.

This book took about two years to come together—not

two years of nonstop writing, but a process that stretched across seasons of doubt, healing, questioning, and rediscovery. There were months where I set it aside completely because I wasn't sure what I was trying to say anymore.

Then came the car accident.

Confined to my bed, all I could do was rest, pray, and watch movies. One afternoon, I put on Patch Adams. In one scene, Robin Williams washed his face in a sink, and I heard Dante's line for the first time: "Midway upon the journey of our life, I found myself within a dark wood, for I had lost the right path."

Those words didn't just hit me—they found me.

I'm a deep thinker by nature, so the idea of the "dark wood" didn't need explanation. I already knew it intimately. I was living it: the confusion, the drifting, the fear, the loss of direction. That single line shifted everything. Suddenly, the structure of this book became clear.

This wasn't supposed to be a self-help guide. It was supposed to be a pilgrimage. A descent and a rise. A journey from survival to surrender. From wandering to purpose.

Dante's Inferno became the metaphor that matched my own soul's journey.

The closer I drew to God, the clearer everything became. This book wasn't about me anymore—it was about what God wanted to reveal through me. It became a testimony. It became a reminder that our identity is not defined by pain, failure, or fear, but by the One who never loses us, even when we lose ourselves.

So if you are reading this right now, hear me clearly: You are loved. You are seen. You are valued. Your story is not over.

If I could sit across from you right now, I would tell you this: Every journey—every transformation—begins with one small decision: to turn the page.

As you read, let these words remind you that your life is not random, your pain is not wasted, and your purpose is unfolding in ways you can't yet see. God has been with you in every dark wood, every silent night, every lonely road.

I am deeply grateful to the Holy Spirit, who gave me peace when nothing else could, and without whom this book would still be unfinished.

These pages were written with tears, prayers, conviction, and hope. A hope that endures through pain and blooms through purpose. A hope that I pray settles into your heart as you join me on this journey. Thank you for walking through the dark wood with me as you read this book.

Acknowledgments

There are several people that I would like to acknowledge and thank for their support and examples and roles in my life and this book. And I would like to start with special thanks to my father, my pastor, and Jesus.

* * *

My father, Thomas—You have meant an incredible amount to me throughout this entire process. When I look back at the journey that brought this book to life, your presence is woven through every step of it. You believed in me long before the pages were organized and before the chapters found their voice. That kind of belief is rare, and I don't take it for granted. Thank you for always being there—for the encouragement, the steady guidance, the quiet confidence you've had in me, and the way you always seemed to know when I needed a push and when I needed grace. You've played a bigger role in this than you realize, and I'm truly grateful.

* * *

Pastor Alfred & Akiba Watts—You were there for me through many seasons when I was walking through the dark wood and confusion, fear, and uncertainty were clouding my path. Your prayers, wisdom, and compassion helped me find light when I didn't even know where to look. You and Akiba are truly amazing people, and I thank God for placing you both in my life. Your love and guidance left a mark that time can't erase, and I'll always be grateful to you two.

"The strength of the lion tamer lies not in the fact that he is stronger than the lion but in the fact that the lion thinks that he is."

—Alfred D. Watts

* * *

My Lord and Savior Jesus Christ— People may read this and think it sounds cliché, but I truly don't care. I mean every word. When I say God wrote this book, I mean it. Every page was prayed over. Every paragraph was birthed by the breath of God. I was simply the fingers He used to type the words. This book was written and rewritten until I made sure every word was from You. Until You blessed every story and every section.

If a life is changed through this book, it won't be because of me. It will be because the One who transforms hearts spoke through me.

Thank you, Father, for choosing me as the vessel. It was only by abiding in You that I made it this far. With all my heart, I thank You and give You all the glory.

It was always You, Lord. Always the Holy Spirit. All glory belongs to You.

* * *

I am also grateful to many other people who have loved and supported me. If it weren't for all of you, this book would not exist. Each of you has shaped my journey in ways seen and unseen, contributing to the person I am and the one I'm still becoming.

To my mother who is no longer with us. I forgave you a long time ago. I love you a lot and I cannot wait to see you again.

To my other mom, Doreen— Your kindness and grace have shown me what family truly means. Love you.

To my sisters and brother-in-law— Michaelle, Melissa and Jose

To the friends & mentors of my past—John "Mook" Gibbons (Wu-Tang Management), Pastor Todd and Leslie Foster (COTR, Cornerstone Christian Center), Pastor Marcus and Saundra Rooks (Cornerstone/CCC), Pastor Rick Hocker (Freedom Fellowship). Thank you for your love and mentorship. You all have meant so much to me and my walk with God.

To my friends—Roderick Little (from Newton, NC), John Gibbons, LaRon Conaway, Manny Abreu, Ed Reid, Brandon Holmes, Mack, Johnny Vargas, LZ, Joel "Akurit" Ortiz, Uriah Peterson, Miguel Vazquez, Luis Vazquez, Tracey Brown Petry, Pilar Biggio, and anyone I forgot. I love you all. Thank you so much for your support.

To the Chihuahua—Ти покликаний робити великі справи. Я завжди віритиму в тебе.

The greatest journey you will ever take is the one that leads you back to yourself.

Anonymous

Introduction

I Am My Biggest Stranger

Somewhere along the journey of life, many of us wake up and realize we don't truly know ourselves—and perhaps we never have. The person in the mirror, the choices we make, the fears we hide—they can feel foreign. We become strangers to our own hearts, minds, and potential. And the longer we avoid that stranger, the louder the sense of distance grows. *I Am My Biggest Stranger* is about facing that realization. It's about those quiet moments when you wonder: "Who am I, really? And how did I get here?" and "Who am I meant to be?"

Maybe it creeps in slowly—subtle at first, almost imperceptible. A few corners of your life begin to feel unfamiliar, like walking into a room you've known for years and realizing something's changed. The furniture feels slightly out of place. The light falls differently. The walls seem narrower—or colder.

Small routines start to feel hollow. Conversations feel rehearsed. The moments that once brought joy now feel muted. And beneath it all, there's a quiet ache—a distance you can't quite name—as if the life you're living has become a shadow of the one you once imagined.

Or maybe it strikes suddenly—a shock, a loss, a betrayal, or a quiet moment of despair where everything you believed about yourself cracks open. The version of yourself you've been relying on, shaped to fit expectations or survive, suddenly feels foreign. You look around and wonder how you got here, how you let yourself drift so far from the person you thought you were—or the person you hoped to become.

Either way, that stranger has been there all along. Quietly. Patiently. Waiting. Whispering. Daring you to notice. Not to shame you but to remind you that a part of you has been left behind, neglected, or silenced. That stranger is real. That stranger is yours. And finally, that stranger is calling you to turn, to pause, and to meet them.

This book does not offer all the answers—and it was never meant to. Life doesn't come with a manual, and neither does self-discovery. Some pages may feel like devotionals, grounding you in simple truths. Others may read like personal reflections, a window into my own journey that mirrors pieces of yours. And some pages will offer exercises, questions, or prompts designed to pull you deeper into your own story. The variety is intentional. Because the journey back to yourself is not uniform: it bends, it shifts, it loops. It rarely moves in straight lines.

This uncertainty mirrors the process itself: Self-discovery is messy, layered, unpredictable. You may uncover clarity in one area of your life only to feel lost in another. You may take one step forward only to feel like you've taken two steps back. Some days the path feels illuminated, and other days it feels hidden in shadow. That doesn't mean you're failing—it means you're alive, human, and in the middle of becoming.

There is no checklist that guarantees you will suddenly know yourself. There is no neat formula that instantly bridges the distance between who you are and who you long to be. But there is a path. It is not rigid; it is not the same for everyone. It is a path of noticing the subtle stirrings inside you, questioning the stories you've always believed, feeling what you've tried so hard to numb, and confronting the truths you've avoided.

This path asks for honesty, not perfection. It requires courage, not certainty. And as you walk it—sometimes stumbling, sometimes running, sometimes crawling—you begin to see that the very act of showing up to yourself, again and again, is the work. That is the way home.

Here, you will find honesty and vulnerability—not the polished kind we often present to the world, but the raw kind that asks you to sit with yourself as you are. You will be invited to confront the habits, thoughts, and fears that have quietly shaped your life and made you a stranger to yourself.

Some of these habits are easy to recognize: patterns of avoidance, the endless cycles of overthinking, or the way we overcomplicate life as a way to distract ourselves from what really matters. Others are more subtle, almost invisible—like the fear of being truly seen, the hesitation to name your deepest desires, or the reluctance to face truths that might change the way you live. And then there are the voices, the inner whispers that say, "You're not enough," "You don't belong," or "You'll never change."

This book will not shame you for those patterns, nor will it demand perfection. Instead, it will shine a light on them—not a harsh light meant to expose, but a gentle one meant to reveal. It will help you see yourself with clarity rather than distortion, with compassion rather than judgment. Because only when you see yourself clearly can you begin to walk in truth.

This is not a book about "fixing" yourself or trying to become some polished, idealized version of you—that version is a stranger too, built from other people's expectations, comparisons, and impossible standards. Chasing that image only keeps you further away from who you really are.

Instead, this book is about meeting the stranger you've been avoiding. The one who is not perfect but real. The one who is messy, complicated, brilliant, contradictory, and deeply human. The part of you that laughs too loudly, feels too deeply, questions too much, or carries scars you'd rather hide. This stranger is not your enemy—they are the part of you that has been waiting the longest to be seen.

To meet them is not about achieving perfection but about choosing honesty. It's about giving yourself permission to be exactly as you are, even when that feels uncomfortable or unpolished. Because the truest version of you is not flawless—it is authentic. And authenticity is where healing, growth, and freedom begin.

Expect to wrestle with questions that don't have easy answers—the kind that linger long after you've asked them, echoing in your thoughts as you go about your day. Questions that unsettle you, stretch you, and demand more than surface-level responses.

Expect to explore the space between who you are right now and who you long to become. Sometimes that distance will feel small, a matter of a few steps. Other times, it will feel like a canyon—wide, daunting, impossible to cross. But in naming that distance, you begin to map the way forward.

Expect to challenge the narratives you've carried for years, the labels that have defined you, the doubts that have whispered, "You're not enough." These stories may have shaped your choices, your identity, even your relationships. Confronting them won't always feel comfortable—but it will feel liberating. Because once you see them clearly, they lose their power to control you.

This book is for the quiet moments—the nights when the house is still but your mind is loud, the mornings when you wake already feeling out of place, the long drives where silence feels heavier than words. It is for the crowded rooms where you shrink into the background, for the conversations you replay over and over, wishing you had said something different.

It is for those moments when you catch yourself drifting, half-there but not really present—when you know something is missing and you ache for a deeper connection with yourself.

Along the way, I will ask questions—some simple, some impossible. Each is an invitation to pause, to reflect, to engage with yourself in a way you may not have in a long time. You don't need the "right" answer, because there isn't one. Sometimes your response will come quickly; other times it may surface days later, lingering in the back of your mind until it's ready.

The only requirement is honesty—not the polished honesty you offer others, but the raw kind you often keep hidden even from yourself. These questions are not tests to pass but doorways to walk through, each one leading you closer to the stranger you've been avoiding.

Yes, it may be uncomfortable. You may feel resistance, fear, shame, or even anger rising up as you face the parts of yourself you've neglected or hidden. That discomfort is not failure—it is a sign of truth. It is the body and soul signaling that you are stepping into territory that matters.

Growth is never painless. It strips away illusions, dismantles defenses, and exposes wounds we'd rather keep bandaged. But it is always necessary. In that raw, unsteady space, the stranger inside begins to feel less like an enemy to be silenced and more like a long-lost part of you—aching to be acknowledged, longing to be known, waiting to be welcomed home.

In the pages that follow, you'll notice that parts of this journey are inspired by Dante's *Inferno*—not as a theological doctrine, but as a mirror for the inner world. In Dante's classic poem, he travels through the nine circles of Hell, each one representing a different form of human struggle—pride, greed, lust, anger, and more. But beneath the imagery and symbolism, there is something deeply relatable: a descent into the *self*. A confrontation with what has been hidden, avoided, or corrupted.

The journey through the *Inferno* isn't just about punishment—it's about awareness. It's about facing the darkness within, not to stay there, but to *move through it*. And in the same way, this book invites you to descend into your patterns, your pain, and your past with the promise that, on the other side, there is transformation.

Each circle we explore will not be a condemnation but a reflection. A way of naming the parts of ourselves we've locked away, denied, or misunderstood. Like Dante, we will not stay in the dark. But we *must* pass through it if we ever want to rise.

You may begin to notice subtle shifts: patterns you never recognized before, quiet truths surfacing where silence once lived. You may feel forgiveness stirring—for the ways you've ignored yourself, silenced your needs, or settled for less than you deserved. And slowly, almost imperceptibly, small changes emerge in your actions. Not from a sudden revelation or a magical solution but from the steady practice of attention and awareness.

It is in this noticing that you begin to return to yourself. You start to speak your own language again—the rhythm, the voice, the heartbeat that has always been within you, waiting patiently to be remembered. In that recognition, the stranger within becomes less distant, and you begin to feel at home in your own skin once more.

Ultimately, *I Am My Biggest Stranger* is an invitation to turn toward yourself with curiosity, courage, and compassion. An invitation to stop running from the stranger within and instead face your own truths with unflinching honesty.

When you do, you may be surprised at what you discover. You may see not only the pieces of yourself you've overlooked but also the patterns of the life you've been living on autopilot—the choices you've made out of fear, the dreams you've set aside, the versions of yourself you thought you had to be.

But alongside those realizations, something else emerges: possibility. The possibility of living with greater clarity. The possibility of aligning who you are with who you are becoming. The possibility of belonging fully to yourself at last.

This book does not promise easy answers. It offers something more enduring: a path back to yourself.

There is no timeline, no finish line, no perfect destination. There is only the path—the quiet, unfolding journey of noticing, naming, and embracing the stranger within. Step forward with curiosity. Step forward with courage. Step forward with compassion. The stranger has waited patiently, not to punish or shame you, but to be acknowledged. Now is the time. It's time to meet them—and in doing so, to finally meet yourself and be the person you were always meant to become.

In the middle of the journey of our life, I found myself in a dark wood, for the straight way was lost.

Dante Alighieri, *Inferno*, canto I

Chapter 1

Entering the Dark Wood

The Dark Season

Have you ever found yourself in a season of life where nothing seems to move in your favor—where it feels as if everything is happening to you, not for you? When life feels unfair, and depression, anxiety, or doubt begin to creep in and take root?

Perhaps you've lived that way for years, quietly carrying the weight. It might be constant, or it might come in waves, pulling you under when you least expect it.

Sometimes you don't even know how you got there—only that you're in a place you don't want to be. Other times you know exactly how you arrived, but no matter how hard you try, you can't seem to climb out. You struggle to see the good. You struggle to learn from it. And deep down, you're left wondering whether there's a way back to yourself.

Dante's Exile and the Birth of a Journey

In the early 1300s, an Italian poet named Dante Alighieri knew that exact feeling. He wasn't writing from a life of ease. Dante was deeply involved in the turbulent politics of Florence, a city divided by rival factions that fought not only for power but for influence over every aspect of daily life.

Imagine a world where politics divides the people like never before. I know, that must be so hard to imagine in America. But I have a tiny suspicion it'll be easy if you try.

That same division also existed back then in Florence. When his faction lost, Dante was exiled and stripped of his home, his friends, and his place in the society he loved. Alone and wandering, he carried grief, betrayal, and despair, and he was forced to make sense of a life that had turned upside down.

Out of this political and personal turmoil came one of the greatest works of literature the world has ever known: The Divine Comedy. Written as a journey through the afterlife—Hell, Purgatory, and Heaven—the poem is both an allegory and a mirror of the human condition. It explores the consequences of choices, the nature of virtue and vice, and the path toward self-understanding. Dante's exile and his feelings of dislocation and loss gave him the insight to map a journey that resonates centuries later, showing us how the darkest trials can illuminate the truths of the soul.

Dante's World in Turmoil

To understand the depth of Dante's journey, you have to step into the turbulence of fourteenth-century Florence. This was not just a city; it was a battlefield of ideologies. Political factions like the Guelphs and Ghibellines fought fiercely, and even the Guelphs split into rival camps—White and Black Guelphs—that were each vying for control.

Dante was a member of the White Guelphs, who sought to limit the influence of the pope in Florentine affairs. When the Black Guelphs seized power with papal backing, Dante found himself on the losing side. He was exiled in 1302, condemned never to return under threat of being burned at the stake if he did.

The Emotional Landscape of Exile

Imagine being torn from everything you know: your home, your friends, your purpose, and the identity that once anchored you. One day you belong; the next, you're a stranger everywhere you go. That was Dante's reality. Exiled from Florence, the city he loved, he wandered from town to town across Italy, dependent on the kindness of others, a guest in homes that were never his own.

But Dante's true exile wasn't measured in miles. It was an exile of the soul—a separation from belonging, from peace, from the life he thought he had built. The world he knew was stripped away, and what remained was silence, self-reflection, and the haunting question that every wounded soul eventually asks: "Who am I now that everything I depended on is gone?"

He had lost his place in society, his status, and even the trust of those he once called allies. But in that wilderness of displacement, something sacred was forming. The external exile mirrored an internal one—a journey through grief, doubt, and rediscovery. It was in this place of broken identity that The Divine Comedy was born.

In the loneliness of exile, Dante found something the world could never give him: clarity. He began to see that the journey wasn't about punishment, it was about purification. The roads between cities became roads between worlds—from despair to faith, from confusion to revelation. His wanderings were not wasted time; they were sacred preparation.

Exile has a way of stripping us down to essence. It reveals what's false, what's fragile, and what's eternal. In that emptiness, Dante met himself—not the poet, not the politician, but the man who had to face his own darkness before he could ever lead others toward the light.

Because exile, whether physical or emotional, is never the end of the story. It is the soil where purpose takes root—where identity is refined, and where the soul learns to walk not by sight but by faith.

The Loss That Deepened the Darkness

Dante's exile wasn't the only thing that broke him. Years earlier, he had lost Beatrice, the woman he loved but could never have. She was married to another man and died young, leaving him with a grief that never left his soul. In her, he saw purity, wisdom, and the reflection of God's beauty on earth. When she was gone, that light went out. Combined with the exile that stripped away everything else he loved, including his home, his reputation, and his sense of belonging, Dante found himself standing in the ruins of everything that once gave his life meaning.

That's where the dark wood began. Not in a physical forest but in the space between heartbreak and purpose—the place where despair whispers that life has lost its color. Dante wasn't wandering through trees; he was wandering through memory, regret, and longing. The Divine Comedy begins there, in the intersection between loss and longing—where a man realizes that love must become something greater than desire if it's ever going to heal him.

Parallel Paths: My Own Beatrice

When I first read about Beatrice, I understood Dante in a way that few men ever could. He loved her deeply, yet he never truly had her. Their connection existed somewhere between reality and eternity—a bond more spiritual than physical, more eternal than temporal. When she was gone, her absence became his compass. Every word he wrote afterward carried her shadow, and every step through Hell was haunted by her memory.

I had my own Beatrice—let's call her Linda. Like Dante, I never had a real relationship with her, but her presence left an imprint on me. She was a reminder of what could have been—the kind of connection that quietly reshapes you, even from a distance. When life started to come apart after an accident that changed my direction, I understood what Dante meant by the dark wood. It wasn't exile from a city—it was losing my sense of peace, purpose, and who I thought I was meant to be.

Just as Beatrice became Dante's reminder of divine love—the kind that calls you to grow beyond yourself—Linda became that mirror for me. I used to joke with her that she was my own personal Yoda. I loved her, and I couldn't explain why. I felt connected to her in a way that defied logic.

Her role in my story wasn't to stay; it was to awaken something. God used her to show me that I needed to face what I had buried: the loneliness, the pride, the fear, the need for validation. Like Beatrice, she appeared not to complete my story but to redirect it.

Dante's journey began with losing Beatrice. Mine reignited in a similar way—through my accident and also by my realization that sometimes God allows certain people to walk into our lives not to stay but to start something in us. A transformation. Some loves are meant to build homes; others are meant to build you.

When you finally trust God and release what was never meant to stay, that's when God steps in. That's when grace starts its work, pulling you out of the dark wood and into the chain of grace.

The Chain of Grace

Before Dante ever stepped into the gates of Hell, Heaven had already moved on his behalf. In canto II, the Virgin Mary intercedes out of mercy, sending Saint Lucy, the symbol of divine light, to awaken Beatrice. Lucy, moved by compassion, calls upon Beatrice, who represents divine love, to act. And Beatrice, radiant with both tenderness and authority, commissions Virgil—the voice of reason—to guide Dante through the darkness.

It's one of the most fascinating moments in The Divine Comedy because it reminds us that divine love always moves first. Before Dante ever cries for help, Heaven is already organizing his rescue. Every layer of grace works in harmony: mercy stirs compassion, compassion awakens love, and love sends guidance.

Reason (Virgil) doesn't appear by accident; it's dispatched by Love itself. Guidance descends not because Dante earns it but because Heaven refuses to abandon a wandering soul. Even when he's lost, terrified, and paralyzed by confusion, unseen forces are already at work preparing the path, arranging the help, and lighting the way one step at a time.

It's a portrait of divine order—grace moving quietly behind the curtain long before we realize we need it. Just as Dante's journey began with a heavenly chain of intercession, ours often begins the same way: mercy moves, love responds, and light descends into our darkness.

The Call of Virgil

When Beatrice sends Virgil, she isn't sending perfection—she's sending wisdom. Virgil represents human reason, logic, and discipline—the tools God often uses before faith is fully restored. Sometimes Heaven answers our prayers with people who don't look divine but carry divine purpose: a counselor, a mentor, a friend who holds us accountable. Virgil reminds us that reason can lead us back to grace when emotion has blinded us.

Why We Begin in Hell

For a large number of chapters in this book, we will journey through the same circles of Hell that Dante encountered in Inferno. Why focus only on Hell? Because the struggles, temptations, and "monsters" Dante faced—pride, anger, lies, hatred, lust, and despair—mirror the obstacles we confront in our own lives. Each circle represents a shadow of the human experience, a pattern or impulse that can keep us estranged from ourselves and from the lives we were meant to live.

By exploring these nine circles, we are not chasing punishment or fear—we are recognizing the parts of ourselves that have gone unexamined. We confront the ways we live in Limbo, the self-hatred we hide, the anger we project, and the pride that blinds us. In doing so, we begin to untangle the chains that have held us back and we take the first steps toward becoming the people we were always meant to be.

Meeting the Dark Wood

Dante opens his poem by admitting he's in a jam—a dark wood. He's lost, alone, and weighed down by fear, confusion, and despair. This isn't just a forest; it's a wilderness inside his own soul. He's stuck, unsure of the path forward, surrounded by shadows and monsters he must face before he can even think about climbing toward the light.

In theology, the dark wood is more than depression or confusion—it's the space where God allows the old self to die so something eternal can emerge. It's the silence before calling, the confusion before clarity.

When Dante writes "the straight way was lost," he isn't just saying he lost direction—he's admitting that he lost alignment with truth. That's where every transformation begins: when you finally realize your map no longer works.

Naming Our Own Night

We all know what that dark wood feels like. It's the nights when anxiety won't let you sleep, the mornings when depression makes even getting out of bed a struggle. It's the memories that keep replaying when no one else is around, the unresolved anger, the bitterness, the unforgiveness that won't let go. It's the shame and regret you try to bury, only to find it rising again. It's being in a crowded room and still feeling utterly alone. It's when God's presence in your life feels distant, when you don't feel His movement like you once did.

No more bursts of joy—just long, heavy days and even longer, heavier nights.

Where the Work Begins

This is exactly why I'm bringing up the dark wood so early in this book. This is where the real work begins. This isn't a book about easy answers. If you truly want to confront your struggles and discover who you are, this is where you need to be. You must put yourself in the dark wood, if you aren't already there.

The demons you need to face live in the ugliness of life: in the depression, the doubt, the fear you've been avoiding. Yes, you're going to have to go there.

You may think you hate where you are. That's the best place to start! If this book makes you feel uncomfortable at times, good. That's exactly where you need to be. We'll be discussing deep topics and there may be some triggers for some of you. But we will get through it together.

Stepping into Darkness to Find Light

Like Dante, you can't start the journey toward growth and light by ignoring the darkness. You have to step into it, wrestle with it, and come out with the scars and strength that prove survival. Because only by entering the darkness can you begin to discover the light.

Dante didn't just sit in his dark wood and hope it would disappear. He faced it head-on, even when he had no clear path forward. Lost, scared, and alone, he didn't immediately see the mountain of light he would eventually climb. Instead, he confronted the chaos around him, step by step, with help along the way.

He was guided first by Virgil, the Roman poet who represented reason, wisdom, and human strength. Virgil didn't carry Dante out of the darkness. He showed Dante the way, helped him understand the dangers and monsters around him, and taught him how to navigate through them. Dante had to walk the path himself—confronting fears, witnessing horrors, and making choices about who and what he would trust.

Dante's journey through the dark wood was far from easy. Terrifying beasts, confusing paths, and moments that could have made him turn back confronted him at every step. Yet he pressed on, learning that the darkness itself held lessons—insights about fear, courage, and the choices that would define who he would become.

Jesus Is Present in the Dark Wood

Do you know who else is in the dark wood, fighting for you if you let Him? It's Jesus. You can call on Him right there in the shadows. He's already waiting for you.

David wrote in Psalm 139:8, "Even if I make my bed in hell, You are there." That's the truth of it. He will never leave you nor forsake you. His Holy Spirit is your Comforter and your Guide. Even when you can't feel Him beside you, He's watching.

I think back to my own dark wood seasons—the homeless shelter, the nights on the street searching for a place to rest or something to eat, my very first time living alone with no one I knew around. In every one of those moments, it was just Jesus and me. Somehow, I knew everything would be okay. I believed God would send help—and He always did. Even when I doubted, He came through.

Help doesn't always arrive with angels and trumpets. Sometimes it looks like a therapist, a pastor, or a kind stranger who takes an interest in your life. But behind them all stands God's faithfulness. Even when you think He's forgotten you, He's already working things together for your good.

Faith doesn't always show up in bright moments; sometimes it shows up under flickering lights, in places that smell like fear and bleach. One of those nights still stands out vividly in my memory—a moment that tested both my faith and my identity.

A Night in the Shelter

On my eighteenth birthday, my father kicked me out of the house. I moved in with my sister, but we fought constantly, and she eventually kicked me out too. I bounced between her place, the homes of friends from church, and wherever else I could find a couch to sleep on. When I wore out my welcome, I would go back to my sister's—only for the cycle to repeat itself. All the while, I was just trying to finish high school.

Standing in line outside a shelter near my school was one of the strangest moments of that whole experience. I had my backpack, my Bible, and more fear than I wanted to admit. The line was full of men who smelled of sweat, cigarettes, and lost time. I kept telling myself I didn't belong there, even though, in that moment, I did.

Out of nowhere, a drunk man turned to me, eyes glassy. "Hey Bobby," he said, like we were old friends. "I got your back. Last night was rough, but you handled yourself good." I froze, not bothering to tell him I wasn't Bobby. There was no point. In that strange, unsettling moment, I realized how easily I could vanish into someone else's story.

When the shelter doors opened, the light inside was harsh and the smell was a mix of bleach, body odor, and desperation. They checked my bag, let me keep my Bible, and I handed over everything else. I'd slipped a pen from my school folder into my pocket earlier that day, just in case I had to stab someone in the throat if it came down to it.

The bunks were stacked tight, metal frames with thin mattresses. I took the top bunk, held my Bible, and kept the pen under my blanket like a hidden weapon. The showers were just a row of open stalls, no privacy. I waited until it was almost empty and got in and out quickly, avoiding eye contact.

That night, I lay awake listening to the sounds of the shelter—snores, coughs, whispers in the dark. I barely slept, but somewhere in that uneasy silence, I realized something: this wasn't the end of my story. It was just a moment that would refine me, not define me.

By morning, they kicked us all out into the cold. I grabbed my backpack and walked straight to Waterbury Adult Education, where I was finishing my diploma. I was hungry and exhausted, but I kept going. That night taught me that survival isn't a sign of weakness; it's proof of strength. Faith doesn't always pull you out of the fire—sometimes it keeps you standing in it.

That night didn't define me. It refined me.

The Fork in the Road

Maybe right now, you're in your own dark wood. There's a fork in the road ahead. One path offers the easy escape—the quick fix that dulls the pain but never heals the wound. Take that road, and you'll meet the same monsters again and again. They don't disappear; they follow you.

The other path is harder. It hurts. It's the one where you face the demons you've been avoiding and where you fight the spiritual battles that have waited too long. One path gives quick comfort but no peace. The other brings temporary pain but lasting victory.

The choice is yours. Will you keep running from the dark wood, or will you stay, face your giants, and discover the strength only God can give?

What the Dark Wood Teaches

The lesson is clear: the dark wood is not a place to escape from. It is a place to walk through. To survive it, you need guidance, awareness, courage, and persistence. You have to face the monsters, make decisions in the shadows, and keep stepping forward even when the path isn't clear.

Dante shows us that the journey through darkness is as important as reaching the light. Growth, understanding, and resilience are forged in the struggle—not after it. Many of us miss this point because the darkness is so painful.

And this is where many fall: when they take the easy road.

What happens when you take the easy road is subtle, almost invisible at first. It feels like relief. The weight lifts for a moment, and you tell yourself that you made the right choice.

You took just one sip, watched just one scene of pornography, took a drug to numb the pain or slept to ignore it. You avoided the pain. You avoided the fight. But what you don't see is that you've just fed your giants.

Each time you choose comfort over courage, the giants grow stronger. Fear learns your patterns. Pride builds another wall. Addiction, lust, anger, or whatever monster you're running from learns how to wait you out. You think you're keeping it quiet, but you're really keeping it fed.

The easy road always promises peace, but it only provides silence, the kind that's temporary and deceptive. You can distract yourself and bury yourself in work, money, or relationships, but the giants stay alive beneath the surface. And every time you avoid the battle, they multiply.

Before long, the same giants that once whispered start to roar. They show up in new disguises—different faces, same roots. The same fear, the same insecurity, the same hunger for approval. What you don't conquer, you repeat. What you don't face, you feed.

The dark wood teaches us that victory doesn't come from running—it comes from remaining. It comes from trusting that God is in the shadows with you, sharpening your faith and strengthening your spirit. The very place you want to escape is often the ground where your courage is forged.

Reflection Questions: Entering the Dark Wood

Before you move forward, pause. This book isn't meant to be read passively; it's meant to be *walked through*. Every chapter reveals something about the world around you, but it also reveals something deeper: the world within you.

That's why each section ends with reflection questions—not as homework, but as ***heart work***. These aren't tests; they're invitations. They're moments to sit with the Holy Spirit and ask, "What are You trying to show me here?"

If you truly want to grow through this journey, get a notebook or journal. Don't just think through these questions—*write* through them. There's power in putting thoughts to paper; it slows your mind, anchors your emotions, and allows God to speak between your sentences.

You'll find that some answers come quickly, and others unfold over time. Don't rush them. Some questions aren't meant to be solved; they're meant to be *sat with*.

Use these reflections as checkpoints along the path, reminders that transformation doesn't happen by reading words, it happens by *responding* to them.

So before you turn the page, take a breath. Ask God to meet you here. And begin the conversation.

Exercises

1. **What is your current "dark wood"?**
   What area of your life feels confusing, painful, or directionless right now?
2. **When did you first notice something wasn't right?**
   Was there a moment, event, or feeling that made you realize the "straight path" had been lost?
3. **What giants have you been avoiding?**

Name one fear, habit, memory, or belief that you've been afraid to face.

4. **Who or what has God used to awaken you?**
   Is there a person, loss, moment, or season that stirred something deeper in you—like Beatrice or Virgil in Dante's journey?
5. **What would it take to stop running and start walking forward, one honest step at a time?**
   What's one practical decision you can make this week to face the discomfort rather than avoid it?

The tragedy of life is not that it ends so soon,
but that we wait so long to begin it.

attributed to W. M. Lewis

Chapter 2
Living in Limbo

Inferno: *Confronting Your Inner Sins*

Limbo doesn't look like Hell the way we picture it. In Dante's world, there's no fire. No screams. No obvious suffering. No demons with pitchforks, no rivers of lava. Just stillness. Stillness that dulls the senses and numbs the soul.

On the surface, it looks peaceful: like a city stuck in dusk. The sky doesn't darken, but the sun never rises either. There's no violence, just stillness. And that stillness is the curse.

In Dante's telling, this is where the "almost" souls dwell—the ones who lived moral lives but never pursued truth. They weren't evil. They just never moved.

That's what makes Limbo so dangerous. It doesn't destroy you with pain—it numbs you with comfort.

You start out visiting for a season... and then you unpack.

The longer you stay, the less you dream. The less you pray. The less you expect. You settle for decent. For safe. For "good enough." You say things like:

- "I'll do it next year."
- "I'm fine, just tired."
- "I'm just going through a phase."

But deep down, something in you knows the truth: You stopped climbing. You stopped growing.

And now, you're not falling... but you're not flying either.

Welcome to the land of "almost." Here, we start our descent not just into a story but into a mirror of the human soul. Guided by Virgil, Dante's journey through the *Inferno* is more than ancient poetry—it's a path we all walk when we dare to confront what lies beneath our surface. Each of the nine circles of Hell is not just a medieval vision of the afterlife but a reflection of our own struggles with anger, lust, greed, envy, pride, and despair, the forces that can quietly rule our lives if we never choose to face them.

In the chapters ahead, we'll walk through each of these circles. We'll begin in Limbo, the First Circle—the land of "almost," where souls linger in longing. From there, we'll face the storms of lust, the cold slush of gluttony, the crushing weight of greed, and so on, until we reach the deepest circle of treachery. Each circle will hold up a mirror to our own lives, inviting us to see more clearly and to recognize the patterns we must break.

But first, let's step into that First Circle. Let's linger in Limbo and understand what it means to live in the land of "almost," where the greatest danger isn't suffering but the slow fading of purpose.

Limbo: The First Circle—The Land of "Almost"

There's a deep sadness that hangs over Limbo. Philosophers like Aristotle, Socrates, and Plato dwell here, alongside great poets like Homer—figures Dante deeply admired. These souls aren't suffering physically; their torment is the quiet ache of emptiness. They are forever aware of the light of Paradise but can never reach it. They live in eternal "almost." They almost made it. They almost reached fulfillment. They almost became whole. Yet in the end, despite their brilliance and virtue, their spiritual fulfillment was incomplete, leaving a longing that can never be sated.

And that's what makes Limbo so haunting. It's not just the place for those who never believed—it's the home of those who stopped moving. Not everyone in the dark wood runs from their pain, and not everyone fights their way through it. Some just stay. Call it the third option. They build a home in the shadows and call it safety. They stop chasing purpose and start managing survival.

That's what Limbo is—not punishment, but paralysis. The refusal to move. You're not climbing toward light or falling into darkness; you're just standing still, hoping life will change on its own.

But in that stillness, something begins to die. Dreams shrink. Convictions fade. You stop praying, not because you've lost faith, but because you've stopped expecting anything to happen. You tell yourself you're fine, and maybe you are, but you're not alive.

That's the danger of Limbo: It doesn't kill you quickly; it numbs you slowly. It's not hellfire that keeps you there—it's comfort's whisper. The longer you stay, the quieter your calling becomes, until one day you can't even hear it anymore.

The people in Limbo don't run and they don't fight. They simply stop. And when you stop long enough, the dark wood starts to look like home.

That's What Limbo Is: The Land of "Almost"

Now here's the part that should hit you: How many people today are living in their own Limbo? How many of us drift through life without real purpose, without clarity, without connection to something greater? We're not out there committing great evils. We might even live respectable lives. But deep down, we know we're coasting. We're showing up, but we're not fully alive.

Limbo isn't punishment—it's paralysis. It's the quiet comfort of mediocrity disguised as peace. It's scrolling through life instead of living it, mistaking motion for progress, and mistaking busyness for purpose. You can hold a job, pay your bills, smile for photos, and still be stuck in Limbo because your soul isn't moving.

People in Limbo don't scream for help, they whisper "Maybe tomorrow." They convince themselves that someday they'll start—the book, the business, the healing, the forgiving—but someday never comes. And slowly they stop noticing that they've settled for "almost." Almost happy. Almost free. Almost healed.

Limbo is dangerous because it doesn't feel like suffering—it feels like safety. You're not falling anymore, but you're not climbing either. You've built a home halfway up the mountain and convinced yourself that the view is enough. But comfort can be a coffin when growth is calling your name.

The truth is, Limbo doesn't take your life, it numbs it. It keeps you breathing but not becoming. It's the space where dreams collect dust, purpose gets postponed, and faith fades into habit. And unless you decide to move, to step out, to rise, and to risk, you stay trapped in the illusion that you're living when you're actually only existing.

Because God didn't create you for *almost.* He created you for *all.*

Living in Limbo

Living in Limbo is being a stranger to yourself. It's when you silence your deeper longings because comfort is easier. It's when you go to work, pay the bills, and smile at the right times, and yet at night you lie awake thinking, *Is this really all I am?*

Limbo asks hard questions:

- "Are you living with direction, or are you just existing?"
- "Do you know your 'why,' or are you drifting?"
- "Are you truly alive, or are you stuck in the 'almost' of life?"

Dante places Limbo at the very start of Hell for a reason. Before you can face lust, anger, greed, or any other monster, you must face this truth: Life without purpose is its own kind of death.

And here's the uncomfortable part: Some people stay in Limbo forever, in this life and beyond. They never take the risk of really knowing themselves. They never ask the hard questions. They never leave the shadows of "almost."

But you? If you're reading this, you're already different. You're already restless enough to search. You're already refusing to stay in Limbo. That means you're ready to step out of "almost" and into the difficult, messy, but meaningful journey of becoming who you were meant to be.

Who You Really Are

So the question remains: *Who are you?*

Who you ***really*** are is not determined by your current situation, your feelings, or your failures. If you didn't know that, now you do. Your true identity is already inside of you, but the only way you'll start to live in that truth is if you discover it for yourself.

You can open your Bible and read verses that say you are "more than a conqueror in Christ" (Romans 8:37). And that's true. But let's be honest: If you've never conquered anything in your life, if you've spent years feeling defeated, empty, and stuck, those words won't mean anything to you yet. How can you believe something you've never experienced?

Here's the mistake people make: They think if they just repeat the right words (affirmations, positive quotes, even scripture), then somehow those words will magically make them into someone new. But let me ask you: Has anyone ever built a meaningful life by chanting sentences to themselves? No.

What actually happens is this: Words spark thoughts, thoughts spark decisions, and decisions create action. And it's only through action that you begin to see results. Those results are what finally allow you to believe what you've been saying all along.

Yes, fill your mind with truth. Yes, declare who God says you are. But never forget that faith without works is dead. You don't just speak your way into becoming who you were meant to be—you step into it through action, discipline, and persistence. You must act your way out of Limbo.

And the victories don't have to be huge. Small wins stack. Maybe you take a course. Maybe you clean up your finances. Maybe you give your children more of your time so they can live fuller lives. Maybe you finally show up for yourself in one simple, practical way. All of that has a snowball effect and soon you find that you are constantly moving forward with true intention and unwavering action.

This Is What Gets You Out of Limbo

Those small victories matter. Each one is a battle won—not over the world, but over the part of you that wanted to quit. Each step isn't just movement, it's momentum. It proves you're no longer stuck in place.

Progress isn't measured by distance; it's measured by direction.

Limbo begins when you stop moving forward. When you accept "almost" as your address. Almost alive. Almost healed. Almost happy. But never fully stepping into the life you were built for.

In Dante's *Inferno*, the souls in Limbo weren't bad people. Many were moral, intelligent, even admirable. But they lacked one thing: They never pursued their purpose. They stayed safe. They stayed comfortable. They stayed *ordinary* when greatness was calling.

That's what "almost" does—it traps you in a life that looks fine on the outside but feels empty on the inside.

We all know that place:

- "I almost chased that dream..."
- "I almost told the truth..."

- "I almost healed that part of me..."
- "I almost became who I was meant to be..."

"Almost" is where potential goes to die.

So ask yourself: "Where am I still living in 'almost'?" And more importantly, "What is the one step I can take today to move beyond it?"

Because healing doesn't happen by accident. Growth doesn't come from comfort. God doesn't reveal your purpose while you're hiding from yourself.

If you're going to know who you really are, God will show you the parts you'd rather skip—the wounds you ignored, the habits you rationalized, the lies you believed just to survive.

Seeing them isn't shame—it's strategy.

Acknowledging the ugly isn't the finish line—it's the doorway.

When you finally face the truth, you stop living halfway alive. You stop settling for "almost." You start becoming the person God designed, not the version fear tried to edit.

That's how you climb out of Limbo: One honest step. One uncomfortable decision. One small victory at a time.

The Arrival of Reason

In Dante's Limbo, he meets Virgil, the Roman poet who becomes his guide. Virgil represents reason, wisdom, and the limits of human understanding. He can't save Dante's soul, but he can lead him forward.

And that is the quiet mercy of Limbo: Even in the land of "almost," God sends help.

Guidance doesn't always come with fireworks or angels.

Sometimes it shows up as clarity. A moment of self-awareness. A conviction in your chest that whispers, "There has to be more than this."

That's where reason steps in.

Reason says:

"This isn't working anymore."

"I can do better than this."

"I'm tired of feeling stuck."

It calls the soul out of denial and into direction.

Virgil couldn't redeem Dante, but he could walk with him until grace took over. He could help Dante rise from survival into pursuit.

Reason is often the first sign that you are waking up. You are not healed yet, but you are hungry for change.

When your soul grows restless enough to seek truth, God meets you there and leads you forward, one step at a time.

Escaping the Land of "Almost"

Here's the uncomfortable truth: You can't stay in Limbo forever. You either choose to climb toward the light or you eventually slip further down into the next circle.

Because life doesn't stand still. You're either moving forward or you're falling back.

And what's waiting below Limbo? Desire without direction. The storm of lust—not just sexual desire, but any craving that controls you. Because when you live in "almost," your soul starts searching for substitutes. Numbing pleasures. Quick fixes. Distractions that feel like life but leave you emptier than before.

That's why Limbo is dangerous. It feels harmless, like you're just drifting. But drifting always leads somewhere. If you don't grab hold of purpose, the current of life will drag you into storms you weren't ready for.

So ask yourself again:

- "Am I living with intention, or am I drifting?"
- "Am I building, or am I numbing?"
- "Am I alive, or am I stuck in 'almost'?"

You were never created to live in "almost." You were created for more. But the choice is yours: Stay in Limbo, or take the next step.

Even in Limbo, grace is waiting. It waits for movement, for the moment you stop settling and start searching.

Exercises to Escape the Land of "Almost"

Remember to get your notebook out and write your thoughts out on paper.

1. Define Your "Almost"

Write down one area of your life where you've been saying, "I almost did..." or "I almost started..." What's holding you there? Fear? Comfort? Uncertainty? Name it. Clarity breaks paralysis.

2. Name the Substitute

Every "almost" is sustained by a substitute—something that keeps you numb enough to stay.

Ask: "What do I reach for when I don't want to feel stuck?" (Scrolling? Food? Busyness? Validation?)

Awareness is the first step toward freedom.

3. Reignite Desire with Direction

Desire isn't evil—it's energy misdirected. The goal isn't to kill desire but to reclaim it and reroute it toward something meaningful.

You might not know your full purpose yet, and that's okay. But here's where we begin:

"What is one thing you feel drawn toward that feels life-giving, helpful, or healing for you or others?"

Write it down. Then break it into one small step you can take this week.

Small obedience still builds big momentum—even when you're not 100 percent sure where the road leads.

4. Make a Covenant with Action

Sign your name beneath this statement:

"I choose movement over comfort. I choose purpose over distraction. I will not live in 'almost.'

Put the date. This makes it real.

5. Ground Yourself Daily

Every morning this week, ask:

- "What am I building today?"
- "What am I avoiding?"
- "Who does God say I am becoming?"

That last question brings the spiritual grounding that keeps the climb intentional and God-centered.

Closing Thought

You've taken the first step. You've begun to see the patterns—the distractions, the fears, the false identities—and you've chosen awareness over avoidance. That choice alone makes you different from most.

But every awakening is followed by a test. Once the light flickers on inside, the shadows begin to move. The moment you decide to grow, the forces that once kept you comfortable will try to pull you back. That's how transformation always begins: with resistance disguised as desire.

The path ahead will not tempt you with obvious evil but with pleasure, comfort, and control—the illusion that something outside of you can fill what only God and purpose can complete. This is where many souls lose their way.

And so begins the next stage of the journey—the storm of lust. Where craving masquerades as connection, where the search for love turns into addiction, and where you'll learn that freedom doesn't come from satisfying desire, it comes from mastering it.

Love has no wings, but is an angel. Lust has no horns, but is a devil.

Matshona Dhliwayo

Chapter 3

Lust: The Storm of Desire

Dante's Entry into the Second Circle

When Dante enters the Second Circle of Hell, the air itself changes. The calm silence of Limbo vanishes and is replaced by a violent, moaning wind that never ceases. The storm roars through the darkness, carrying cries that rise and fall like waves against invisible cliffs. It isn't just a storm of air—it's a storm of souls. Every gust carries human voices, and the sounds of longing and regret are entwined into one unending wail.

The winds howl, twisting and tossing the damned like leaves caught in a hurricane, and they spin without rest or direction. They are swept upward, slammed downward, and driven across the black sky in an endless cycle of motion that mirrors the desires that once ruled their hearts.

These are the souls consumed by lust, men and women who allowed passion to replace purpose, who chased what felt good until it became their god. Their bodies burned with desire in life; now their spirits are driven by a wind they can never escape.

There is no ground to stand on here. No moment of stillness. The storm does not punish; it exposes. It reveals what it feels like to be mastered by craving, to be blown wherever impulse takes you. Each soul becomes a reflection of its own restlessness—a being that cannot stop moving because it never learned how to be still.

The Second Circle is smaller than Limbo, but it is heavier and darker. The walls seem to pulse with the sound of thunder, and even the light, if you can call it that, flickers like a heartbeat in distress. Dante shields his face from the wind, his cloak whipping against his body as he clings to his guide, Virgil. Every step forward feels like walking into resistance, as though the storm itself wants to pull him into its madness.

And yet, within the chaos, Dante begins to see forms—countless figures swirling through the air, tangled together by invisible cords of desire. Lovers, strangers, betrayers, all bound by the same invisible hunger. Their faces are both beautiful and tormented, marked by the echo of what once felt like love but in reality was obsession. Their suffering is not just physical—it's emotional and spiritual. They are forever chasing what they can never reach.

Dante watches one soul reach for another, their fingers nearly touching before the wind hurls them apart. The movement repeats endlessly—the grasp, the separation, the longing. It's a cruel mirror of the very thing that damned them: the pursuit of fulfillment through desire without discipline.

The storm does not discriminate. Kings and peasants, poets and warriors—all are equal here. Their titles, wealth, and power have been stripped away, leaving only the truth of what they loved most. And in this circle, every false love is revealed for what it was: an addiction to pleasure, not a devotion to truth.

As Dante gazes into the whirlwind, a realization begins to form: This storm is not just around him, it's within him. It's the same storm that lives in every human being: the restless hunger for what will never satisfy, the longing to be filled by something fleeting. And as the winds rage, he begins to understand the first great lesson of the Inferno: that Hell is not a place we are sent to—it's a state we create when we allow desire to rule our soul.

From Limbo to the Storm of Lust

Limbo is the land of "almost"—the quiet drifting, the numb existence where nothing moves but time. Lust is what happens when that numbness demands to feel something again. When you've been asleep too long, even pain feels like proof you're alive.

That's the danger of "almost." When purpose is missing, pleasure becomes the substitute. The soul starts chasing anything that feels like life and provides the rush, the thrill, the hit of dopamine that says, "I still exist." But every time you reach for more, it leaves you emptier than before.

Lust isn't born in fire, it's born in silence. It starts where direction ends. When your spirit drifts long enough without purpose, desire slips in and offers one. It tells you, "This will fix you. This will make you whole." But that's the lie that keeps the storm alive.

So Dante's descent makes perfect sense. After Limbo comes the wind; after drifting comes the spin. The soul that once floated aimlessly now twists violently in craving, chasing what it can never hold.

Why Lust Comes Second

There's a divine order, even in descent. Limbo represents numbness—a soul asleep, drifting without purpose. But when the numbness starts to break, the heart panics and reaches for sensation.

That's why lust follows Limbo: When we lose direction, we try to feel instead of heal. The silent ache of emptiness turns into the desperate chase for meaning through pleasure. The tragedy is that the search for feeling often leads us further from the source of true life. Desire, when divorced from purpose, becomes motion without direction, and that's the essence of the storm Dante walks into.

Francesca and Paolo: A Love That Became a Storm

Among those captured in this circle, two figures drift closer, clinging to each other as much as the storm allows. Their names are Francesca da Rimini and Paolo Malatesta.

Francesca begins to tell her story. She was married for political reasons to Paolo's brother—a marriage without love, only strategy. In her loneliness, she found Paolo. At first, it was friendship. Then one day they sat together reading the tale of Lancelot and Guinevere. When the story described the forbidden kiss, Francesca and Paolo looked at one another and gave in. That one kiss became an affair. Desire grew unchecked until it consumed them. When they were discovered, they were killed.

Now, in death, the storm of lust that controlled them in life sweeps them endlessly.

As Francesca speaks, Dante is overwhelmed. Her voice is tender, her grief raw. She doesn't sound like a monster; she sounds like a human being who loved and lost control. Dante is so struck with sorrow that he collapses to the ground.

The Mirror of Francesca: Compassion and Warning

When Dante hears Francesca's story, he's undone by compassion. Her words are soft, her pain is familiar, and her love feels tragically human. It's easy to pity her, and maybe even to understand her. But that's what makes her story dangerous. Because in her sorrow, there's also self-deception. Francesca blames love for her downfall, but what she really worshiped was desire.

She says, "Love, that excuses no one loved from loving in return, seized me so strongly." But love didn't seize her—lust did. She confuses passion for purpose, emotion for truth. And Dante, moved by her pain, nearly falls into the same trap. His pity becomes a mirror for our own tendencies to romanticize our sin and to dress rebellion in the language of love.

That's the warning hidden in this circle. We can be so enchanted by the beauty of our feelings that we justify what's destroying us. We say things like: "I just couldn't help it." "It felt too real to be wrong." "God knows my heart." But every time we excuse our choices with emotion, we trade freedom for bondage.

Francesca's story reminds us that unchecked compassion can become compromise. Dante's tears are noble, but if he stays in that pity too long, he risks being swept into the same storm. The moment we sympathize with sin more than we seek to overcome it, we begin to drown with it.

Her tragedy isn't that she loved too deeply; it's that she

loved without discipline, without alignment, without truth. Love without truth leads to ruin; truth without love leads to cruelty. The balance of both is what redeems the soul.

So when Dante collapses, it isn't just grief for her, it's recognition. He sees in Francesca the same human weakness that lives in all of us: the longing to be seen, the hunger to be loved, the willingness to surrender our values to feel alive again.

That's what makes this circle so haunting: Francesca isn't just a woman in a poem. She's every person who ever mistook craving for connection. She's a reflection of the part of us that knows better but still reaches for the forbidden kiss.

A Warning and a Mirror

Francesca and Paolo are not just characters—they are a warning and a mirror held up to the human heart. Their story reveals what happens when desire is allowed to steer without wisdom. They didn't set out to destroy themselves; they were swept by a passion they never questioned, and in the end it became their prison. The winds that fling them endlessly through the dark are simply the outward expression of the inward storm they never learned to control.

But their story also shows us something else: We are not powerless. Desire itself isn't the enemy—misplaced desire is. The storm begins when we chase the immediate feeling instead of the ultimate truth. When we want love without commitment. Pleasure without purpose. Connection without responsibility.

Every person knows that pull. That hunger. That moment where you stand at the edge of a choice and convince yourself, *just this once*. We've all felt that wind starting to lift us off the ground.

But unlike Francesca and Paolo, we still have time to choose differently. To pause. To face ourselves honestly. To confront what we're really seeking beneath the surface of longing. To take action that aligns who we are with who we want to become.

Transformation doesn't require perfection; it requires direction. Desire becomes destructive when it drags us. It becomes divine when it leads us upward.

The storm will always be there. The question is whether we let it throw us or whether we learn to walk, step by step, toward a deeper kind of love.

Modern Storms of Lust

Dante saw souls tossed by a raging wind, never able to rest. If he were writing *Inferno* today, he wouldn't need to look far to find that same storm. He'd see it glowing from a phone screen at midnight. He'd see it in the endless scroll of comparison, in the dopamine surge of a like, a swipe, a view, a message that means nothing yet feels like everything.

Today, lust rarely hides behind curtains or alleyways. It hides in plain sight, dressed as connection. We chase pixels and attention like oxygen, convincing ourselves that stimulation equals satisfaction. We lust for more: more followers, more money, more attention, more affirmation that we matter. We've mistaken noise for love, and the pursuit of instant pleasure for peace.

The same winds that carried Francesca and Paolo now blow through Wi-Fi signals and streaming feeds. They whisper, "You deserve this. You need this. Just one more scroll, one more glance, one more hit." But the truth hasn't changed in seven centuries: Every time we reach for false intimacy, the storm grows stronger.

This is the modern inferno: a storm that doesn't always destroy the body but does erode the soul. It keeps us busy, distracted, restless, and never satisfied. And like Dante's souls, we find ourselves spinning endlessly, chasing the illusion of connection while forgetting what real love even feels like.

The Mirror of Lust: How It Reflects Us

But here's where the story gets uncomfortably close to us. Lust isn't just about sex. It's any craving that takes the driver's seat in your life. For some, it's relationships. For others, it's money, food, attention, status, or even the hunger to always be right. It's that restless urge that whispers, "If I just had this, I'd finally be fulfilled." But the second you grab hold, the craving only grows stronger.

That's why the storm is the perfect punishment for lust. It's not just judgment—it's a mirror. The storm shows us what unchecked desire feels like: restless, never satisfied, forever searching, never at peace.

The question is: "What storm are you letting rule you?"

Because the difference between freedom and the whirlwind is simple: Either you master your desires or they master you.

The Anatomy of Lust

Lust doesn't start as fire; it starts as a whisper. It begins quietly, in loneliness, boredom, or pain. When the soul feels empty, the mind starts looking for shortcuts to relief. That's where lust walks in, promising comfort without commitment, pleasure without purpose, intimacy without effort.

But that promise always comes with a trap. The first time you give in, it feels harmless. The second time, familiar. Before long, it becomes your default response to stress, sadness, or silence. What once felt like a choice becomes a reflex, and that's how the storm begins.

The pattern always follows the same loop: Desire → Justification → Indulgence → Guilt → Numbness → Repeat. You tell yourself, "It's not that bad" or "I can stop whenever I want." But every time you rationalize it, you reinforce the chains that hold you. Each indulgence strengthens the storm until it feels bigger than you are.

Here's the truth: Lust never satisfies the need that created it. It only deepens the emptiness. It's a counterfeit comfort—a cheap copy of what your soul is really craving. You're not looking for another thrill; you're looking for connection, purpose, and peace. Lust gives you a moment of escape, then leaves you right where it found you, only emptier.

And the worst part? The more you feed it, the less you feel. The storm dulls your spirit until what once convicted you now feels normal. That's how spiritual death begins—not in one dramatic fall, but in a slow surrender to the small compromises that steal your soul piece by piece.

Identifying Your Storm

Is pornography wearing you down? Sex addiction? Food addiction? Social media obsession? Obsessive shopping? Alcohol? Take a moment and ask yourself which craving is holding on to you right now. What storm is whispering in your ear?

All of these cravings have one thing in common: They are vices keeping you from truly knowing who you are.

If you try to become the person you were always meant to be without confronting and conquering these things, you'll always second-guess yourself. You'll never live a fully free life. And when you aren't true to yourself, you can't fully impact or help change anyone else's life.

After all, the foundational purpose for each of us who live for God is to allow the life and love of Jesus to be lived through us so that all who see our lives will glorify God. How can we strive forward for that purpose if we refuse to confront what's keeping us from evolving into our true self?

The Validation Trap: What We're Really Chasing

When you strip back every craving, every addiction, every bad habit, and every moment where lust pulled you, underneath it all is usually a desire to feel worth something. We don't lust because we're evil. We lust because we're empty.

We want to feel chosen. Desired. Seen. Important. Enough.

That's why lust wears a thousand faces. For some people, it's sex; for others, it's attention, praise, alcohol, money, status, likes on a post, a text back, a late-night "You up?" Anything that confirms: "You matter. Someone wants you. You're not alone."

But here's the difference that determines whether we rise or fall:

Healthy Validation	Unhealthy Validation
Confirms your identity	Tries to create your identity
Comes from God and self-worth	Comes from people and performance
Strengthens confidence	Breeds insecurity
Encourages authenticity	Encourages compromise
Grows love	Grows lust
Adds to your life	Controls your life

Unhealthy validation always demands a payment:
Your boundaries
Your dignity
Your peace
Your purpose
And the cost only gets higher.

Because the attention that boosted you one day becomes the approval you're *desperate* for the next. The hit wears off faster each time. The storm spins harder. And slowly, without even realizing it, we begin building our worth on the shifting winds of other people's opinions.

That's how we lose ourselves.

Understanding the Lust for Validation

Before we begin the exercise on seeking validation, it's important to understand the nature of validation itself. When we rely on external validation for our self-worth, we often set ourselves up for disappointment. If our self-esteem is anchored in others' opinions, we may find ourselves feeling down or even depressed when that validation isn't met.

This pattern can create a cycle where we constantly seek approval, and when it's not received, we may fall into deeper emotional lows. By recognizing this tendency, we can begin to shift our focus inward and build a healthier, more resilient sense of self-worth.

In the following exercise, we'll explore how to recognize these patterns and begin to find validation from within.

Exercise: Revealing How You Seek Validation

Get your notebook or journal out. Sit with them for a moment—not to shame yourself, but to face the truth head-on.

When do I crave validation the most? Loneliness? Stress? Boredom? Fear?

Who am I secretly trying to impress? A crush? An ex? Strangers online? My dad? My past self?

What am I afraid will happen if nobody notices me? That I'll feel invisible? Forgettable? Unworthy?

What behavior do I keep repeating just to feel wanted? Messaging someone I shouldn't? Dressing for attention? Posting for likes? Buying to feel valuable?

How does it leave me feeling afterward? Better? Or emptier?

Write the answers down. Stare at the reality of them. This is how you weaken lust's power—with honesty.

What Healthy Validation Sounds Like

Instead of:

"Tell me who I am."

It becomes:

"I know who I am, and I choose relationships that respect that."

Instead of:

"Notice me."

It becomes:

"I already carry value, so I don't have to earn it."

Validation isn't a sin. But the source matters.

Attention can hype you. But identity can hold you.

The goal isn't to need nothing. The goal is to crave the right things and love that doesn't require you to betray yourself to feel it.

And that shift—from searching for worth to living from worth—is what begins to calm the storm.

How to Defeat the Storm

So what's the answer? How do you defeat these issues and claim real victory? There is no magical, one-size-fits-all answer. I told you at the beginning that this wouldn't be easy, because the steps are personal to you.

Maybe for one person, it's seeing a therapist; for another, it's finding an accountability partner. It could be daily prayer, scripture reading, or a combination of these. The point is, you have to find the actions that work for you, because everyone's path to overcoming these vices is unique.

For me, the breakthrough came when I stopped sitting in the pain and started contributing beyond it—writing, creating, putting my energy into something that strengthened me instead of draining me. I was writing for years before I ever started this book. I found healthy ways to express what I was feeling, and in that process I learned to validate myself.

The point is this: You must go into battle with these challenges. You can't just hope they disappear on their own. You have to face them head-on, fight, and win. Every small step counts, every victory matters, and every action builds momentum toward freedom.

The storm of lust isn't defeated by wishing it away; it's conquered by intentional, disciplined action that reshapes your life and your soul.

Personal Reflection: My Own Storm

Years ago, I ran adult parties in New York City. They were exclusive, high-end events designed to draw in Wall Street executives—men with money, influence, and secrets. The goal wasn't just entertainment; it was strategy. I planned to use these gatherings as a gateway into real estate deals. The women who worked the room weren't just dancers—they were part of the plan. I wanted them to charm the men, offer "dances," and start casual conversations that revealed clues about their businesses, habits, marital status, and weaknesses.

My vision was simple: Learn their secrets, understand their patterns, and eventually use that knowledge to build powerful connections. Power, after all, isn't always about muscle or money—sometimes it's about access. I wanted that access. I wanted to know what made these men tick. And it worked—at least at first.

But the truth is, the whole thing was built on something dark. It was manipulation. It was evil. And even though I eventually found legitimate ways to fund my real estate deals, the damage had already begun.

The very world I thought I was using... started using me. What began as a business strategy slowly shifted into something else—something that grabbed hold of me. Surrounded by models, glamour, and constant temptation, I wasn't focused on connections anymore. I was feeding cravings I didn't even know I had. The attention, the lust, the validation—those things became the real goal. And what started as a calculated way to gain power became an addiction to pleasure.

The truth is, my downfall wasn't just lust for sex; it was lust for money, for power, for connection, for validation, for feeling seen and wanted. I thought the physical encounters would fill the void inside me, but they only widened it. Each new experience brought a rush that faded faster than the last, leaving me emptier than before. I wasn't seeking pleasure; I was chasing meaning in all the wrong places.

I did all this while my wife was home sleeping, thinking I was out networking. That's how deep the deception went. I justified it because I told myself it was for business. But deep down, I knew I wasn't chasing deals anymore—I was chasing desire. My lust for sex, power, and validation had overtaken my life, and it cost me the very thing I once claimed to be building it for: my marriage

You may be surprised by me telling you such personal details. I'm far from perfect. I'm just like you—facing the same temptations, fighting my own battles. Writing this book doesn't make me any different.

I depend daily on the grace of God, and I face my monsters head-on. I'm brutally honest with myself because that's how you win when you're all by yourself with no one to pray for you or stop you from making the wrong decisions.

That's what real growth looks like: learning how to stand when no one else is holding you up.

The Bible Says David Encouraged Himself in the Lord

When scripture says, "David encouraged himself in the Lord" (1 Samuel 30:6, KJV), it wasn't written from a mountaintop moment; it was in the ashes of Ziklag. His home burned. His people wanted to stone him. Every voice around him spoke of defeat. But instead of collapsing, David turned inward—not to his ego, but to his God. He found strength, not because his situation changed, but because his focus did. That's what it means to encourage yourself in the Lord: to choose faith when feelings fail, to draw courage not from the crowd but from the Creator.

If you want victory, you must understand something people rarely admit: Transformation is lonely.

You can be married and still feel isolated. You can be in a room full of people and still feel invisible. You can have friends and still feel like nobody truly knows you.

That loneliness doesn't mean you're broken; it means God is separating you from who you were so He can introduce you to who you're meant to become.

Most people stay stuck because they wait for someone to save them, encourage them, or believe in them first. But sometimes God removes every voice around you so the only one left is His.

When you can encourage yourself, you become unstoppable. Not because everything gets easier but because your faith stops depending on who stays and who leaves.

This is where warriors are built—in the quiet. In the tears no one sees. In the battles no one applauds. Your greatest strength won't come from who shows up for you—it will come from the moments in which you choose to rise anyway.

True victory is found when you confront the truth about who you currently are and choose to rise above it every single day so you can meet the stranger within yourself. Everybody goes through it. That's why I wrote this book.

Lust, I learned, isn't just about sex. It's about any craving that consumes your clarity and hijacks your purpose. It's the hunger for more—more attention, more success, more control—that never truly satisfies. It's the storm Dante wrote about, a whirlwind that carries you wherever it pleases until you forget why you ever started moving in the first place.

That storm of desire isn't just Dante's metaphor—it's

very real. It's in the patterns we repeat, the habits we can't break, the cravings we try to ignore but that shape our decisions. And the more we give in, the more the storm grows.

The Redemption: Turning the Storm into Fuel

Every storm that once tried to destroy you carries the same energy that can rebuild you. The fire that burned you can also refine you. Lust itself is not the enemy; disordered desire is. When desire is brought back under truth, it becomes power.

God never told us to kill desire. He told us to redeem it. Desire is the spark that builds nations, births art, creates families, and fuels purpose. It's the same force that drives you to reach higher, love deeper, and create something that lasts. But when that energy becomes disconnected from purpose, it turns destructive. The goal isn't suppression—it's transformation.

The passion that once chased temporary pleasure can become the passion that builds something eternal. When aligned with faith and discipline, desire becomes holy ambition. It becomes the drive to serve, to create, to lead, and to give. The Bible never calls for apathy; it calls for alignment. Paul wrote, "Flee youthful lusts, and pursue righteousness, faith, love, and peace" (2 Timothy 2:22). The energy doesn't vanish. It's redirected.

For years, I believed I had to kill my desires to be righteous. But when you deny what God placed in you, you also deny the strength that can heal others. God doesn't want dead hearts. He wants disciplined ones. When your desires are filtered through purpose, they become fuel for your calling.

Maybe your storm is lust, greed, control, or pride. Whatever it is, it can be sanctified. What once enslaved you can become your greatest testimony—the story that brings light to those still caught in the whirlwind. The very place that brought shame can become the source of your strength.

Redemption isn't pretending the storm never happened. It's learning to use its wind to lift your sails. It's standing where you once fell and saying: "This is where God met me. This is where I changed."

You don't have to curse your past. You can consecrate it. The same cravings that once led you astray can now drive you toward purpose—to love, to build, to heal, to create. Desire, when purified, becomes devotion. Passion, when disciplined, becomes purpose.

That's what it means to turn the storm into fuel. You no longer run from your desires. You harness them. You no longer bow to the wind. You ride it. And in that, the storm no longer owns you. It propels you.

The Lie of Lust

I had to face something hard: Chasing fulfillment through lustful ways was a lie. Lust gives you a moment that feels like satisfaction, but the moment always ends. And when it does, it leaves you emptier than before. That's the thing about vices: They whisper, "This will make you happy. This will complete you," but their real goal is to keep you stuck.

They keep you circling in the storm: endlessly searching, never resting, never fulfilled. They promise escape while quietly tightening the chains. Lust convinces you that the next moment, the next thrill, the next person will finally make you whole... but they never do.

Because lust doesn't fill the void—it feeds it.

Faith, Action, and Self-Awareness

And here's where faith, action, and self-awareness intersect. I had to take responsibility. I couldn't just pray or hope for change; I actually had to do the hard work. I sought accountability, confession, therapy, and guidance. I had to rebuild what I didn't know I had lost: the ability to love unselfishly, the ability to connect without using others to fill a void, the ability to respect myself enough to stop seeking validation in all the wrong places.

The moment I started choosing action over indulgence, the storm began to lose its grip. I learned that desire isn't inherently evil—it's neutral energy. When left unchecked, it can become destructive, spinning you endlessly like the winds in Dante's Second Circle. When harnessed and aligned with purpose, desire can fuel passion, creativity, and meaningful connection.

The Two Paths of Desire

Think about it: Every craving or vice you face has two paths. It can either rule you like the storm-tossed Francesca and Paolo, leaving you spinning endlessly and never at peace, or you can confront it, understand it, and redirect it toward something that builds you instead of breaking you. That's how true freedom is won.

The Purpose of the Battle

I know one thing for sure. Your purpose is not to just live a great life. We all are put on this earth to contribute to one another's lives in a productive way. The only way you can truly contribute on a meaningful level is if you have conquered your own demons.

The storm is real, yes, but so is the possibility of mastery. And mastery doesn't come from luck or luck alone. It comes from discipline, courage, honest reflection, and consistent action. It comes from staring your cravings in the face, naming them, and refusing to let them define you.

I had to learn to love differently—not just to seek love, but to give it in a way that was unselfish, patient, and real. That's what broke the cycle. That's what finally gave me a taste of peace and a sense that the storm wasn't eternal. I began to understand that the more I sought validation and fulfillment outside of myself, the more I was trapped in the storm. The more I cultivated self-respect, love, and purposeful action, the calmer the winds became.

The Final Challenge

So I ask you again: What storm are you letting rule your life? Where are your desires spinning out of control? And what is the first action you can take today to stop being tossed like a leaf and start steering your life with intention?

Because the difference between being swept away forever and finding freedom is action. Small victories. Daily choices. Honest reflection. Discipline. And the courage to choose love—the unselfish, transformative kind—over the fleeting satisfaction of lust.

Facing Your Storm: A Second Circle Exercise

The Second Circle isn't just Dante's story or my story—it's your story too. That storm of lust, of unchecked desire, exists in many forms today: pornography, sex addiction, food addiction, social media obsession, obsessive shopping, alcohol, or even a hunger for control, attention, or validation. Whatever your "storm" is, the way out is the same: awareness, action, and accountability.

Remember to write your thoughts out on paper. Here are practical exercises to start steering your life out of the whirlwind:

1. **Identify Your Storm**
   Write down the cravings, habits, or vices that consistently control your decisions or distract you from your purpose. Be honest, even if it's uncomfortable. If you're unsure, ask yourself:
   - What am I seeking outside myself to feel fulfilled?
   - What patterns keep me spinning in circles, never satisfied?
2. **Trace the Root**
   Every desire has a reason. Ask:
   - Why do I chase this?
   - What am I avoiding by giving in?
   - What emptiness or longing am I trying to fill?
3. **Name the Consequences**
   Write down the real costs of letting this storm rule your life. How has it impacted your relationships, your health, your self-respect, your time, or your peace of

mind? Seeing the truth on paper makes the storm less abstract and more conquerable.

4. **Decide Your First Action**

   Action is the only way to start mastering the storm. Choose one tangible step today. Examples:

   - Schedule a therapy session or counseling appointment.
   - Find an accountability partner or mentor.
   - Commit to daily prayer, journaling, or scripture reading.
   - Set practical boundaries with your triggers (social media, alcohol, certain people or situations).
   - Replace destructive habits with constructive ones (exercise, creative work, time with loved ones).

5. **Track Your Wins**

   Every small victory counts. Write down your successes—even tiny ones—to remind yourself that the storm can be slowed, tamed, and eventually mastered.

6. **Reflect and Adjust**

   At the end of each week, reflect:

   - Where did I feel the storm trying to pull me back?
   - Where did I act instead of giving in?
   - What's the next step I can take to stay on course?

Remember: Mastery over desire isn't about perfection—it's about consistent, disciplined action. The storm may howl, but each step forward, no matter how small, is a battle won. You are capable of breaking free. You are capable of stepping out of the whirlwind and into a life of freedom, purpose, and self-respect.

The Calm After the Storm

When the winds finally quiet, you realize they were never meant to destroy you—they were meant to reveal you. Every gust, every fall, every moment you thought would break you was really shaping you. The storm stripped away the illusions, the masks, and the lies you told yourself. What's left is something real—someone stronger, humbler, and more honest.

Peace isn't the absence of desire—it's the mastery of it. When desire bows to truth, chaos gives way to clarity. You stop running from your reflection and start recognizing the person you were created to be.

The calm after the storm isn't silence—it's sacred stillness. It's the moment your soul exhales and says, "I made it through."

You're not the same person who entered this circle. You've walked through the winds and found your footing. You've faced what tried to own you, and now you stand not as a survivor but as someone reborn in purpose.

But even when the storm quiets, the hunger remains. The soul that once chased sensation now begins to crave satisfaction—not just to *feel*, but to *feed*. This is the next temptation: the feast that never fills, the comfort that slowly consumes. And so, as the wind fades, Dante steps forward into the Third Circle—where appetite becomes addiction and indulgence takes the throne.

Gluttony is not just about eating too much; it's about the endless craving for more that can never be satisfied.

inspired by writings of C. S. Lewis

Chapter 4

The Storm of Desire and the Hunger Within

From Storm to Hunger

Once you've faced the storm of lust—that restless craving that pulls at your heart and mind—you might think the hardest part is over. But Dante's journey reminds us that there are many ways the soul can be trapped. Just beyond the whirlwind of desire lies another danger: gluttony, the endless hunger that consumes without satisfaction.

In the Third Circle, souls lie in filth, pelted by icy, relentless rain. Their punishment mirrors their lives: They sought pleasure in excess and chased comfort, indulgence, and instant gratification. They didn't seek balance or meaning; they only sought more. They were never satisfied, and in death that emptiness follows them, unrelenting and eternal.

Dante's Encounter: The Mirror of Appetite

When Dante and Virgil step into the Third Circle, the air grows heavy, thick with decay. The ground is dark mud, soaked by an unending cold rain that smells of rot. Above them, thunder rumbles with no lightning to follow—there is only the sound of endless appetite crashing down from the sky. This isn't fire and fury like other parts of Hell. This is the weight of indulgence—a slow, choking misery that buries everything it touches.

Out of the darkness, a monstrous figure appears—Cerberus, the three-headed hound of Hell. Each head snarls and drools, tearing at the air, clawing at the souls lying in the filth. His three mouths snap and howl, but they never close long enough to be fed. Cerberus doesn't just guard the gluttons; he is their sin made flesh. Each head represents a hunger that can never be satisfied—one for food, one for pleasure, one for comfort. He rakes at the damned with his claws, ripping at their swollen bellies as they cry out, but he does not kill them. He torments them with the reminder that desire without discipline becomes self-devouring.

Dante watches in horror as the rain turns the ground into a swamp of decay. The souls wallow in it, blinded by the same indulgence that once blinded them in life. They didn't seek evil for evil's sake—they simply never knew when to stop. Pleasure became their identity. Appetite became their master. Now, their punishment mirrors their condition: forever full, yet never satisfied.

Among them, one figure lifts his head to speak—a man Dante recognizes. His name is Ciacco, a Florentine once known for his wealth and indulgent lifestyle. In life, they called him "Ciacco the Hog." His body, bloated and broken, sinks into the muck as he speaks. But his voice is strangely clear, almost gentle, as if he's finally seeing truth after a lifetime of denial.

He tells Dante that Florence has become sick with greed and division, that the city's soul mirrors his own decay. His gluttony wasn't just about food—it was about more. More wealth. More comfort. More influence. More of everything. His words reveal a brutal truth: Personal indulgence always ripples outward. What destroys one man's soul eventually infects the world around him. When people only feed themselves, communities collapse.

Virgil listens in silence. Dante feels pity—not the shallow kind, but the kind that aches with recognition. Because what he's really seeing isn't just Ciacco. He's seeing himself, his own potential to become trapped in comfort, in distraction, in excess. He realizes that gluttony doesn't begin in the body—it begins in the soul when we stop hungering for truth and start hungering for escape.

As the rain continues to fall, Dante turns away from Ciacco, heavy with understanding. The Third Circle isn't about punishment; it's about revelation. It's the mirror that shows us what happens when our appetites consume our purpose. When we feed our cravings more than our calling. When we choose to fill instead of to grow.

Ciacco's decay isn't only physical, it's spiritual rot born of apathy. He reminds us that what we feed grows, and what we feed on eventually defines us.

That truth lingers like the taste of spoiled sweetness. Dante moves forward with Virgil, the rain still pounding, the mud clinging to his feet. But this time, the weight he feels isn't just from the storm—it's from the realization that unchecked comfort can damn a soul just as surely as unchecked desire.

The Modern Face of Gluttony

Think about your own life. Gluttony isn't just overeating; it's any form of overindulgence that dulls your awareness, steals your energy, and keeps you from living fully. Maybe it's food, alcohol, binge-watching, shopping, screen time, or constant consumption of content that leaves you restless and unfulfilled. The common thread? You're chasing something outside yourself instead of facing what's inside.

The lesson is clear: Unchecked indulgence is as imprisoning as the storms of lust. The soul that cannot regulate desire, whether for pleasure, comfort, or distraction, remains trapped. You might be almost fulfilled—temporarily satisfied—but you will never be truly free until you recognize the patterns and take action.

The Call to Action

Just as with lust, action is the key to freedom from gluttony. Awareness alone isn't enough. You must set boundaries, replace destructive habits with constructive ones, and intentionally pursue what nourishes your body, mind, and spirit. Every small step toward moderation, discipline, and presence is a victory and a way to reclaim your freedom and step out of the cycle of excess.

As Dante moves deeper into Hell, each circle challenges him—and us—to confront different shadows within our lives. Lust shows him the chaos of desire; gluttony reveals the emptiness of excess. Both demand attention, both demand action. And both remind us: If we want to live fully, we cannot ignore what controls us.

So take a moment and reflect: Where are you overindulging? What comforts, pleasures, or distractions have you allowed to rule your choices? And what's the first step you can take to reclaim balance, control, and clarity in your life?

The Psychology of Comfort: Why We Run Instead of Heal

Gluttony doesn't begin with the act of consuming too much. It begins with the moment our soul whispers: "I don't want to feel this."

Comfort becomes the most tempting when we are tired, stressed, anxious, or ashamed. Our brains reach for dopamine, the quick hit that says, "You're okay for a moment. Stay here."

But that moment never lasts.

Comfort was designed by God to restore us and to refill strength and peace. But when we use it to avoid discomfort, silence, or truth, comfort becomes a cage disguised as care.

The soul craves healing, but the mind seeks escape.

Instead of facing what hurts, we find ourselves reaching for distractions:

- Another plate
- Another scroll
- Another purchase
- Another nap
- Another show
- Another drink

Not to grow... but to forget.

This is where the quiet danger lies: Comfort stops being a gift and becomes a substitute for purpose.

We call it self-care, but deep down we know it's self-dulling.

Dante's Third Circle exposes that truth: Gluttony isn't about pleasure—it's about protection through avoidance.

Because when our heart doesn't know what to do with pain, it will always try to feed it instead of heal it.

When the noise of excess fades, what remains is not fullness but the quiet question: What are you really feeding?

Unknown

Chapter 5

Escaping the Third Circle: The Cost of Comfort and the Discipline of Freedom

The Silence After the Storm

When the craving quiets and the storm begins to fade, we tell ourselves the battle is over. But the silence that follows gluttony can be just as dangerous as the storm itself. It's in that silence that habits hide and comfort begins to whisper again: "Just one more."

Freedom doesn't come when the storm ends—it comes when you choose a new way to live once the rain stops. Gluttony isn't simply about consuming too much; it's about forgetting what true nourishment feels like. You start feeding the ache instead of the soul, mistaking numbing for healing until the line between the two disappears.

To move forward, you must learn to tell the difference between what restores and what only distracts—between nourishment and numbing.

Nourishment vs. Numbing: What Are You Really Feeding?

When comfort becomes our escape, we must learn to tell the difference between what brings healing and what brings hiding. Not every "comfort" comforts—some only silence the symptoms while the deeper wounds grow. The real question isn't *what* you're consuming, it is *why*.

Because what you feed determines what grows inside you.

Nourishment vs. Numbing

Nourishment	Numbing
Heals the root	Hides the root
Fills the body with strength	Fills the moment with escape
Rest to recover	Sleep to avoid reality
Eating to fuel life	Eating to silence emotion
Silence for clarity	Noise for distraction
True connection	Cheap attention
Movement for energy	Stillness that weakens
Presence in emotion	Avoidance of emotion

Numbing doesn't make the hunger go away, it just teaches the soul to starve quietly. Nourishment requires patience and intention, but it leads to growth, strength, and peace.

The Seduction of Excess

Excess is clever. It doesn't attack—it invites. It promises

relief, escape, and satisfaction… and then slowly steals all three.

It always begins innocently:

- One more slice.
- One more drink.
- One more episode.
- One more scroll.

But "just one more" always turns into too much.

Excess doesn't shout, it whispers: "You deserve this. You've earned this. This will make you feel better."

And maybe for a moment, it does.

But afterward? The pleasure fades and the emptiness remains.

Excess doesn't fill a void. It creates one.

Because when comfort becomes consumption, consumption becomes control.

And that's the silent tragedy of gluttony: You don't notice you're drowning until the weight of your own choices pulls you under.

The Feast That Became a Funeral

There's a story from ancient Rome about a young emperor named Elagabalus whose hunger for pleasure became his undoing. He was barely eighteen, surrounded by power, gold, and admiration, but none of it was enough. Every day, he searched for a new sensation, a new indulgence, a new way to feel alive.

His feasts became legend. Historians say he once hosted banquets where the food was served on plates of gold, where guests sat among flowers that rained down from the ceiling until they couldn't breathe. The air was so thick with perfume that people fainted. Elagabalus laughed, calling it divine luxury.

But behind the laughter was fear, the same fear that hides in every overindulgent soul: *What if the pleasure runs out? What if the silence comes back?*

The emperor's appetite grew wilder. When food and wealth stopped exciting him, he turned to shock—darker games, crueler amusements, endless excess. His empire began to rot from within, mirroring the decay in his own spirit. His guards eventually killed him—not out of rebellion, but because of exhaustion. Even those who benefited from his indulgence couldn't bear its weight anymore.

He died surrounded by everything he ever wanted, and yet he was utterly empty.

Elagabalus's story isn't ancient history; it's human nature. It's what happens when pleasure becomes a god and purpose becomes an afterthought. His banquet was his prison, his crown a chain.

That's the same truth Dante saw in the Third Circle: Gluttony isn't just overeating, it's overliving without meaning. It's when you keep consuming because you've forgotten how to be still. The feast always becomes a funeral when you stop feeding your soul.

And for most of us, the banquet isn't made of gold or wine—it's made of distractions. The endless scrolling, the late-night cravings, the emotional comfort we pull from screens or food or noise. It's how we keep from hearing the one sound we fear most: our own thoughts.

Because behind every pattern of excess is avoidance—not hunger, but hiding. And that's where Dante's rain turns cold.

The Weight of Avoidance

The uncomfortable truth is this: Most patterns of excess aren't really about pleasure—they're about protection. We reach for comfort not because we're greedy but because we're afraid. Afraid to feel pain. Afraid to face regret. Afraid to sit in silence long enough to hear what our soul is really trying to say.

Avoidance wears the mask of indulgence. Gluttony is simply the physical form of an internal escape.

When Dante enters the Third Circle, he isn't just witnessing punishment—he's witnessing paralysis. The souls here aren't chasing new sensations anymore. They're stuck in the mud of what they refused to confront. Every cold drop of rain represents a moment they chose numbness instead of healing—now multiplied into eternity.

That's what avoidance does. It doesn't erase pain—it delays it. It buries it under distractions until the weight becomes unbearable. The food, the scrolling, the noise—they're never about hunger. They're about running from the truth that something inside us needs attention.

I learned this the hard way. My deepest burden wasn't overeating or overspending, it was the constant effort to stay numb. I thought I was managing life, but I was only managing my pain. Every time I postponed healing, the cost grew heavier, like another drop filling the flood.

Avoidance doesn't demand much—only your strength, your awareness, your future. It convinces you that survival is peace and that denial is progress. And just like the souls buried in Dante's rain, you eventually wake up wondering how the storm began.

But here's the rescue line: Facing pain doesn't break you—avoiding it does.

The moment you turn toward what hurts, the weight begins to lift. The mud begins to dry beneath your feet. And for the first time, you realize something powerful: Every drop that once drowned you can also wash you clean.

The Anatomy of Gluttony

Gluttony isn't defined by what we consume; it is defined by what we neglect.

It begins quietly. Not with the loud storms of lust but with a subtle ache inside that whispers, "Something is missing." When we ignore that ache, we look for the quickest way to silence it.

First comes **Discomfort**—a restless dissatisfaction you can't quite name.

Then **Distraction**—the quick fix: a bite, a binge, a purchase, a scroll.

Then **Dependence**—when relief becomes routine and routine becomes "need."

Then **Detachment**—awareness dulls and life runs on autopilot.

Finally comes **Decay**—not of the body, but of purpose. A slow fading of the hunger for what truly matters.

That's the anatomy of gluttony: a descent that looks peaceful on the outside while the soul rots quietly within.

Where lust craves excitement, gluttony craves ease. Where lust devours for thrill, gluttony consumes for relief. One burns, the other numbs.

The souls Dante saw buried in the rain were not villains—they were the victims of their own comfort. They stopped reaching. They stopped growing. They settled for feeling "okay" instead of becoming whole.

Their punishment—a cold, constant rain—isn't violence. It is numbness made eternal.

A life without hunger for purpose becomes a life without movement.

But here's the hope buried in that mud: The moment you recognize the pattern, you can break it.

Awareness is the first awakening. Intention is the first step out of the rain.

The Modern Rain and Filth

Gluttony in life isn't just measured by calories or money spent. It's measured by where we give our power away to something that cannot sustain us. It's in the hours spent scrolling while life passes by, the late nights numbing pain with food or drink, the constant need for stimulation to avoid silence.

These are the rains and filth of Dante's Third Circle made real in modern life: heavy, unrelenting, and cold. The answer—and the way out—is intentional, disciplined action. It is choosing awareness over autopilot, presence over distraction, and nourishment over indulgence.

The Cost of Excess

And it's not just your spirit that pays the price. Overindulgence often shows up in our physical health too. Whether it's the weight we carry, the sluggishness we feel, or the way our bodies struggle with illnesses like diabetes, gluttony leaves a mark that we can't ignore.

So ask yourself: Where am I letting excess rule my life? Where am I chasing comfort or distraction instead of facing the parts of me that need to grow? And most importantly, what one action can I take today to reclaim myself from the cycle of overindulgence?

Because every storm conquered, every chain broken, and every step taken toward moderation is a victory. It proves to your soul that you are stronger than your cravings, wiser than your impulses, and capable of living a life that is not "almost," it is fully alive.

Breaking Free from the Third Circle

Recognizing the emptiness of excess is only the beginning. Awareness cracks the door, but action is what pushes it open. Dante didn't stop at observing the rain and filth of the Third Circle—he kept moving. And so must we.

So how do you break free from the weight of gluttony and from the overindulgences that drain your energy, dull your mind, and steal your freedom? The answer isn't found in a quick fix. It comes through deliberate, consistent steps.

The first step is awareness. You cannot change what you refuse to name. Take an honest look at your life. Where are you overindulging? Food? Screens? Shopping? Alcohol? Work? None of these in moderation are destructive, but when they rule you, they rob you of life. Write them down. Say them out loud. Naming them is the first blow against their power.

Once you've named the indulgence, the next step is to uncover the trigger. What drives you back to the same excess over and over again? Is it boredom? Stress? Loneliness? Habit? These cravings don't come out of nowhere. They're signals pointing to something deeper inside of you. When you can see the trigger, you can begin to heal what lies beneath it.

Then set one boundary. Not ten. Not twenty. Just one. If your struggle is late-night scrolling, set a cutoff time for your phone. If it's overeating, commit to one meal a day that's clean and intentional. If it's alcohol, limit yourself to a set amount. Don't try to change everything at once—start with one clear boundary. Small victories build the strength for larger ones.

But here's the key: Boundaries without replacement collapse quickly. You cannot simply strip away an indulgence and leave emptiness in its place. That emptiness will demand to be filled, and if you don't choose what to fill it with, the old habit will return. Instead, replace indulgence with nourishment. Go for a walk. Journal. Pray. Call a friend. Read. Choose something that strengthens instead of weakens. The goal isn't deprivation—it's transformation.

This is where accountability becomes vital. Excess thrives in secrecy. Tell someone you trust about your battle. Share your boundaries and your goals. Let them check in with you. You don't need an army, you just need one trusted voice who reminds you of who you are and who you are becoming.

And in the process, practice ***presence***. Before you give in to that familiar craving, pause for one moment and ask yourself: "Do I really want this, or am I avoiding something?" That pause is powerful. It cuts through autopilot and forces you to confront the truth: Indulgence never satisfies the hunger of the soul.

Celebrate the small wins. But if you struggle with eating too much, just know it isn't a good idea to celebrate with chocolate cake. Find healthy rewards.

Don't wait until you're completely free to rejoice. Every time you choose discipline over indulgence, every time you win a single battle, you're rewriting your story. You're proving to yourself that you're stronger than the craving, wiser than the impulse, and capable of living beyond excess.

And here's the deeper truth: Excess is always a mask for a greater hunger. The endless consumption is only a shadow of what your soul truly longs for. Maybe it's purpose. Maybe it's love. Maybe it's clarity. Maybe it's God. But no amount of indulgence will ever fill that hunger. Only facing it directly and tending to it intentionally will finally satisfy it.

So ask yourself: "Where am I letting excess rule my life? What am I truly hungry for? What one action can I take today to reclaim myself from the cycle of indulgence?"

Remember this: The storm of gluttony doesn't end in a single moment. It ends choice by choice, step by step, day by day. And every decision you make in the direction of freedom is proof that you are no longer trapped in the rain and no longer buried in the filth. You are moving forward. You are reclaiming your life. You are becoming whole.

Reflection Questions:

- In what areas of your life do you notice overindulgence or excess?
- How do these patterns of indulgence impact your overall well-being, both physically and mentally?
- What emotions or triggers often lead you to seek comfort in excess?

Practical Exercises:

- **Identify Triggers:** Spend a few minutes journaling about moments when you felt the urge to overindulge. What were you feeling or experiencing at that time?
- **Set One Boundary:** Choose one indulgence to address and set a simple, clear boundary. For example, if it's late-night snacking, decide on a specific time to stop eating.
- **Replace with Nourishment:** Make a list of positive, fulfilling activities that can replace the indulgence. For instance, instead of binge-watching, try a relaxing walk or reading a book.
- **Accountability Partner:** Reach out to a friend or family member and share your goals. Set up a weekly check-in to discuss progress and challenges.

Action Plan:

- **Daily Check-In**: Each day, take a moment to reflect on your choices and acknowledge small victories.
- **Weekly Reflection:** At the end of each week, review your progress. What worked well? What challenges did you face? Adjust your plan accordingly.

From Hunger to Possession

When the rain finally slows, the silence feels strange, almost holy. For a moment, the soul believes the storm has ended. The craving quiets, the appetite softens, and there's peace in the pause. But hunger, if left unhealed, doesn't disappear. It evolves.

What once whispered "I need more to feel alive" begins to murmur "I must keep what I have, or I'll die." The open hand that once reached for comfort begins to close into a fist. Desire turns to fear. Appetite becomes possession. And that's where the next descent begins.

Because when we no longer seek to consume, we start to hoard: affection, attention, control, money, power, even faith itself. We cling to anything that promises safety. But the tighter we hold, the heavier it becomes. The very things we cling to start to pull us down.

This is where Dante walks next—into the Fourth Circle, where the souls of the greedy roll their burdens in endless futility, each crash echoing the truth they never faced: You cannot carry both peace and possession.

The rain fades behind Dante. The ground hardens beneath his feet. The hunger of the body gives way to the hunger of the soul, and the journey continues, downward, into the weight of wealth and the illusion of control.

Nothing is enough for the man to whom enough is too little.

Epicurus

Chapter 6

Greed: The Fourth Circle

The Descent into Greed

After leaving behind the rain and filth of gluttony, Dante and Virgil descend deeper into the infernal spiral, to the place where the stench of excess gives way to the heavy clatter of stone. The air grows thick and oppressive, weighted by the echo of endless toil. The light is dim, not because of smoke or shadow, but from the dull reflection of countless stones grinding against one another—symbols of burdens no soul can ever set down.

Here, in the Fourth Circle, the damned are divided into two warring halves: the hoarders and the wasters. Their punishment is eternal opposition—an endless collision of greed in its two extremes. One group strains forward, rolling their heavy stones with desperate effort, crying out, "Why hoard?" The other group pushes back, just as frantically, shouting, "Why waste?"

Round and round they go, colliding in futile rhythm—a cycle of accusation without progress, of motion without meaning. Each impact echoes the same truth: Both sides are trapped by the same disease—obsession with possession. Whether they clung too tightly or spent too freely, their lives revolved around the same false god: *more*.

Now condemned to push their weight forever, they circle endlessly in the dark, locked in a parody of life's pursuits—striving without rest, gaining nothing, forever consumed by what once consumed them.

We may not roll stones in the dark, but our lives aren't that different. We push deadlines, debt, and expectations, circling the same routines—working harder, earning more, buying bigger—and calling it progress. Yet the motion never satisfies because the motive was never peace.

What Is Greed

Greed isn't always loud. It often hides behind ambition, achievement, and the illusion of progress. It can look like success on the outside but feel like suffocation on the inside. It's the whisper that says: "One more deal, one more raise, one more step—then you'll finally be enough." You never are.

This is where desire turns into weight—when the pursuit of more becomes the chain that drags the soul beneath what it once thought it could control.

Greed doesn't always appear as darkness; sometimes it dresses itself as discipline. It convinces you that constant striving is noble, that rest is weakness, and that your value depends on results. Beneath that drive is fear—the fear of not being seen, not being safe, not being enough. It's subtle. It masquerades as progress while running on anxiety. You tell yourself you're building a future, but you're really trying to fill a void. The more you gain, the emptier it feels, because greed doesn't feed the soul—it starves it.

True ambition serves purpose. Greed serves pride. And when pride is your motivation, peace becomes impossible.

The Mirror of Greed

It isn't always about money. It's about control, identity, and the illusion of security. It's the quiet belief that if you can just gather enough, own enough, or achieve enough, then the restlessness inside will finally settle. But it never does.

For some, greed shows up as hoarding—clinging to resources, time, or opportunities out of fear that there won't be enough tomorrow. For others, it shows up as wastefulness—spending, consuming, or discarding as if nothing truly has value. And for many, it hides beneath comparison—always measuring life by what others have rather than by what already exists within.

At its core, greed is the lie that says, "I am what I own." It convinces you that worth is something you can buy, that fulfillment is something you can hold, and that peace is found in possession. Yet the more you gather, the more the hunger grows. That's why the souls in this circle push their stones endlessly—they are trapped in the futility of chasing what can never satisfy.

The truth is, greed has nothing to do with how much you have and everything to do with how much has you. It's not measured in wealth but in attachment. The hands that clutch too tightly eventually close themselves off from receiving anything real.

We live in a world that rewards accumulation and calls it success. But no amount of achievement can quiet an unhealed soul. Greed doesn't whisper "more" because it wants growth; it whispers "more" because it fears loss. And fear can never create freedom.

The Psychology of Greed

Psychologists often describe greed as a form of fear—a quiet panic that whispers, "What if I lose what I have?" or "What if I never have enough?" It isn't always about money. More often, it's about control, safety, and self-worth. Beneath the surface of every craving for more lies a wound that says, "I'm not secure unless I can control the outcome."

From a neurological standpoint, greed is fueled by the brain's reward system. Every achievement or acquisition releases dopamine—the same chemical that fuels addiction. The problem isn't the dopamine itself; it's how easily it becomes tied to external rewards. Over time, the pursuit of more becomes less about need and more about the next "hit." Success becomes the new substance, and busyness becomes the high.

It's why the wealthy can feel poor and the successful can still feel empty. The more you feed greed, the hungrier it becomes. Like a fire, it expands with every log you throw into it, consuming what it was meant to warm.

Modern psychology connects this cycle to insecurity and comparison. When you don't feel enough within, you start trying to fill the space without. You chase validation, attention, or achievement—not out of joy, but out of the fear of being unseen. You start measuring your worth by movement, not meaning.

But no matter how much you collect, the void never closes. That's because greed isn't a hunger of the body—it's a hunger of the soul. And the soul cannot be fed by what the hands can hold.

The only way to break this cycle is to recognize it for what it is—not ambition, but avoidance. Greed is often an attempt to run from stillness—the place where truth waits. When you stop chasing and finally sit in silence, you realize what you were truly hungry for wasn't wealth or recognition—it was peace.

Modern Faces of Greed

In our world today, greed doesn't always wear gold or diamonds. Sometimes, it wears hustle. It looks like the man who never rests because he's afraid to lose momentum. It looks like the woman who buys what she doesn't need to prove she's doing fine. It hides in comparison, perfectionism, and the silent competition of social media.

We've built a culture that rewards exhaustion and calls it ambition. We glorify busyness as if rest were laziness. We measure our worth in numbers—followers, salaries, square footage—and we call it progress. But often, what we call progress is just another form of bondage.

The modern world has mastered the art of keeping us chasing. New upgrades. New goals. New distractions. The language has changed, but the lie remains the same: "If you just get this one more thing, then you'll finally feel complete." And like every lie, it keeps us running in circles.

Technology has turned greed into a rhythm—scroll, compare, desire, repeat. Every image and advertisement whispers that what you have isn't enough. Your phone becomes a mirror reflecting everything you lack. But the problem isn't what you see—it's what you start believing.

Even our ambition can betray us. There's a difference between working hard and being driven by fear. One builds purpose; the other builds pressure. You can be passionate and still peaceful—but when you're consumed by the chase, peace becomes impossible.

The tragedy of modern greed is that it often hides behind good intentions. You tell yourself you're doing it for the family, for stability, for freedom. But if you lose your peace in the process, you've traded your soul for an illusion.

Greed today isn't about wealth alone—it's about distraction. It keeps you so focused on more that you forget what matters now. It steals presence, turning life into a blur of goals without gratitude.

To live free in this world, you have to see through its noise. You have to be bold enough to stop scrolling, stop comparing, and stop chasing shadows. Because true wealth isn't found in the next thing—it's found in noticing the things you already have.

My Own Stone

I chased status like it was oxygen, convinced that if I didn't keep climbing, I'd suffocate. My excitement—my identity—was tied entirely to achievement. If I wasn't winning, I wasn't worth anything.

I believed that "making it" would fix my life—even my marriage. I imagined success would bring happiness, a home far from New York, a fresh start. But when my wife didn't want that future, instead of facing the truth, I tried to buy a different one. I hid money. I spoiled myself. Luxury became therapy. Success became anesthesia.

The day I landed exclusive listings for twenty-three luxury units in Williamsburg, Brooklyn was my first real taste of power. I'd been promoted from rental agent to senior project manager practically overnight. I structured it so I didn't have to sell a single condo myself. My focus was on getting more listings while senior brokers handled the day-to-day sales.

Every time they closed, I got a nice cut. I had never sold a home or condo in my life—I just knew how to talk a good game. In fact, no one ever realized that about me—certainly not the developers who kept trusting me with their listings. The only people who knew were my broker and myself.

And I had no shame. I ran meetings on my own—full presentations breaking down sales data and market trends like I'd been doing it for years. Whatever they wanted—feasibility studies, area comps, details on competing projects, or concession strategies—I had it ready. One developer even told me I was one of the most knowledgeable agents he'd ever met. I learned it all, except for one thing: how to actually sell.

When that first $13,000 landed, I told my wife about $3,000 of it. The rest I kept—not out of necessity, but out of ego. *If I can do this once, I can do it forever*, I thought. The delusion wasn't in the money—it was in the belief that the money could fill the void.

But every win disappeared like mist. Achieve, celebrate for five seconds, then panic about the next one. It was never enough. I wasn't driven—I was running. Running from the silence, running from my emptiness.

When I started building homes, nothing changed. Sell the house, erase the debt, chase the next high. The finish line always became another starting line. There was no destination, only motion.

That's the bitter truth of greed—it promises fullness but leaves you thirsty. It's drinking salt water. You keep going back for relief that can't exist.

And the worst part? You think you're climbing, but you're really just pushing the same stone in circles. That was my Fourth Circle. My own private Hell: motion without meaning.

I wasn't punished by God. I was punishing myself, believing the next dollar would validate me, that more would finally make me enough.

But the day I stopped running, just long enough to feel the emptiness instead of burying it, I realized something: Freedom doesn't come from acquisition but from release. Abundance doesn't come from holding tighter but from letting go. Greed isn't a sin of wealth; it's a wound of the heart.

And healing begins the moment you stop measuring your worth by what you carry and start noticing how light you feel when you finally set it down.

Wealth consists not in having great possessions but in having few wants.

attributed to Epictetus

Chapter 7

The Weight Beneath the Gold: Escaping the Fourth Circle

The Stoics on Greed

The ancient Stoics understood the trap of greed long before our modern world gave it new disguises. They knew that wealth, ambition, and success could easily enslave a man if he forgot his true purpose. To them, the danger wasn't in having much—it was in needing much.

Seneca, one of Rome's wealthiest men, wrote often about this paradox. Despite owning vast estates and being surrounded by luxury, he warned his students that "riches enslave a man if he does not know how to use them." He practiced voluntary poverty at times—sleeping on the floor or eating simple meals—not to reject wealth, but to remind himself that comfort was a privilege, not a purpose. "It is not the man who has too little," he said, "but the man who craves more, that is poor."

Seneca understood that the craving itself was the problem. The hunger for more corrodes peace. The moment your happiness depends on what you can gain, you've already lost control of your soul.

Epictetus, born a slave and later freed, lived on the opposite end of wealth and privilege, yet he taught the same truth. He owned almost nothing, but he was rich in contentment. To his students, he would say, "You may be rich in gold and poor in peace. Wealth does not bring freedom; only discipline of the soul does."

His message was clear: True freedom has nothing to do with possessions. It is the ability to remain unmoved by loss or gain. A man who can lose everything and still stand tall is richer than the man who owns the world but trembles at the thought of losing it.

The Stoics believed that greed begins the moment that desire forgets its boundaries. The antidote isn't to reject success but to master it—to own without being owned. Wealth can serve you or enslave you. The difference lies in whether your hands are open or closed.

The Currency of Validation

I was seventeen when I learned that greed doesn't always wear a suit or carry a briefcase. Sometimes it wears insecurity and smells like cheap cologne and minimum wage.

I was working the register at a local discount store, surrounded by fluorescent lights, long lines, sticky floors, and the constant beep of barcodes that felt like a countdown to nowhere. Every day I watched thousands of dollars pass through my hands, and something inside me whispered, "They won't miss it. You deserve more than this."

At first, it was small. A few bills tucked away. A justification here, a rationalization there. I told myself it was harmless—I was underpaid anyway. I wasn't stealing. I was *balancing the scales.*

But that's how the enemy works. It always starts with a whisper.

And then came the rush.

I started giving out twenties like it was Halloween candy. Friends would stop by my house, and I'd peel a bill off like I was some neighborhood legend. I'd say, "Here, get yourself something," and they'd laugh and call me "boss." I liked that word—boss. It sounded like respect, but it gave me the wrong kind of validation.

People started asking if they could run errands for me. I was seventeen. I had no errands. But I still hired friends to "help" with things I didn't even need help with—carrying boxes, running fake tasks, finding excuses to hand out cash—just to keep the illusion alive.

In my head, I wasn't a scared kid behind a register anymore; I was running an operation. I was somebody.

The more I gave away, the more powerful I felt. I was feeding off the attention, off the image. I'd walk into school with crisp sneakers, a few new shirts, and the kind of confidence that comes from money you didn't earn. My friends thought I was up, but really I was sinking.

Greed always comes with a receipt.

That day finally came. I was halfway through my shift when it all caught up with me. I was heading upstairs to clock out for lunch when my supervisor stopped me. His tone was calm—too calm. He asked me to sit down. On the small TV in front of us, grainy footage played from the security cameras. There I was, my own hands exposing me, one bill at a time.

My chest tightened. My throat went dry. Every excuse I rehearsed in my head sounded smaller than the sound of my own heartbeat. They didn't yell. They didn't need to. The evidence was enough.

After a long silence, they called the police. When I emptied my pockets and laid out over two thousand dollars, taken in less than three hours, I saw the shock in their eyes. My own heartbeat drowned out every sound. I didn't even have time to process what was happening.

Then came the radio chatter. The metallic click of handcuffs. The sting of cold steel biting my wrists.

Walking down the stairs past my co-workers was worse than the cuffs. No one said a word, but every stare felt like a mirror. They weren't just watching me—they were seeing *through* me.

The ride to the station was quiet. No words, no explanations. Just the hum of the patrol car and the weight of shame sitting heavier than any chain. When we arrived at the station, they processed me and put me in a holding cell that smelled like regret. I sat on the metal bench, staring at the wall, thinking about how quickly "easy money" had turned into the most expensive mistake of my life.

But I wasn't sorry I did it. I was sorry I got caught.

Hours later, the bail bondsman drove me to my house, where my sister wrote the check for my bond. I paid her back with my check from work. She didn't say much, and she didn't have to. Her silence said everything.

That was the night the giant of validation fell silent for the first time. I realized I hadn't been chasing money; I'd been chasing worth. I wanted to feel seen, powerful, in control. But sitting there in that cell, stripped of everything, I saw myself for what I was: empty, scared, and lost.

Greed had promised me freedom. But all it gave me was chains.

The Parable of the Rich Fool

In Luke 12:16–21, Jesus tells the story of a wealthy farmer whose land produced an abundant harvest. The man stood before his overflowing barns and asked himself, "What shall I do? I have no place to store my crops."

Then he decided, "I will tear down my barns and build bigger ones, and there I will store all my grain and my goods. And I'll say to myself, 'You have plenty of grain laid up for many years. Take life easy; eat, drink, and be merry.'"

But that very night, God said to him, "You fool! This very night your life will be demanded from you. Then who will get what you have prepared for yourself?"

Jesus ends the parable with a sobering truth: "This is how it will be with whoever stores up things for themselves but is not rich toward God."

The message isn't a condemnation of success—it's a warning about self-centered accumulation. The man's fatal mistake wasn't that he prospered; it was that he believed his prosperity existed for himself alone. He measured his life by how much he could store, not by how much he could share.

It's the ultimate image of spiritual short-sightedness. He built bigger barns, but he never built a bigger soul. He planned for years ahead, but not for eternity. He thought comfort was peace and possessions were security. But what he built for protection became his prison.

The rich fool's barns are no different from the stones Dante's souls push in the Fourth Circle. Both represent endless effort in service of a false promise—the belief that *more* will make you safe. Yet both stories end the same way: with the realization that all the *more* in the world can't buy contentment.

I was that man once. Maybe not with barns but with ambition. I built more, bought more, chased more, thinking it would finally quiet the ache. But just like that farmer, I was feeding an appetite that only grew hungrier the more I satisfied it.

When Jesus called the man a fool, it wasn't to shame him, it was to awaken him. To remind him that everything we hoard will one day belong to someone else, but what we give will always belong to eternity.

Connecting to Dante's Fourth Circle

The parable of the rich fool mirrors Dante's Fourth Circle perfectly. Both reveal the same tragic irony—souls who mistake accumulation for achievement, comfort for peace, and possession for purpose.

The rich farmer in Jesus's story is a modern reflection of those condemned souls rolling their stones through the darkness. His barns are his stones. His labor, though successful, never ends because it's driven by a hunger that can't be satisfied. The more he stores, the emptier he becomes.

In Dante's vision, the hoarders and the wasters are locked in an eternal collision, each blaming the other for their misery, yet both enslaved by the same desire—*more*. They move in constant motion but never make progress. That is the punishment of greed: to live forever chasing what can never be caught.

The rich man believed comfort was the reward for hard work. He thought peace could be purchased by accumulation. But when God called him a fool, it wasn't because he had wealth—it was because he mistook wealth for worth. He built bigger barns, but not a bigger heart.

I've been there. I may not have pushed a stone or built a barn, but I've known what it feels like to work without peace—to chase success while losing myself in the process. Greed isn't always loud or obvious. Sometimes it looks like long hours, constant striving, and endless justification. It tells you you're being responsible when, in truth, you're being consumed.

That's the hidden torment Dante captured: the soul in motion that never moves forward. The man who's always busy but never fulfilled. The woman who achieves everything but never feels whole. The professional who builds an empire yet feels empty inside.

Greed turns life into a treadmill—constant effort, no arrival. It replaces joy with anxiety, gratitude with comparison, and freedom with fear. The circle never ends until you step off and face the truth: That peace was never waiting at the finish line. It was waiting in the stillness you avoided.

The souls of the Fourth Circle believed they could create meaning through motion. But meaning isn't found in movement—it's found in alignment. Until your heart and your purpose move in the same direction, every victory will feel hollow.

The Cost of Greed

Greed steals more than wealth—it steals joy. It robs you of peace long before it ever touches your possessions. It's not just a moral flaw; it's a spiritual sickness that reshapes how you see the world and the people in it.

It begins quietly, with small compromises. You start measuring worth by numbers—money, followers, titles, square footage. You start confusing your *net worth* with your *self-worth*. You become restless, even when life looks good on paper. And soon, the very things you thought would make you happy begin to own you.

Greed doesn't just take from your wallet; it takes from your soul.

It steals gratitude, because you're always focused on what you don't have instead of what you do. It erodes relationships, because people become tools for profit instead of souls to be loved. It blinds purpose, because your life becomes about accumulation rather than meaning.

In time, it warps your identity. You start chasing outcomes instead of growth. You see people as competition instead of community. You start believing that slowing down means losing, when in truth it's the only way to breathe again.

Dante's Fourth Circle reveals that greed and wastefulness are the same disease in different disguises. One hoards out of fear of losing, the other spends to prove control, but both are enslaved to the same illusion. Life isn't about grasping or squandering; it's about stewarding.

Greed is the illusion that you can buy peace without surrendering control. But peace can't be purchased—it has to be practiced. The only way out isn't through having more; it is through learning to need less.

When you finally stop trying to own everything, you discover that the greatest wealth is found in gratitude, contentment, and faith. Greed builds prisons out of abundance. Gratitude builds freedom out of simplicity.

But every descent in Dante's journey has a counterpart, and every shadow reveals a hidden light.

The Spiritual Contrast: Contentment

If greed is the hunger that never ends, contentment is the quiet table where the soul finally eats and feels full. It doesn't mean giving up on ambition or refusing growth; it means learning the difference between striving and straining. Greed grasps; contentment receives.

Contentment is not the absence of desire; it's the absence of dependence. It's the moment when you stop saying, "I'll be happy when," and start saying, "I'm grateful now." It's understanding that peace doesn't wait on outcomes—it grows in obedience, gratitude, and trust.

In Philippians 4:11 (NIV), Paul said, "I have learned to be content whatever the circumstances." That word "learned" matters. Contentment isn't natural—it's practiced. It's forged through seasons of lack and seasons of abundance until you realize that neither defines your joy.

When you live in contentment, money becomes a tool instead of a master. Success becomes a blessing, not an identity. The noise of comparison fades, and gratitude takes its place. You stop chasing the illusion of more because you finally see what's already enough.

Contentment doesn't dull your ambition; it purifies it. It shifts your drive from ego to purpose, from proving something to becoming something. It turns work into worship and possessions into opportunities for stewardship.

In the stillness of contentment, you discover what greed always hides—peace isn't found in control but in surrender.

The Way Out

If you want freedom from the weight of greed, you must take intentional steps to loosen its grip. Greed is not broken by guilt; it's broken by gratitude, generosity, and awareness. The moment you stop grasping for more and start giving from what you already have, your heart begins to heal.

1. **Practice Gratitude Daily:** Write down what you already have—peace, health, family, faith, or purpose. Gratitude shifts your focus from scarcity to abundance. It reminds you that joy doesn't depend on what's next; it depends on what's now.
2. **Give Generously:** The fastest way to defeat greed is to give. Give your time, your money, your energy, your kindness. Every act of giving weakens greed's control over your soul. Generosity doesn't deplete you; it restores you.
3. **Live with Intention:** Ask yourself regularly: "Do I own this, or does this own me?" If a possession, habit, or pursuit begins to control your peace, it's not worth the weight. Simplify what no longer serves who you are becoming. Freedom is found in focus, not excess.
4. **Redefine Wealth:** True wealth isn't measured in possessions but in purpose. It's not what you can count; it's what counts. Wealth is time with loved ones, peace in your mind, joy in your home, and the freedom to serve God without fear.

The Fourth Circle reminds us that possessions were never the enemy—it's the attachment to them that enslaves the soul. The endless pushing of stones mirrors the endless cycle of wanting, getting, and wanting again. But that cycle can be broken.

You don't have to live that way. You don't have to let greed or wastefulness define your story. Freedom is possible—not in grasping more, but in releasing what was never meant to define you.

Because in the end, the question isn't "How much did you gain?" but "How much did you give? How much did you love? How much of your life was spent pushing stones, and how much was spent lifting others?"

A Story of Generosity

Not long after I started letting go of my old habits, I met a man who changed how I understood wealth. He didn't have much to his name—his shoes were worn, his car barely ran, and his home was simple—but he had a kind of peace I couldn't explain. He carried himself with ease, as if life had already given him everything he needed.

One afternoon, while sitting outside a diner, he noticed a woman digging through her purse at the counter, realizing she didn't have enough cash to pay for her meal. Without hesitation, he stood, walked over, and quietly paid for her food. No speech. No attention. Just a simple act, done in silence. When I asked him later why he did it, he smiled and said, "If I waited until I had more, I'd never give at all."

That line stayed with me. *If I waited until I had more, I'd never give at all*. It reminded me that generosity isn't about what's in your wallet—it's about what's in your heart. The man had nothing extra, yet he lived like he had everything that mattered.

For so long, I had convinced myself that I would give more when I had more, that once I reached a certain level of success, I'd start helping others. But generosity isn't something you grow into; it's something you choose. It's a mindset, not a milestone.

That moment changed me. I began to see giving not as loss but as liberation. Every time I gave, I felt lighter. Every act of generosity broke another chain that greed had wrapped around my heart.

True generosity doesn't measure the size of the gift—it measures the size of the heart that gives it. And when you give freely, without expectation, you discover a truth greed never tells you: that in releasing, you receive more than you ever imagined.

Exercises to Break the Grip of Greed

Greed loses its power when you bring it into the light—when you slow down long enough to see how it has been shaping your thoughts, your habits, and your peace. These exercises are designed to help you shift from clutching to trusting, from hoarding to stewarding.

1. **Identify Your Stone**

Take a quiet moment this week and write down the stone you keep pushing—the thing you believe will finally make you feel safe, successful, or seen. Maybe it's money, control, validation, or approval.

Then ask yourself: "What has this cost me?"

Awareness is the first crack in greed's foundation.

2. **The Gratitude Reversal**

Each morning, instead of asking what you need, list three things you already have, things money can't buy: peace, health, relationships, faith, purpose. Gratitude doesn't deny ambition; it refines it. It teaches the heart that abundance isn't something you chase, it's something you notice.

3. **The Generosity Challenge**

Give something away that you've been holding onto tightly—not just money, but also time, energy, or attention. Buy a meal for someone who can't repay you. Share your skills freely. Call someone who needs encouragement instead of scrolling for validation. Every act of giving loosens greed's grip a little more.

4. **Simplify One Space**

Choose one area of your life to declutter this week—your closet, your desk, or your digital space. As you let go of what you don't need, quietly repeat: "I release what no longer serves who I'm becoming." Physical simplicity creates mental and spiritual clarity.

5. **Redefine Wealth**

Write down your personal definition of wealth—one that has nothing to do with numbers.

For example:
Wealth is peace in my home.
Wealth is time with my son/daughter.
Wealth is freedom to serve God without fear.

Keep this definition visible. Let it become your new measure of success.

Soul Check

- What would it look like to live as if you already have enough?
- Who could you bless today without expecting anything in return?
- If God asked for the thing you value most, could you give it up?

Greed doesn't die through guilt—it dies through gratitude and trust. The more you open your hands, the lighter your soul becomes.

Key Takeaways: Reflections from the Fourth Circle

Greed disguises itself as progress, ambition, or even responsibility. It doesn't always look destructive—it often looks productive. That's why it's so dangerous. It convinces you that constant striving is noble while quietly draining your peace.

The souls in Dante's Fourth Circle aren't just cautionary figures from a poem; they're mirrors of us when we lose sight of what truly matters. Their endless struggle—pushing stones that never rest—represents the modern chase for more: more money, more recognition, more validation. It's the cycle of working harder but never feeling closer to peace.

If you take anything from this circle, let it be this:

- **Greed isn't about what you have**. It's about what has you.
- **More doesn't equal peace.** The appetite for more never ends because it feeds on emptiness, not abundance.
- **Gratitude is greater than gain.** When you're thankful, you're free.

- **You don't escape greed by earning less.** You escape it by wanting less.
- **True wealth is measured in peace, not possessions.**

Greed promises power but delivers slavery. It offers fullness but brings hunger. The moment you realize that peace comes not from gaining but from releasing, you begin to climb out of the Fourth Circle.

Freedom doesn't start with more—it starts with enough.

Closing: The Weight Beneath the Gold

The deeper I went chasing wealth, the heavier my soul became. Greed wasn't just about possessions—it was about control. And when control becomes your god, peace becomes your sacrifice. I didn't see it then, but every deal that fell through, every delay, every person who questioned my methods—it all started stirring something darker inside me.

That's the hidden cost of greed: When you live to control outcomes, you grow angry when life doesn't obey. The same hands that once clutched at money began to clench into fists. My ambition, once dressed in confidence, started wearing the mask of irritation, pride, and resentment.

I had climbed the ladder, only to find myself face to face with something worse than failure—bitterness. The stones of greed had become fuel for a deeper fire burning within me. And just when I thought I had conquered the weight of wanting more, I discovered that greed was only the surface of something deeper.

Because beneath the glitter of success, there was anger—the frustration of never feeling enough, of constantly reaching and never arriving. The more I tried to control life, the more I resented it for not obeying my will. I wasn't just exhausted—I was becoming hardened.

That's where the descent continued. Because beneath greed's golden surface lies something darker still.

And that's where the Fifth Circle begins—anger.

Anger is an acid that can do more harm to the vessel in which it is stored than to anything on which it is poured.

attributed to Mark Twain

Chapter 8

The Fire of Anger: The Fifth Circle Is When Rage Rules You

The Descent into the Fifth Circle

And so we enter the Fifth Circle of Anger. The air clings to the skin like a fever. Beneath the surface, something thick and black exhales—bubbles bursting with the sound of swallowed words. Voices rise, some raging, others muffled, as bodies thrash in a slow, brutal wrestling that never ends.

Only after the stench of the place settles in do you realize where you are: the River Styx, a swamp of fury where anger doesn't flash and fade. It festers.

Here, wrath rules everything. The loud and the silent alike are trapped in its current: one half above the surface, screaming and striking, the other submerged beneath, stewing in bitter quiet. It's not chaos for chaos's sake; it's justice shaped like a mirror. These souls didn't fall here because they were angry once—they fell because they built their lives around it.

The wrathful believed rage made them strong, that fury proved they cared. But now they swing endlessly at ghosts that never fight back. Their strength became their sentence.

The Fifth Circle isn't just a place; it's a state of being. It's what happens when you never learn to let things go, and when every grudge, every insult, every "I'll show them" moment piles up until you're stuck waist-deep in the muck, fighting shadows that don't even know your name.

The Nature of Anger

Anger wears many faces. Sometimes it's loud—shouting, slamming doors, or breaking things just to feel something break other than yourself. Other times it's quiet—a slow simmer that hides behind polite smiles, heavy silences, and fake "I'm fine" responses. Whether explosive or suppressed, both are rooted in the same thing: pain left unprocessed.

You can dress anger up in confidence, disguise it as passion, or justify it as justice, but underneath it's still the same—an emotional response to a feeling of being wronged, unseen, or powerless. And when that emotion goes unchecked, it doesn't stay contained; it seeps into every corner of your life.

Unchecked anger is like acid—it eats the container before it touches anything else. It drains energy, clouds judgment, and poisons relationships. It makes small issues feel enormous and blinds you to reason. Before long, you're not reacting to what's in front of you, you're reacting to everything that came before it.

Modern life gives us endless fuel for this kind of fire. We live in a world that rewards outrage. People argue online like gladiators in digital arenas, not realizing they're just swinging at ghosts. Drivers honk, curse, and rage at strangers they'll never see again. Couples sleep beside each other but live worlds apart, both convinced the other is to blame.

We've mistaken anger for strength, but it's really just strength in disguise—borrowed power with a steep interest rate. It feels good for a moment, but it costs you peace, clarity, and connection.

The truth is, anger isn't always evil. It's human. But when it becomes your default response, it stops protecting you and starts imprisoning you. Like the souls in Dante's Fifth Circle, you end up thrashing in your own swamp, fighting shadows that never tire and wounds that never heal.

The Trap of Unchecked Anger

Anger's got a funny way of making smart people look stupid. It's the one emotion that convinces you you're in control—right before it proves you're not.

Take Joe: Great guy. Hard worker. Calm most of the time, until he gets behind the wheel. One day, he's driving home from work, minding his own business, when someone cuts him off in traffic. Happens every day, right? But not to Joe. Not that day.

Joe takes it personal—like the guy didn't just change lanes, he insulted his entire family tree. So he hits the horn, rolls down the window, and yells something that probably violates three commandments. Then, to make his point, he speeds up just enough to pull alongside the guy, ready to give him *the look*.

But when he gets next to him, the other driver isn't angry. He's singing—full-on concert mode, windows down, eating a donut. Powdered sugar everywhere. Not a care in the world.

Joe, meanwhile, looks like he's training for a stress test. He's gripping the wheel, veins popping out, heart rate in the triple digits. And that's when it hits him: The other guy isn't suffering. He is.

That's the trap of anger. It's like drinking poison and waiting for someone else to get sick. You think you're teaching them a lesson, but they're not even enrolled in your class. You're the only one losing peace, and probably your voice.

The guy went on with his day; he probably finished that donut, and maybe he hit another high note in his car concert. Meanwhile, Joe spent the next hour replaying the whole scene in his head, getting mad all over again.

That's how anger works: It doesn't end when the moment ends. It stays with you, looping the same argument in your mind, feeding off your energy. It makes you feel powerful for a second but leaves you drained for days.

I should know. In case you haven't figured it out, I'm "Joe."

The Deception of Anger

I used to think my anger protected me, but really it was protecting the pain I refused to face. Anger became my armor, but underneath it was fear, rejection, and the belief that if I stayed mad, I'd stay safe. The truth is, anger doesn't shield you; it isolates you. It builds walls where healing was supposed to happen.

Anger never fixes anything. It doesn't make people respect you more, it doesn't prove your point, and it definitely doesn't make traffic move any faster. It just makes you miserable and gives your blood pressure something to brag about.

The Bible says, "Human anger does not produce the righteousness that God desires" (James 1:20, NIV). And it's true. Anger might feel righteous, but it rarely is. It's more like a toddler with a hammer—it might have purpose, but it doesn't have aim.

And that's how most of us live: angry at people who aren't even paying attention, while peace drives right by.

When Dante crossed the River Styx, he saw souls clawing and striking each other in the murky waters—each one certain their fury was justified, each one blind to the truth that no one was listening. They weren't winning anything; they were just sinking. Their anger had become their eternity.

That image has always stayed with me, because that was me too. I wasn't screaming in a swamp, but I was still thrashing in my own version of it: replaying old arguments, reliving past offenses, holding grudges that only poisoned me.

Anger doesn't just pull you under; it convinces you that you're still in control while you're drowning.

Modern Anger: The Swamp Reimagined

In today's world, the swamp looks different, but it's everywhere. It's the man pounding on his steering wheel in traffic, veins bulging as if rage could move cars faster. It's the comment section online where insults fly like stones across the Styx. It's the couple in silent tension, saying nothing but carrying years of unspoken resentment. It's the co-worker smiling on the outside but boiling inside.

Dante's swamp still exists, only now it hides behind car windows, screens, and polite small talk. The form has changed, but the poison is the same: uncontrolled emotion consuming peace from the inside out.

When Anger Consumes

Anger comes in many forms. Explosive rage, smoldering resentment, and self-directed fury all stem from the same root: surrendering power to emotion instead of mastering it. When anger drives decisions, it corrodes relationships, clouds judgment, and steals energy.

The souls in the Fifth Circle are mirrors of this truth. Their eternal struggle in the Styx shows what happens when anger is left unchecked: It consumes and traps the soul. Dante saw it as an endless war—bodies colliding, shouting, clawing through the mud. But he was really showing us the inner war we fight every time we refuse to let go.

Unchecked anger steals life quietly but destructively. It damages relationships, distorts reality, drains energy, and clouds judgment. Like the Styx, anger can be dark, murky, and suffocating. The longer you dwell in it, the harder it is to see the way out.

Modern Life and the Fifth Circle

Modern life has its own Fifth Circle. Arguments that escalate instead of resolve, grudges replayed in the mind, frustrations with work, family, or society—these are all fires that consume attention, energy, and peace. They leave you trapped, struggling in a swamp of your own making.

Freedom from wrath doesn't come from ignoring it. It comes from mastering it. Recognizing triggers, pausing before reacting, expressing emotion constructively, redirecting energy into something productive, and forgiving without excusing behavior are the ways to transform destructive energy into something that strengthens rather than diminishes.

Rage's False Promise

Rage promises power, release, or justice, but it delivers exhaustion, regret, and isolation. Left unchecked, it magnifies conflict instead of resolving it. It consumes thoughts, erodes relationships, and traps the soul in cycles of resentment and shame.

The trigger could be something as simple as someone cutting you off on the road while you are driving. You want to kill that person in that moment. You have visions of pulling them over and beating them with a baseball bat or something. That may not be how you think but it's definitely crossed my mind. I'm not ashamed to say it either. I have victory over that because I've taken the steps to overcome it. When something like that happens now, I laugh it off and remind myself that in five minutes I won't even be thinking about that guy. And it's true. It happens that way every time.

My Story: Living with Anger

Anger has always been one of my strongest temptations. Not in a violent way, but the kind that rises up when you feel misunderstood, disrespected, or falsely accused. I used to believe that reacting with intensity proved I was strong, and that defending myself at all costs meant I was in control.

But here's what I eventually learned: Anger doesn't make you powerful—it makes you predictable.

I thought I was standing up for myself. But really, I was surrendering control to whatever—or whoever—pushed my buttons. And anger always collects a payment: peace, relationships, clarity, and sometimes opportunities.

Scripture says, "Human anger does not produce the righteousness that God desires" (James 1:20).

For a long time, I didn't understand that. Now I do.

Anger disguises itself as strength, but it's really a trap that keeps you locked in past wounds, reacting instead of rising.

Walking Through the Fire

Like many of you, I've walked through this fire personally. I've felt the sting of resentment, the weight of grudges, and the flare of explosive anger. At first, anger felt like power, a way to assert control in a chaotic world. But over time, it became a trap. Every moment spent stewing, every insult hurled, every internal battle of "why me" chained me more tightly. The fire of wrath wasn't warming me—it was burning me from the inside.

As Dante watched the wrathful thrash and sink, he didn't turn away. He learned from their struggle, and so must we. The point isn't to condemn anger but to confront it, to see what it reveals about the human heart. Only then can we rise above the same waters that drowned the souls in the Fifth Circle.

The Stoics called anger "a brief madness," and I understand why. It clouds judgment and blinds reason. You say things you can't unsay. You do things that echo long after the emotion fades. It's not strength—it's surrender disguised as control.

That's when I began to understand the Fifth Circle on a deeper level.

The Stoics on Anger

In addition to describing anger as a brief madness, the Stoics believed anger was the most dangerous of all emotions because it disguises itself as strength. Seneca wrote that anger is like a falling rock—a force that cannot be called back once it starts.[1] To them, wrath wasn't power; it was loss of control, the mind surrendering its throne to emotion.

They didn't deny that injustice exists—they simply refused to give it their peace. Marcus Aurelius taught, "When you are offended at someone's fault, turn to yourself and study your own failings. Then you will forget your anger."[2] To the Stoic, the goal was not suppression but *mastery*—to transform the initial heat of offense into clarity, patience, and discipline.

Anger, they said, begins as a spark of perception: Something happens, and we judge it as an injury. But the moment we attach ego to that judgment, the fire spreads. Wisdom lies in the pause between the event and the reaction. Epictetus urged that if someone irritates you, you should realize that your judgment about the event is what disturbs you, not the event itself.[3]

What the Stoics understood—and what Dante dramatized in the Fifth Circle—is that the real enemy isn't the offense; it's the attachment to it. Every time you replay the insult, you relive the injury. The Stoic way was to meet insult with integrity, injury with understanding, and offense with

---

1 Paraphrased from Seneca, *De Ira* (On Anger), book 1.

2 Marcus Aurelius, *Meditations*, book 10.

3 Paraphrased from Epictetus, *Enchiridion*, 5.

self-control. Not to excuse wrongs but to refuse to become them.

When you practice that pause, that sacred moment between impulse and action, you begin to reclaim mastery over yourself. The swamp no longer owns you; you learn to walk across it with reason steadying each step.

Anger Is a Swamp

The Fifth Circle shows that anger is a fire that can burn from the inside if left untended. But fire, when controlled, can also warm, light, and transform. It can illuminate the way forward, forge resilience, and provide energy for creation rather than destruction.

In this swamp, the souls thrash endlessly, a reminder that when anger rules, it enslaves. Yet every moment of awareness, every deliberate act to transform or release the anger, is a step out of the mire. Control over wrath is not just an absence of violence—it is a reclaiming of freedom, clarity, and peace.

God's forgiveness is not just a casual statement; it is the complete blotting out of all dirt and degradation of our past, present, and future.

Billy Graham (paraphrased)

Chapter 9

Forgiveness and the Fire Redeemed

The Purpose of Anger

Not all anger is destructive. There's a kind that doesn't burn—it builds. Scripture shows that anger can be a signal of justice, courage, and conviction when it's rooted in love rather than pride.

Even Jesus displayed anger when He drove the money changers from the temple (John 2:13–17). His wrath wasn't reckless; it was righteous. It wasn't about ego or offense; it was about protecting what was sacred. Ephesians 4:26 (NKJV) says, "Be angry, and do not sin." In other words, anger itself isn't the problem—it's what you do with it that matters.

Righteous anger calls us to act when we see injustice, cruelty, or hypocrisy. It can fuel change, inspire courage, and strengthen boundaries. The key is motive: Is your anger driven by love for what's right or by a desire to punish?

Used properly, anger becomes passion. It's the fire that compels you to speak truth, defend the vulnerable, or correct what's wrong. It can move you to have hard conversations, set healthy boundaries, and confront sin—starting with your own.

When anger is filtered through wisdom, humility, and prayer, it transforms from a weapon into a tool for healing and growth.

Changing It

Changing it begins with recognition: noticing when anger rises, naming it, understanding its source. Is it fear? Injustice? Hurt? Once identified, it loses some of its power. Then comes the choice: How will you respond? You can lash out, simmer silently, or redirect the energy toward something constructive. The difference is enormous. A controlled response transforms fire into warmth, energy into action, and pain into insight.

Forgiveness

Forgiveness is another key. Not as a gift to others but as liberation for yourself. To forgive doesn't mean condoning what was done or pretending it didn't hurt; it means refusing to remain shackled by the past. Bitterness binds, while release frees.

What most people miss is that forgiveness isn't a feeling—it's a decision. It's not about waiting until the pain fades; it's about choosing freedom while the wound still aches. You can't always control what people do to you, but you can decide what you carry. Unforgiveness is like dragging a chain that only you can unlock, and the key has been in your hand the whole time.

Holding a grudge feels powerful at first. It convinces you that you're protecting yourself or getting even. But over time, it turns into poison: It hardens the heart and drains joy. Scripture says, "See to it that no bitter root grows up to cause trouble and defile many" (Hebrews 12:15). That root doesn't just grow in your relationships; it grows in your spirit, twisting into resentment that eventually strangles peace.

Forgiveness isn't weakness; it's strength under control. Jesus showed us that on the Cross when He said, "Father, forgive them, for they know not what they do" (Luke 23:34, ESV). He didn't wait for an apology. He didn't require justice first. He forgave because He understood that holding on would keep the wound open but letting go would set the world free.

And maybe that's the lesson: Forgiveness isn't about making someone else worthy of mercy, it's about keeping your own heart from becoming the next circle of Hell. Every time you choose to release bitterness, you reclaim a bit of your peace. Every time you let go, you rise a little higher out of the swamp.

Forgiveness doesn't erase memory. It reclaims meaning. It turns pain into perspective, wounds into wisdom, and scars into strength. It doesn't rewrite your story—it redeems it.

The Hidden Hurt Beneath Anger

Anger can be a signal—a flare fired from the heart to warn that something deeper is broken. It often points to unmet needs, violated boundaries, or a sense of betrayal. When you learn to listen without letting anger dictate your behavior, you can respond with wisdom instead of instinct.

Beneath most anger is pain. Someone ignored your worth, rejected your love, or took something sacred from you. Anger becomes the mask that hides the wound—it's easier to wear fury than to face grief. But when you slow down and name the pain beneath it, the fire cools and clarity follows. You begin to see that anger wasn't meant to destroy you; it was meant to reveal where you're still bleeding. That moment of honesty becomes the beginning of healing.

Dante understood this better than most. His map of Hell isn't only about punishment; it is about reflection. Each circle mirrors a way the human soul tries to live without grace, a different attempt to avoid facing truth. When we cling to bitterness or refuse to forgive, we don't just stay in one circle—we build new ones around ourselves. These new circles can mix elements from every one of Dante's circles and trap you all over again.

Forgiveness isn't forgetting or excusing what happened. It's choosing not to let the wound become your identity. I know how hard that is, especially when you loved someone deeply and they didn't respond the same. That kind of pain cuts deep, and it can twist into bitterness, resentment, or even hate if you're not careful.

Here's the truth: Holding on to anger only hurts you. It's like drinking poison and hoping your enemy will die. The person who wronged you may never change, but you don't have to keep letting their actions define your life. Moving on doesn't mean you didn't care—it means you value your future peace more than your past hurt.

So How Do You Respond?

Channeling anger through action is essential. Anger left unexpressed corrodes from the inside, but when directed with intention it becomes fuel. Physical activity, creative work, advocacy, service, or disciplined practice—each of these can become a vessel for transformation. The goal isn't to suppress the fire but to shape it. Go for a run. Write until the words stop trembling. Build something. Pray with intensity. Turn your energy into motion, not destruction.

When you take action, you begin converting chaos into clarity. The same fire that once burned bridges can forge strength when aimed toward purpose. What once drove you to shout or withdraw can now drive you to create, to heal, to grow. The energy doesn't disappear; it evolves. It becomes movement, art, courage, and conviction.

Anger handled well can clear the fog. It can sharpen your focus, expose what truly matters, and reveal what's been ignored. Every time you respond to anger with awareness instead of reaction, you reclaim a part of yourself that emotion once held hostage.

Each step—recognition, choice, release, and transformation—is a reclaiming of self. It's how the swamp becomes navigable. You may never drain it completely, but you learn to walk across it without sinking. Over time, the fury that once ruled you becomes wisdom and a reminder of your strength, not your shame.

You will still feel anger rise in moments of injustice, betrayal, or disrespect. But now you'll know what to do with it. You'll breathe, you'll pause, and you'll ask, "What is this trying to teach me?" And then you'll move—forward, not backward.

The swamp of anger may never fully disappear, but by learning to navigate it, you move from being controlled by fury to using it as a force for clarity, growth, and purpose. The path is neither easy nor quick, but every deliberate step, every pause before reaction, every choice toward healing, every moment you refuse to be ruled by rage is a victory over the chains that once bound you.

That's how redemption begins—not in silence or denial, but in discipline and direction.

Anger As a Force

Anger is a force. It can protect, signal, and energize, but it can also enslave. Every time you lash out, stew in bitterness, or hold a grudge, you give away a piece of yourself. The swamp teaches us that uncontrolled wrath is never harmless. It corrodes your relationships, clouds your judgment, and keeps you trapped in cycles of resentment and regret.

But when understood, anger becomes a compass. It points toward what matters—toward injustice, violation, or pain that demands attention. Beneath every spark of anger lies something sacred: a boundary crossed, a value ignored, a fear unspoken. When you pause long enough to listen, anger becomes less of an enemy and more of a messenger.

So ask yourself: "Where am I letting anger rule me? What swamps have I built in my own life by holding onto bitterness, resentment, or frustration? Who have I punished in silence while secretly poisoning my own peace?"

The Sacred Pause

The first step is awareness. Watch for the sparks—those moments when irritation, frustration, or rage begin to rise. Notice the sensations in your body: the tightening of the chest, the shallow breath, the clenched jaw. Anger speaks through the body before it ever reaches the mind. Journaling, reflection, or quiet meditation can help you recognize the triggers and patterns. Ask yourself, "What is this anger really about? Am I angry at someone else, or at myself? Is it about the present moment, or something much older that I've never healed?"

Next, create space. The pause is sacred. Even a few seconds between stimulus and response can change everything. That pause is where wisdom lives. When you breathe, you break the chain—the automatic reaction that turns emotion into destruction. In that space, you regain authority over yourself. You are no longer just reacting; you are choosing.

Then dig deeper. Anger is almost always a signal pointing to something unresolved within you. Ask yourself what need, fear, or boundary is being threatened. Maybe it's the need to be respected, heard, valued, or safe. Maybe it's the fear of loss, rejection, or betrayal. When you uncover the truth beneath the fire, you begin to understand its purpose.

Once you understand the root, choose your action. Healthy expression matters. Write it down. Talk to someone you trust. Move your body. Redirect the energy toward something constructive. Paint, pray, build, lift, run, serve. Let movement cleanse the static. Transformation begins when anger stops being a weapon and starts becoming a tool.

Remember, anger itself is not evil—it's energy. Fire can burn, but it can also warm. What matters is where you aim it. The goal is not suppression but mastery. Suppression hides it. Expression without intention harms others. But mastery transforms it.

You transform anger when you use it to protect what is sacred, to defend what is right, or to set boundaries that honor your peace. You turn wrath into wisdom when you let it illuminate what you've ignored rather than incinerate what you love.

And when you begin to see anger this way, you no longer fear it. You respect it. You listen to it. You let it guide you toward growth. Because sometimes the things that make you angry are the very things God is trying to heal.

Forgiveness Means Letting Go

The hardest step is release. Forgiveness is not about the other person—it's about freeing your own soul. It's about loosening the grip that pain has on your heart. When you forgive, you are not excusing what happened, you are choosing not to be imprisoned by it any longer. You stop letting the memory of the wound dictate the direction of your life.

Forgiveness is not weakness. It is strength under control. It's the quiet decision to stop rehearsing the offense in your mind and to stop giving energy to the moment that hurt you. Because every time you replay the story, you relive the pain. And as long as you relive it, you can't move forward.

Let go of grudges, resentment, and the desire to punish. Ask yourself honestly: "What chains am I holding onto that keep me stuck in the swamp? What memories still have emotional power over me? What anger do I keep close because I've mistaken it for protection?" Forgiveness is the act of unclenching the fists of the soul.

And when you finally release, something sacred happens. The space once filled with bitterness becomes available for healing. Peace rushes in like clean air after a storm. You begin to see the person who hurt you—and even yourself—through the lens of compassion rather than contempt.

Letting the Fire Refine

Finally, transform. Let the energy of anger drive you to rebuild and to set boundaries, improve yourself, and act with intention. Transformation doesn't mean pretending it never happened. It means refusing to let what happened define you. It means saying, "Yes, it broke me for a time, but it will not bind me forever."

Every small victory, every time you respond instead of react, every moment you choose patience over rage and compassion over resentment is a step out of the mire. These are the unseen triumphs that strengthen your spirit.

Anger will always exist; it's part of being human. But mastery over it is possible. You learn to notice its rise without becoming its prisoner. You learn to let it burn clean—to refine, not consume. Awareness, boundaries, healthy expression, forgiveness, and transformation create a path to freedom.

Each choice you make is a step out of the swamp—a reclaiming of your peace, your purpose, your self-respect. Every time you choose understanding over judgment, love over bitterness, and release over control, you prove to yourself that you are stronger than your impulses, wiser than your past reactions, and fully capable of living with clarity, grace, and peace.

Forgiveness is not the end of the journey—it's the threshold to a new one. It's the moment you stop being a victim of your story and start becoming the author of your future.

Reflection Exercises

- When does anger rise in my life, and why?
- Am I angry at the situation, the person, or myself?
- What small action today can redirect this energy toward growth and positive change rather than destruction?

- Who or what do I need to forgive to reclaim my freedom?

Exercise 1: Naming the Fire

Write down three situations (past or present) that trigger deep anger or resentment.

For each, answer:

- What exactly am I angry about?
- What expectation was violated?
- What deeper emotion sits beneath this anger—fear, rejection, shame, helplessness?

Purpose: Awareness dissolves power. When you name the true source of anger, it loses its control over you.

Exercise 2: The Mirror Test

- Think of a person you've held anger toward.
- Ask: "What about them mirrors something unresolved in me?"
- Be brutally honest. Sometimes the traits we hate most in others reflect what we've refused to confront in ourselves.

Purpose: This turns judgment into growth. Anger can reveal your own blind spots.

Exercise 3: Transforming the Energy

- Choose one ongoing source of anger.
- Instead of reacting, channel that energy into a positive, disciplined action—walking, writing, praying, building, or creating.

- Note how your body and emotions shift when anger becomes motion.

Purpose: Energy redirected becomes empowerment.

Exercise 4: The Forgiveness Ledger

- Draw two columns: "Who I Need to Forgive" and "What I Learned."
- Write one name per day until the list is complete.
- For each person, note what that pain taught you about your boundaries, values, or strength.

Purpose: Forgiveness isn't permission—it's freedom.

The swamp is never gone. But mastery means walking through it without being consumed. It means reclaiming the power that anger once held over you and learning to move through life with calm, clarity, and purpose.

Closing: Rising from the Swamp

Anger is a strange teacher. It shows you what you care about, but if you're not careful, it'll also teach you how to drown. The swamp of wrath isn't some far-off place; it's the argument you can't stop replaying, the bitterness you nurse before bed, the moment you decide being right is worth more than being at peace.

But here's the grace in it all: Once you learn to walk through that swamp without sinking, you discover something powerful—you can't control what people do, but you can control what you carry. Every time you choose peace over pride, stillness over shouting, forgiveness over fury, you rise a little higher.

And maybe that's what Dante was really showing us: The goal isn't to escape Hell; it's to stop building it.

As Dante and Virgil climb out of the swampy chaos of anger, they approach something darker—quieter, but just as deadly. The next circle isn't filled with fists or fury; it's filled with minds closed off to truth.

If wrath is fire turned outward, heresy is that same fire turned inward—beliefs so rigid they burn from the inside. In the city of Dis, walls of iron separate the living from the light. Down here, pride doesn't roar, it reasons. It justifies. It calls rebellion wisdom.

In the next chapter, we'll leave the noise of anger behind and step into the city of the self-righteous—the place where conviction hardens into arrogance and the heart forgets how to listen.

Certain people have crept in unnoticed... who pervert the grace of our God into sensuality.

Jude 1:4 (ESV)

Chapter 10

The Sixth Circle: Heresy (City of Dis)

The Tombs of Reason

The air shimmers with heat as Dante steps into the city of Dis. Rows of burning tombs stretch into the distance, each one glowing like a furnace of thought. Inside them lie the souls of the heretics—those who had minds so brilliant that they mistook their own light for God's. Their intellects have turned inward until the fire that once illuminated now consumes.

The city of Dis burns, but it is not the fire of chaos. It is the fire of thought—reason heated until it glows. And yet, there is something colder than flame here. Because when conviction burns long enough, it calcifies. The heat of pride eventually freezes into certainty.

The tombs are open when Dante passes through, but after the Final Judgment, they will be sealed forever. That detail is crucial: It shows that even in damnation there's still the illusion of openness, of argument, but in the end, their reasoning will lock them completely away from truth.

This circle represents a deeper kind of tragedy. The souls here are not monstrous; they are thinkers, philosophers, visionaries. But they mistook intellect for divinity. They believed enlightenment was the same as salvation. The city of

Dis—walled, fortified, guarded by fallen angels—mirrors their own minds: proud, fortified, closed off from grace.

In life, they burned for their opinions; in death, their opinions burn them. The fire doesn't come from outside—it comes from within. Their brilliance, once their glory, is now their torment.

The fires of anger fade, but the journey doesn't cool—it changes form. The swamp quiets, but not in peace. The shouting stops, not because the rage has ended, but because the rage has evolved.

Down here, Hell starts thinking. What was once pure reaction now becomes reason. The heat of impulse gives way to the cold logic of pride. The air thickens—not with smoke this time, but with certainty. Every scream becomes a statement. Every blow becomes a belief.

The descent slows, deliberate now. The chaos of wrath feels almost honest in hindsight, because at least in anger you could feel. At least there was passion, movement, noise. But this next place? It's quiet. Organized. Intellectual rebellion wearing the mask of enlightenment.

Dante steps out of the swamp, the mud dripping away from his feet. Ahead rises the city of Dis, its iron walls glowing faintly like the embers of dead conviction. The gates tower high, guarded by fallen angels, their silence heavier than any roar.

As Dante wrote in *Inferno*, canto X: "Here with the heretics are their followers, of every sect, with more than thou believest, the tombs are loaded."

In the swamp of wrath, you lose control. But in the city of Dis, you seize it and twist it until truth breaks. This is where pride begins to whisper: "You've learned enough. You already know. You are your own light."

And that's the most dangerous lie of all.

The fires of emotion may have burned you, but the frost of intellect will freeze you from the inside out. Here, certainty replaces humility. Faith gives way to philosophy. And reason, once a gift, becomes the very weapon that cuts you off from God.

The descent continues—slower, colder, quieter—into the circle where thought itself becomes the flame. This is where the war moves from the heart to the mind. This is where Hell begins to think.

Every descent begins in noise but ends in silence. In the city of Dis, the shouting stops—not because truth has won, but because pride has taken its place. Heresy isn't born in rebellion; it's born in certainty. It's what happens when the mind decides it no longer needs faith, when reason stops serving God and starts serving itself. I've seen this spirit before—not in Dante's flames, but in boardrooms, pulpits, and even in my own reflection.

From Impulse to Intention

Anger marks the last of the sins of impulse—emotions that take control of the soul. After that, the descent moves into sins of intellect and will. The heretics are found in the Sixth Circle of Hell, inside the city of Dis. This marks the point where rebellion against divine truth becomes conscious and deliberate.

As Dante and Virgil cross into the city of Dis, everything changes. The atmosphere darkens; reason itself becomes corrupted. Here begins the realm of the sins of intellect and will—not passions we fall into, but choices we make with full awareness. In this shift, Hell grows colder and more deliberate. It's no longer about losing control—it's about control twisted into rebellion.

The City of Dis and the Sin of the Mind

The Sixth Circle, where the heretics lie, represents a turning point: the moment the fire of emotion hardens into the frost of intellect. These are not souls who lost control or surrendered to desire; they are those who used their reason to rebel. They did not reject God out of ignorance but out of confidence. They trusted their own minds above mystery, their own logic above faith.

In Dante's world, that rejection is not confusion—it's defiance. It is the deliberate declaration that the unseen is unnecessary and that divine truth can be measured, mapped, and mastered. Here, the intellect becomes an idol, and like all idols it demands worship.

The walls of the city of Dis rise not from stone but from certainty. Every argument becomes a brick; every clever word, another layer of separation. From the outside, it looks like strength. From within, it feels like safety. But to God, it's a fortress of isolation—the mind locking itself away from the very truth it was created to seek.

Turning Grace into License

In Jude 1:4, we're warned that "certain people secretly slipped in—turning God's grace into license." That's how heresy usually begins: not with rebellion that roars, but with reasoning that whispers. It doesn't storm Heaven's gates; it edits Heaven's sentences.

It starts subtle. A small compromise here, a softened truth there. A new "interpretation" that makes obedience optional and holiness flexible. It sounds wise, compassionate even—"God understands," "times have changed," "grace covers everything." And yes, grace *does* cover everything, but it was never meant to cover excuses.

The heretic's pride doesn't always deny God outright; it redefines Him. It reshapes the holy into something more manageable, something that fits within the boundaries of personal comfort. That's what Jude meant by "turning grace into license." It's not rejecting God's love, it's exploiting it.

The danger isn't loud or obvious. It hides behind polished theology, motivational slogans, and even good intentions. It's the voice that says, "Why feel convicted when you can just be comfortable?"

But comfort can become a coffin when truth is buried beneath it. The same grace that was meant to set us free becomes the very thing we twist to justify our chains.

True grace doesn't make sin smaller—it makes redemption bigger. It doesn't erase truth—it fulfills it. Anything less is not grace at all; it's self-permission disguised as faith.

The Heresy of Exception

There's a kind of heresy that doesn't make headlines or stir theological debate. Believers in this heresy don't deny God outright or question His existence, they simply assume they're the exception.

This heresy is the quiet voice that says, "God understands." And while that's true—He does—this voice twists it. It whispers, "God understands, so it's okay." It softens conviction into comfort, and before long sin feels less like rebellion and more like a misunderstanding.

That's how the soul begins to drift—not by rejecting truth, but by reinterpreting it.

We tell ourselves we're different, that God knows our situation, our pain, our reasons. "He knows my heart," we say. And He does. But that's exactly why it matters. Because when the heart starts using God's mercy as an excuse for disobedience, it's not grace we're walking in—it's deception.

Grace was never given to make sin safe. It was given to make redemption possible.

The heresy of exception is subtle. It doesn't rage against holiness; it redefines it. It says, "I'm not rebelling—I'm just being real." But "real" without repentance isn't authenticity; it's apathy dressed as honesty.

We don't face our giants to impress God; we face them to become who He created us to be. Because as long as we live in delusion, we stay in Limbo—strong on Sunday, back in the mud by Monday. That pattern isn't harmless; it's dangerous. It blinds us, dulls conviction, and feeds the very giants we're called to defeat.

The longer you excuse sin in the name of grace, the more it owns you. Soon, grace no longer feels like freedom—it feels like permission.

This is how people stay lost in the dark wood. They aren't trapped by hate but by comfort, convinced that conviction is condemnation and that God's patience means permission. They stop growing because they stop being challenged.

And that's what makes this heresy so dangerous: It doesn't break faith in a moment; it erodes it over years.

The truth is, God does understand, and that's exactly why He calls us higher. His compassion doesn't make excuses for us; it makes a way out for us.

That's the difference between grace and license. Grace says, "Come as you are." License says, "Stay as you are."

One leads to freedom; the other leaves you wandering, justifying the shadows you were meant to escape.

But deception never works alone. There's a force that feeds it—one that knows exactly how to twist truth just enough to keep you still. The enemy of your soul doesn't need you to renounce God; he only needs you to relax.

He wants you comfortable in compromise, convinced that conviction is cruelty and holiness is outdated. His greatest victory isn't rebellion—it's stagnation. Because the moment you stop growing, you start dying. And if he can keep you wandering in circles, mistaking grace for permission, you'll never step into the life God designed for you.

The Heresy of Exception: "Hector"

Hector (name changed) told everyone he met that he was the estranged son of a drug lord, and he sold that lie like it was gospel. Almost everyone believed him. He wanted to rap, but he couldn't. No flow, no rhythm, no message; just noise.

Still, because of his well-crafted lie, he got into rooms most people could only dream of. Red carpet events. VIP lounges. Rappers, athletes, porn stars, hustlers, wannabe moguls, even a few cops who liked to orbit the nightlife. Everyone wanted to be around him because everyone wanted to *feel important*. That was Hector's genius.

You might've even seen him on a talk show, confidently spinning his story. He could sell fiction like scripture, and people bought it without question. I remember him looking me straight in the eye one night and saying, "Mike, I'm the king of lies." And he meant it.

Of course, his story was complete fiction. But he lived it so well that record labels, TV producers, and hip-hop icons believed every word. When rumors started closing in, he doubled down. He flew overseas and filmed himself with one of the real family members of the drug lord just to "prove" his story. To this day, I have no clue how he convinced that person to play along. Maybe Hector should've written a book on persuasion.

But I knew the truth because he once asked me to manage him, and I'd seen a contract he was looking to sign. He told me everything. When I asked what he said to labels that questioned his identity, he always had another lie ready. That was his gift; every truth had an escape hatch.

And still, I stuck around. Why? Because he had connections. A lot of them. And I wanted that access.

This was about a year before I left the music business—a wild, fast, unforgettable chapter of my life. When the money started to dry up, I drifted into real estate by day and adult fetish events by night. Hector was knee-deep in that world too. He partnered with adult stars and hosted high-end swinger parties. Eventually, he wanted us to work together, and I said yes.

I told myself it was business. God knew my heart, right? I wasn't hurting anyone. I was just trying to survive.

Then one night, Hector started talking about expanding into gay adult parties—he said there was more money in it, more buzz. Laughing, half shocked, I said, "That's disgusting. I'm not gay, I don't want to be around that, and I have morals."

That's the moment that exposed me.

I thought I was taking a stand for righteousness, but I wasn't. I was just drawing lines based on *my* preferences, not God's standards. I was fine with swinging, adultery, lies, and greed—but now suddenly I had "morals"? That's how deceived I was.

It didn't take long to realize Hector wasn't just a liar; he was reckless. The kind of reckless that could get people killed. He believed his own stories so deeply that he forgot there were real consequences for pretending to be someone else.

I started to see through him. I suspected the adult stars were the real brains behind the operation, and Hector was just a face. He wasn't smart—he was desperate. And that's what finally made me walk away. Not because I had a moral awakening but because the money didn't add up. He wanted too much of a cut and he had no real talent or brains. That's what stings the most. I didn't walk away out of conviction; I walked away because the profit wasn't right.

He even tried to steal the models that worked for me, but I cut him off before he could. He was foolish, but I wasn't—or at least that's what I told myself. The truth? I wasn't any better.

He might've been competing with Satan for "father of lies," but I was right there beside him chasing money, lust, validation, and calling it survival. I was married, running events at night, then showing up to church on Sunday morning. And somehow I thought that made me okay with God.

But that's the lie that kills slowly: *God knows my heart.*

I told myself I was different. That my situation was unique. That grace covered my hustle. That's what I call the heresy of exception. It doesn't reject God—it just assumes the rules don't apply to *you*.

I wasn't denying truth; I was revising it. I built my own theology, one built on convenience. Grace without repentance. Calling without obedience. A gospel that excused sin because I had "good intentions."

That's the danger of deception: It doesn't sound evil. It sounds *reasonable*. It sounds like "God understands."

And that's what heresy really looks like. It's not always preached from a pulpit. Sometimes it's lived in secret. It's the quiet deal you make with yourself that says, "I'm different. My situation is special."

But it's not.

The truth is, I was living my own gospel. It was one that excused rebellion and called compromise compassion. I turned God's patience into permission, and His mercy into a loophole.

And that's the scariest part about deception: It doesn't feel wrong when you're in it. It feels reasonable.

Looking back, I realize I wasn't just partnering with Hector—I was partnering with deception itself. The devil didn't need to tempt me with evil when comfort and compromise worked just fine.

The Enemy of the Soul

The enemy of your soul wants to keep you in the dark wood, not by destroying you, but by distracting you. He doesn't need to take your faith; he just needs to dull it. He whispers that God has forgotten you, that your best days are behind you, and that there's no point in fighting anymore. He convinces you that comfort is peace, that stillness is safety, and that trying again will only lead to disappointment.

His goal isn't chaos; it's paralysis. Because if he can keep you motionless long enough, your fire will fade on its own.

If he can keep you from moving, he doesn't have to defeat you, you'll do that yourself. And one of his greatest weapons is heresy. Not the loud kind that blasphemes God but the quiet one that convinces you He'll always understand no matter what you choose. The lie that says, "You can do whatever you want, and God will forgive you, so what's the harm?"

That's when he's got you. Not in rebellion but in complacency. Not in rage but in routine.

Because once you stop growing, you start decaying. Once you stop repenting, you start justifying. And when you start justifying, you begin to lose your sense of purpose—the very thing that keeps your spirit alive.

That's how the enemy traps you in Limbo. He makes you believe that change is impossible, that your giants are too big to face, and that grace means you can stay exactly where you are. But grace was never meant to keep you comfortable, it was meant to pull you out.

God promises forgiveness, yes, but forgiveness doesn't cancel consequence. He gives grace to grow, not grace to hide.

The longer you stay in the dark wood, the quieter your purpose becomes until the voice that once called you forward sounds like a memory. That's the enemy's plan: not destruction through hatred, but paralysis through comfort.

And when deception hardens into conviction, the descent deepens from the comforts of compromise to the cold logic of pride.

A Modern Tomb

I think of people like Dr. Allen (name changed to protect privacy), a man I met years ago at a small business conference. Brilliant, successful, and so confident in his own logic that humility had no seat at his table. He didn't believe in faith, not because he'd wrestled with it and found it wanting, but because he believed he'd outgrown it. "I'm not into religion," he said. "I'm into reality." The way he said it, you'd think he had trademarked the word "reality."

He talked like a man who'd cracked the cosmic code—or he did until life cracked him. Years after I met him at that conference, he lost everything in a business collapse, and when I ran into him again, he wasn't the same man. His confidence was gone, and so was his peace. He had answers for everything until life stopped asking the questions he wanted.

That's the essence of the burning tomb. When we build our faith on intellect alone, we end up worshipping our reflection, and reflections make poor saviors. The mind becomes a closed room with no windows, filled with the sound of its own certainty. It's bright, but it's suffocating.

The flames in Dante's vision aren't random punishment; they're precision. They represent the brilliance of human reason, unanchored from humility: intelligence without surrender, insight without reverence. What once illuminated now incinerates.

The tombs remind us that wisdom without grace is still blindness; it is just worded better. The intellect was never meant to replace faith; it was meant to serve it. When reason loses its reverence, it loses its light.

God opposes the proud but gives grace to the humble.

James 4:6 (ESV)

Chapter 11

Brilliance Without Humility: Pride's Cold Logic

The Descent into Pride

Dante is showing us that the fall of the human spirit doesn't only come from weakness or desire; it also comes from brilliance without humility. Once reason becomes its own god, it ceases to illuminate and begins to burn.

So when the journey passes from anger to heresy, it marks more than just another level of Hell. It marks the moment humanity crosses from being enslaved by passion to being enslaved by pride. From there on, every circle of Hell is colder, sharper, and more deliberate because each step downward is a step deeper into the corruption of the mind and the will.

Brilliance Without Humility

Hell isn't filled with fools; it's filled with the confident. The tragedy of the Sixth Circle isn't stupidity; it's brilliance without reverence. These were not aimless souls but sharp minds, articulate thinkers, persuasive voices. They were people who could out-argue anyone, even God.

As the air grows colder in the city of Dis, Dante reveals a new kind of fire: one that doesn't burn the skin but instead burns the soul. This is the fire of intellect unanchored from humility. Reason was meant to illuminate the path to truth, but when pride takes the lead, reason turns its torch inward and burns the hand that holds it.

That's the true horror here: intellect divorced from reverence. The mind becomes both architect and prisoner of its own brilliance. The flames that surround these souls aren't punishment from outside—they're the natural consequence of self-worship. Their ideas burned bright in life; now those same ideas consume them in death.

And this isn't just Dante's world, it's ours. The same spirit appears today in the scholar who mocks belief as outdated, the influencer who preaches self-worship disguised as empowerment, the CEO who measures worth only in profit and control. We celebrate intellect but often forget the soul that's supposed to steer it. The smarter we get, the easier it is to confuse cleverness for wisdom.

Humility isn't the enemy of intelligence; it's the safeguard of it. Without humility, brilliance calcifies. It stops asking questions because it believes it already holds the answers. The moment you stop asking, you stop growing, and when growth stops, pride begins.

We see this every day. Two people arguing online, both certain they're right, neither listening—that's modern heresy in motion. It's not about theology anymore; it's the arrogance of ***certainty without openness.*** The city walls of Dis have just moved to the internet.

In Dante's Hell, pride built walls around the city. In our lives, it builds them around our minds. Once you believe you're always right, correction feels like an insult, learning feels like weakness, and faith feels unnecessary.

The fire that once represented curiosity becomes containment. The same intellect that could have discovered truth ends up defending lies dressed in logic. The soul that once reached for Heaven now debates its existence.

That's the subtle danger of brilliance without humility: It convinces you that understanding something is the same as mastering it and that knowledge can replace awe. But awe is what keeps the mind human. Without it, even light turns cold.

True wisdom bows before mystery. It doesn't try to outthink the divine; it learns to walk with it. The greatest minds in history—Augustine, Newton, Einstein—all carried a sense of wonder that dwarfed their intellect. They understood that knowledge is a door, not a destination.

And that's the choice every thinker faces: to let humility turn knowledge into worship or to let pride turn it into fire. The heretics in their tombs chose the latter. They believed their ideas could replace God and found themselves consumed by the brilliance they once adored.

The Whisper of Pride

Pride doesn't kick down the door, it whispers through the cracks. It's quiet, confident, and convincing. It tells you you're not being arrogant, you're just "thinking for yourself." It tells you you're not rebelling, you're "being authentic." It flatters you with reason, polishes your ego with enlightenment, and before long you're standing in the dark, thinking you've found light.

That's how pride works; it never announces itself as sin. It wears sophistication like armor. It sounds intelligent, self-assured, mature. It doesn't scream "defiance"; it calmly says, "I know better."

The souls in the Sixth Circle didn't end up in burning tombs because they hated God. They ended up there because they replaced Him with themselves. Pride doesn't need to curse Heaven to fall; it only needs to believe it's already there.

The whisper of pride is seductive because it feels empowering. It makes you feel like you've evolved past faith, past humility, past the need for guidance. It gives the illusion of mastery, but mastery without surrender is still bondage.

You see it everywhere today. Pride hides behind confidence in boardrooms, behind certainty in arguments, behind "self-care" that's really self-worship. It's not loud or aggressive anymore—it's curated, filtered, and hashtagged. It doesn't say, "I am God." It says, "I am enough." And that subtle shift is all it needs to replace reverence with self-importance.

Pride doesn't need you to deny truth; it just needs you to redefine it. It tells you that your feelings are facts, your opinions are wisdom, your desires are destiny. It's the oldest lie in the book, and it is still wearing new clothes. The serpent never had to shout; he only had to whisper, "You shall be as gods."

And here's the irony: The more pride convinces you that you're free, the more it enslaves you. You stop growing because you stop listening. You stop learning because you stop doubting. You stop praying because you start believing you don't need to.

Pride is the most dangerous sin because it feels like virtue. It makes rebellion look like maturity and deception sound like logic. You can't fight what you don't think is wrong, and pride never looks wrong when it's dressed in success.

The whisper of pride says, "You've arrived." Humility replies, "You're still learning."

And that's the difference between those who keep rising and those who get sealed in their own tombs.

The Modern Face of Pride

Pride is not loud. It does not shout, nor does it need to. It whispers with confidence, with certainty, and with the quiet conviction that one has already arrived at truth. It is the sin that doesn't feel like a sin because it hides behind achievement, intellect, and self-assurance. It convinces the soul that it no longer needs to reach upward because it already stands high enough.

Heresy in Dante's time looked like theological arrogance; today it often looks like *certainty wrapped in convenience.* It's the ideology that flatters you, the online tribe that never challenges you, the expert who tells you what you want to hear instead of what you need to hear. In modern life, false belief spreads not only from pulpits but also from algorithms, talking heads, and echo chambers that reward being sure rather than being humble. The city of Dis now has broadband.

The Displacement of God

Pride doesn't just elevate the self; it evicts God. It begins subtly, like a quiet rearranging of priorities. One day faith guides you, the next day it's a sidenote, and before long, you're the one making all the rules. It's not rebellion in the traditional sense (no one is shaking fists at Heaven), just a gradual re-centering of the universe around *you.*

In Dante's world, this was the essence of heresy: replacing divine truth with human logic. The heretic's sin wasn't disbelief; it was displacement. They didn't reject the idea of God outright—they simply decided they could define Him better. That's the ultimate irony of pride: It doesn't destroy belief, it rebrands it.

The glutton believed pleasure was the highest good. The wrathful believed their anger was righteous. But the heretic? They believed their own mind was the final authority. They trusted intellect over intuition, logic over love, and in doing so they dethroned the divine.

We still see it today—not in temples or cathedrals, but in boardrooms, newsrooms, and feeds. The modern heretic doesn't need a pulpit; a platform will do. It's the influencer who sells "truth" for clicks, the guru who preaches "your truth" as the gospel, the culture that worships opinion more than wisdom.

And here's the subtle danger: Once the self becomes sacred, everything else becomes negotiable. Morality bends to convenience. Conviction yields to comfort. The Creator becomes a concept, and truth becomes whatever trend gets the most applause.

This is the city of Dis reborn—not walled in stone, but built in pixels and pride. A world where everyone has a voice but few seek wisdom. Where the loudest opinions echo endlessly, drowning out the quiet truth that humility once made audible.

Dante's heretics lay trapped in burning tombs, each flame representing the brilliance of their own reason. In our time, the tombs are metaphorical—glowing screens, curated personas, and closed minds locked inside their own certainty. The fire is still there; it just burns differently now.

That's the cost of displacing God: When you stop worshiping something higher, you inevitably end up worshiping yourself. And self-worship always ends the same way—exhaustion. Because when you are the source of truth, you also have to be its sustainer. You carry the full weight of meaning, identity, and purpose. And no human soul is built to bear that.

So pride doesn't liberate the soul; it burdens it. It promises autonomy and delivers anxiety. It preaches freedom and leaves you enslaved to your own expectations. It tells you that you're enough—until you're not.

That's why the descent from anger to heresy is so devastating. It's not just emotional collapse; it's spiritual inversion. Passion turns to pride, pride turns to control, and control turns to isolation. The heart that once cried out in pain now whispers, "I don't need saving." And that's the greatest deception of all.

In Dante's world, pride is not just arrogance; it is the displacement of God with the self. It is the moment when man's faith in his own power eclipses his reverence for something higher. The glutton believes pleasure is the highest good. The wrathful believe their emotion is righteous. But the proud—the heretics, the violent, the fraudulent, the traitors—believe they themselves are the measure of right and wrong.

When the descent moves from anger to heresy, it's not just a shift in sin—it's a shift in the source of sin. Passion has burned itself out; what remains is the will, hardened and certain. Pride replaces impulse. It gives shape to evil, structure to rebellion, and reason to ruin. That's why, from this point on, Hell becomes colder and more deliberate: Pride strips away emotion and leaves only self-interest.

The Seed of Rebellion

Every rebellion starts as a whisper. It begins not with open defiance, but with a question: "Did God really say... ?" That single seed—doubt laced with pride—was enough to unmake paradise. And it still works the same way today.

Pride is the mind's rebellion against humility. It's not always angry or arrogant; sometimes it's calm, clever, and persuasive. It tells you you're only being "reasonable." It convinces you that dependence is weakness, that submission is small-minded, and that you've outgrown the need for guidance. It flatters the intellect while quietly poisoning it.

That's the sin of the heretic. Not the pursuit of knowledge but the worship of it. They take the tools meant to reveal truth and turn them into idols. They no longer seek wisdom—they seek control. In Dante's vision, their brilliance becomes their own undoing. The very fire that once illuminated now consumes them.

And isn't that what pride always does? It starts with enlightenment but ends with isolation. The mind, convinced of its own mastery, slowly walls itself off until it becomes a kingdom of one. That's why Dante placed the heretics in tombs—because rebellion of the mind always buries the soul.

The seed of rebellion grows strongest in fertile soil—the places where we are most gifted, most confident, most sure of ourselves. It's rarely found in ignorance; it's born in brilliance. It's not the fool who defies Heaven; it's the one who believes he's finally figured Heaven out.

Modern rebellion doesn't wear horns or robes. It wears credentials. It quotes data, not scripture. It trusts its own interpretation of truth more than the source itself. It's the voice that says, "I'm not rejecting God—I'm redefining Him." But the moment you redefine God, you dethrone Him.

Pride doesn't destroy truth outright; it edits it. It bends scripture to fit emotion, twists conviction into preference, and reshapes holiness into something more "relatable." And before long, the soul has built its own theology—one without repentance, without reverence, without God.

That's the heretic's tragedy: They didn't lose faith; they repurposed it. They didn't stop believing; they just started believing in themselves.

And yet, every rebellion that begins with "I know better" ends with the same echoing silence—the sound of a heart that's shut itself off from grace.

So, as the descent continues, Dante's journey turns from the heat of passion to the chill of pride and from the chaos of emotion to the cold logic of rebellion. The fire that once burned bright with feeling now hardens into certainty. What once cried for freedom now demands control. And that is the beginning of every fall—when the mind, convinced of its own light, forgets where the flame came from.

Pride is the mind's rebellion against humility. It is the refusal to bow—not out of hatred, but out of conviction that bowing is beneath you. The heretics embody this perfectly. They are not monsters clawing at Heaven; they are thinkers who stood tall and declared, "We will define the truth ourselves." In life, they believed their light was enough; in death, that light burns them from within.

In a deeper sense, pride is the perversion of creation. The divine gift of free will and reason—meant to elevate humanity—becomes the very weapon that severs it from its source. It is the serpent whispering, "You shall be as gods." And every sin below this circle is just a different way of answering, "Yes."

The Cold Logic of Pride

Fire can destroy, but at least fire still feels. When Dante moves deeper into the *Inferno*, that fire begins to fade—not because sin has been conquered, but because passion has died. The further you go, the colder it gets. Love, anger, desire—all the messy human emotions that once burned with heat—are gone. What's left is pride, pure and polished, stripped of warmth and utterly convinced of its own perfection.

That's the paradox of pride: It begins with brilliance and ends in ice. It promises light but delivers frost. It starts as a spark of independence (*I'll think for myself*) and ends as isolation (*I need no one at all)*. The proud soul doesn't rage; it reasons. It doesn't shout; it analyzes. It doesn't burn with passion; it freezes with certainty.

Pride's logic sounds noble at first. It says things like: "I don't need anyone." "I can handle this myself." "I know what's best." But underneath that confidence is fear—fear of being wrong, fear of being vulnerable, fear of being seen as small. Pride builds walls not to show power but to hide weakness. The problem is that the walls keeping others out also keep grace from getting in.

Cold logic is seductive because it feels safe. Emotion is unpredictable; reason is controlled. But in cutting off the heart, pride also severs compassion. It isolates intelligence from empathy until even truth itself feels mechanical. It's the kind of brilliance that can dissect anything except its own blindness.

This is why the proud can be the hardest to reach. You can reason with the angry and comfort the fearful, but pride resists both reason and comfort. It doesn't fight; it dismisses. It doesn't lash out; it looks down. It doesn't cry out for help; it quietly assumes it doesn't need any.

That's what makes pride so dangerous: It doesn't feel like sin. It feels like control, competence, and composure until life cracks the illusion.

The proud soul isn't wicked in the obvious sense. It's just... done listening. It's too refined for repentance, too logical for faith, too self-assured for surrender. It has nothing left to burn, so it freezes instead.

By the time pride reaches its final stage, it no longer needs to rebel. Instead, it has achieved something worse: indifference. It's not angry at God anymore; it simply doesn't care. And that, in Dante's world—and in ours—is the truest definition of Hell.

That's why Dante's Hell grows colder with each descent. Fire represents passion, and passion still has life in it—even if misdirected, it is human. But pride kills warmth. It turns the soul rigid, unbending, frozen in its own certainty. By the time we reach the lowest circle, where traitors lie trapped in ice, pride has fulfilled its destiny. It no longer burns; it crystallizes. It becomes still, silent, and dead.

The paradox of pride is that it begins with elevation and ends with confinement. It promises the highest freedom and delivers the deepest prison. The heretics in their burning tombs are only the first glimpse of this truth—brilliant minds trapped in their own brilliance, forever surrounded by the echo of their own reasoning.

The Fixed Soul

Pride doesn't just corrupt the heart—it calcifies it. The danger of pride is not just that it sins, but that it ***stops changing***. It convinces the soul that it has nothing left to learn, nothing left to surrender, and nothing left to receive. And once you stop growing, you start dying—slowly, quietly, beneath the weight of your own certainty.

That's what makes the Sixth Circle so terrifying. The souls entombed here aren't raging or writhing; they are fixed. They've become what they believed—unmovable, unteachable, unrepentant. Their brilliance has turned to blindness and their reason to ruin. The flames that once symbolized enlightenment now flicker without warmth, feeding endlessly on themselves.

Hell, in this sense, isn't just punishment—it's permanence. It's not God turning His back on the soul; it's the soul turning its back so completely that it can no longer turn around. Pride locks the door from the inside.

Dante's vision is chilling because it feels familiar. You've met people like this. The ones who can't admit they're wrong. The ones who'd rather lose everything than say, "I'm sorry." The ones whose entire identity depends on being right. That's the modern city of Dis—a world full of fortified egos, echo chambers, and minds that can't be moved.

The fixed soul doesn't need flames; it carries its own. It burns in isolation, consumed by the echo of its own certainty. Every thought circles back to the same conclusion: *I was right*. Every prayer becomes a monologue. Every truth becomes an opinion. In time, the person stops encountering the world and they only encounter themselves.

That's what pride ultimately costs you: perspective. You stop seeing others clearly, stop hearing God clearly, stop recognizing that truth exists outside of your own reflection. Pride whispers that the world revolves around you, and the longer you believe it, the smaller your world becomes. Until finally, it's just you, staring into the mirror, convinced you've mastered everything, unaware that what you've mastered is a cage.

The souls in Dante's Sixth Circle aren't screaming for mercy—they're arguing. They don't beg to be freed because they're still explaining why they shouldn't have to be. That's the ultimate tragedy of pride: It talks even when no one is listening. It reasons itself into ruin.

And that's why Dante calls this level the beginning of the *cold sins*—the point where warmth gives way to rigidity and the soul no longer bends toward grace. Once reason becomes self-contained, it becomes self-consuming. Once the heart stops yielding, it stops beating.

Pride makes the soul incapable of learning. It resists correction, rejects surrender, and despises dependence. It thrives on being right, even when it is wrong. And in Dante's vision, that is the essence of Hell itself: a state where one can no longer change. The damned are not just punished—they are fixed and unable to evolve because pride has calcified their hearts and sealed their minds.

From this moment in the journey onward, every sin Dante encounters—violence, fraud, treachery—will be a deeper manifestation of pride's corruption. The soul that once refused to submit now begins to destroy, deceive, and betray in its effort to preserve its own supremacy. Pride is the seed; every darker sin is the bloom.

The Mirror of the Mind

Every circle of Hell is a mirror. Each one reflects not just what humanity does but how it thinks—the illusions we cling to, the truths we distort, and the lies we defend as righteousness. By the time Dante reaches the Sixth Circle, the mirror has turned inward. It no longer shows the body in motion; it shows the mind in captivity.

The heretics believed they could redefine truth. They used intellect as a weapon—sharp, clever, and convincing. But the more they reasoned without humility, the deeper they sank into delusion. Their brilliance became their blindness and their logic became their prison. That's what happens when you look into the mirror of your own mind too long—eventually, you stop seeing God and start seeing yourself reflected back, nodding in agreement.

In Dante's time, heresy meant theological rebellion—denying the soul, the resurrection, or the divine. But in today's world, heresy often looks like something more subtle: the belief that truth is customizable. That faith can be edited. That morality is flexible as long as you "mean well." It's the modern creed of comfort: *I'll decide what's true for me.*

And yet, that's how the city of Dis is built—one brick of self-assurance at a time. Every wall starts with a single thought: *I know better*. Every tower rises with the belief: *I don't need correction*. Until finally, the walls are so high that light no longer enters. You stop being illuminated by truth and start being flattered by your own reflection.

The mirror of pride is seductive because it doesn't distort—it flatters. It doesn't make you look monstrous; it makes you look magnificent. It tells you that you've evolved past humility, outgrown dependence, and surpassed those who still "need faith." But the moment you start to worship your own wisdom, you've already stepped into the city gates of Dis.

Pride rarely announces itself. It hides in the mind's quiet corners, in the need to have the last word, in the refusal to listen, in the satisfaction of being admired. It tells you that your logic is love, your self-confidence is strength, your control is peace. But if you stare long enough, you'll see what Dante saw: that the mirror doesn't lie—it only reflects the truth you've chosen to believe.

That's the lesson of the Sixth Circle: The mind can be both sanctuary and cell. What determines which one it becomes is not how much you know but how willing you are to kneel.

Because pride will always tell you to stand tall. But grace begins when you're willing to bow.

That's why the transition from anger to heresy is so profound. It marks the birth of deliberate evil—the moment when man stops being a victim of passion and becomes an architect of his own damnation. From here, the descent is not just downward; it is inward, toward the cold, perfect stillness of self-worship.

As we leave the city of Dis and its burning tombs behind, it becomes clear that the journey through heresy is more than a descent into punishment; it is a mirror reflecting the hidden fires within ourselves. Anger shows us the power of passion, but heresy reveals the power of pride—the mind's ability to turn against humility and to elevate certainty above truth. In these circles, the damned are not merely victims of impulse but of will, trapped by their own intellect and the illusion of control.

Reflection: The Inner Descent

This is a moment to pause, to look inward and confront the ways pride shapes your own life. Reflect on times when anger dictated your actions and when reaction overtook reason. Notice where conviction has hardened into rigidity, where certainty prevents learning, and where the mind becomes a prison of its own making. Consider the areas where control dominates and where the fear of surrender masks itself as strength. Visualize the inner landscape of pride versus humility, see the walls that protect yet isolate, and imagine opening just one gate to understanding, compassion, or correction.

Finally, ask yourself where you stand on this map: Are you still driven by passion, or have you begun to justify your pride through logic and certainty? Awareness itself is the first step upward. Just as Dante saw the heretics confined in fiery tombs, you can see where your own reasoning and self-assurance may trap you. The descent into heresy warns that brilliance without humility becomes a fire that burns from within, and yet, reflection and honesty can begin the work of freeing the mind. Let this understanding be both a caution and an invitation: to recognize pride, to question certainty, and to prepare for the next stage of the journey, where choice begins to manifest outward, shaping not only thought but action.

Exercises: Confronting the Fire of Pride

Here are some practical exercises you may want to follow to explore the themes of pride, certainty, and the ways the mind can trap itself. These reflections are designed to help you search for moments where impulse gives way to pride, where certainty becomes rigidity, and where humility can open the gates that pride has closed.

1. **The Mirror of Impulse**. Think back to a time when anger or emotion dictated your words or actions. Then look deeper: What belief justified it afterward? What story did your mind tell to make the reaction feel right? Write down both the feeling and the reasoning that followed. This exercise shows how emotion turns into ideology, how the heart's reaction becomes the mind's defense, and how justification is often the first spark of heresy.
2. **Voice of Certainty.** Write down three beliefs you hold with absolute certainty—not surface opinions, but convictions that shape your view of the world. Next to each one, ask, "What if I am wrong?" and sit with the discomfort. That moment of tension between conviction and humility is the border between the Fifth and Sixth Circles.

3. **Tomb of the Mind**. The heretics in Dante's vision lie trapped in their own thoughts. Take ten minutes and write freely about an idea, memory, or belief that you revisit constantly, something you argue with in your head, then read what you wrote and notice whether it is circular. Ask yourself whether you are reasoning or just reinforcing. That is how intellectual fire turns into a prison.
4. **The Illusion of Control**. List three areas of your life where you try the hardest to stay in control—your emotions, relationships, career, or beliefs. Then describe what would happen if you let go. Consider what it might cost you and what it might free. Pride is often the fear of surrender wearing the mask of strength.
5. **Fire and Ice.** Visualize your inner world when you are proud and when you feel right. Notice if it is fiery, full of energy and certainty, or cold, distant, and detached. Then visualize humility—not weakness, but openness, and write what each one feels like physically. This shows how pride numbs the soul while humility keeps it alive.
6. **The City Within**. Dante's city of Dis represents the fortified mind, with walls built from certainty and guarded by fear. Close your eyes and imagine your own city, then consider what walls you have built to protect yourself from being challenged or vulnerable. Sketch or describe it, then imagine opening one gate and consider what would enter.
7. Finally, the seventh exercise is the **Descent and the Ascent.** Ask yourself where you are on this map. Are

you still ruled by passion, anger, desire, or appetite, or have you begun to justify your pride with logic and control? Write one paragraph answering honestly, without judgment. Awareness is the first step upward.

After completing these exercises, remember: This only works if you have an open mind. It only works if you are not afraid to see the ugliness in yourself and confront that with the loving and well-meaning person of humility you truly are.

Closing: When the Mind Becomes the Battlefield

The city of Dis leaves you with a haunting realization: Hell doesn't begin with hatred—it begins with certainty. The souls in their fiery tombs weren't driven here by impulse; they reasoned their way here, brick by brick, argument by argument. They believed enlightenment was liberation, but it became confinement.

That's the tragedy of pride—it replaces faith with philosophy, humility with logic, and surrender with self-assurance. It builds walls that look like wisdom and towers that feel like strength. But once the mind crowns itself king, the heart becomes the first casualty.

Dante reminds us that sin evolves. What begins as passion in the upper circles—lust, gluttony, greed, anger—hardens into ideology here. Desire cools into certainty. Emotion calcifies into will. And once the soul has convinced itself that it is right, there's no argument left that can reach it.

The flames of heresy burn bright, but beneath their light lies something darker that is stirring—the corruption of power, the twisting of pain into control. Pride was the spark, but violence will be the fire.

And so, as Dante and Virgil leave the burning tombs behind, the ground begins to tremble once more. The air thickens. The glow fades to red. The noise of intellect gives way to the thunder of blood. What was once cold conviction now explodes into chaos.

The descent from pride to violence isn't a fall—it's an eruption. The soul that once said, "I know better," now cries, "I will take what's mine."

And with that, the gates of Dis close behind us and the War of the Seventh Circle begins.

Whoever sows violence reaps destruction.

Proverbs 22:8 (NIV)

Chapter 12

The Seventh Circle: Violence

From Pride to Violence: The Continuum of Corruption

In traveling from the Sixth Circle of Heresy to the Seventh Circle of Violence, one begins to see a continuum of human corruption—a spectrum of pride and choice that moves from the mind inward to the will outward. In heresy, the soul is consumed by intellectual rebellion and the belief that understanding oneself or the universe can replace humility and grace.

Pride masquerades as enlightenment, and in its fire the heretics burn alone, trapped within the brilliance of their own reasoning. Here, hatred is subtle: It is hatred of the truth when it conflicts with ego, hatred of one's own vulnerability, even a quiet self-hatred for weaknesses perceived or imagined.

The passage from the Sixth Circle to the Seventh isn't a sudden drop—it's a slow, inevitable slide. It's the point where thought becomes action, where inner pride hardens into outer harm. What began in the mind as rebellion now erupts through the will as destruction.

In heresy, the soul burns within its own brilliance. It worships understanding instead of truth and intellect instead of humility. The heretic believes knowledge is salvation and that reason alone can replace grace. Pride disguises itself as enlightenment, whispering, "You've outgrown the need to bow." But every flame that burns without reverence eventually consumes its own light.

Here, hatred still hides in refinement. It isn't loud or violent yet—it's quiet, sophisticated, even reasonable. It's hatred of correction, hatred of vulnerability, hatred of weakness, hatred of anything that reminds us we're not gods. It's the mind rejecting mystery because mystery cannot be controlled.

Then comes the shift. The rebellion that once lived in thought now demands expression. Pride that once turned inward now turns outward, clothed in anger, envy, and domination. What was once intellectual arrogance becomes embodied hostility, the idea made flesh, the theory given teeth.

In the Seventh Circle, that transformation is complete. The mind's quiet war becomes the world's open wound. The same pride that blinded the intellect now blinds the conscience. The same self-loathing that whispered in silence now screams through action. Whether directed inward or outward, it's the same force: hatred weaponized.

Here, Dante shows us the final stage of pride's evolution: first rebellion against truth, then resentment of life, and finally violence against creation itself.

The continuum is clear—pride births hatred, and hatred births destruction. What the Sixth Circle conceived, the Seventh Circle executes.

When Hatred Turns Outward

In the Seventh Circle, the corruption that once hid behind intellect now erupts into the open. The flames of pride that burned inward in heresy now ignite the world around them. The soul that once whispered, "I will define truth myself" now shouts, "I will define justice too."

Here, hatred no longer hides in the mind—it bleeds into action. The quiet rebellion of thought becomes the violence of will. The heretic's arrogance becomes the murderer's rage, the oppressor's cruelty, the abuser's control. What began as self-worship now demands sacrifice from others.

Dante shows us three forms of violence, each revealing where hatred takes root: against others, against self, and against God. Each is a mirror of pride turned in a different direction.

Those who spill the blood of others are consumed by domination—the need to prove power through pain. Those who destroy themselves, like Pier della Vigna, are trapped in despair with their pride collapsing inward until it crushes the heart. And those who blaspheme, exploit, or pervert the natural order act out a subtler rebellion: the refusal to honor limits and the belief that they can rewrite creation itself.

In every case, the result is the same—a war against life. Violence is pride made visible. It is hatred with a body, shame with a weapon, despair with a pulse. It doesn't only kill flesh; it corrodes the soul, the home, the community, and the divine image itself.

When pride becomes action, the world bleeds. And in that blood, the truth becomes clear: What we do to others, we are already doing to ourselves.

In the Seventh Circle, the same forces that festered in the mind now erupt into the world. The suicides, like Pier della Vigna, show that hatred can turn inward, destroying the body as the mind becomes a cage of despair. Those who commit violence against others project their hatred outward—anger, envy, and ambition twisting into aggression, murder, and oppression.

Even the blasphemers, sodomites, and usurers reveal a hatred of life's natural order, an aversion to limits, and an inability to honor others, themselves, or the divine. Here, hatred is active, not passive; it is the ego turned outward, seeking to dominate or annihilate.

The Tragedy of Pier della Vigna

Among the twisted trees of the Seventh Circle, Dante meets a soul whose voice pours from a bleeding trunk—a man once celebrated for brilliance, loyalty, and intellect: Pier della Vigna.

Pier was no common sinner. He rose from humble beginnings to become the trusted counselor of Emperor Frederick II—a position of prestige and power. His mind was his kingdom, and through wit and wisdom he built his throne. But with that power came the constant tension of serving two masters: the emperor's favor and his own pride.

When jealousy and political intrigue led to his downfall, Pier was accused of treachery, and he was condemned not by proof but by whispers. The world he had crafted with intellect and loyalty collapsed overnight. His reputation, the very thing he believed gave his life meaning, was destroyed.

And with it, so was he.

Pier turned his brilliance inward, and it devoured him. Unable to live under the shadow of disgrace, he took his own life—an act that sealed his fate in Dante's Hell. There, he is rooted in the Wood of the Suicides, transformed into a tree that bleeds when broken. His voice, once used to advise kings, now cries out only when wounded. The intellect that once elevated him has become his prison, and his body, denied to him, serves as a symbol of the soul that turned against itself.

Pier's tragedy is not just his death; it is his disconnection. He believed his worth was tied to status, approval, and control, and when those things were stripped away, he found nothing left to stand on. His pride couldn't bear humility. His mind couldn't bear imperfection. And so his pride-driven intellect destroyed the vessel it was meant to serve.

What makes Pier's story so haunting is how familiar it feels. His torment may echo through Dante's verse, but it also resonates in boardrooms, classrooms, and quiet bedrooms today in every person who ties identity to performance, value to validation, and meaning to the opinions of others.

We may not hang from the branches of the Wood of the Suicides, but many of us live among its roots—silencing ourselves with shame, strangling our potential with fear, and punishing our own souls for not being enough.

Pier della Vigna reminds us that self-hatred is just pride wearing a mask of despair. When pride cannot stay superior, it would rather destroy itself than surrender to grace.

Pier della Vigna was a man whose life, in many ways, seemed luminous. He rose to prominence as secretary and advisor to Emperor Frederick II, a position of trust, influence, and respect. In the eyes of others, he had power and prestige; in his own mind, he carried an immense burden of expectation and the constant vigilance of a man walking a tightrope between favor and ruin. When accusations of treachery were leveled against him, false or exaggerated, his world collapsed. His honor, the very thing he had devoted his life to protecting, was stripped away in an instant.

Unable to reconcile the weight of public shame with the private pride that had driven his ambition, Pier took his own life. In doing so, he became a literal embodiment of his internal conflict: The mind that once strategized, reasoned, and defended is now trapped as a spirit in an unyielding, twisted tree, a grotesque reflection of his despair. His body, the vehicle of his intellect and action, was denied to him, leaving only a voice that could speak but never act, a reminder that hatred of self—whether born of despair, shame, or pride—is one of the most consuming forces imaginable.

The Psychology of Self-Destruction

When Dante encounters Pier della Vigna, he doesn't just meet a soul trapped in wood—he meets the anatomy of despair. Pier's story is not merely about suicide; it's about the collapse of self under the unbearable weight of pride. He reveals what happens when identity is built on performance and perception instead of purpose and grace.

Self-destruction rarely begins with an act—it begins with a belief. The belief that *worth must be earned*. That failure equals worthlessness. That to fall from grace is to be unworthy of love.

For Pier, and for so many like him, pride and shame are two sides of the same coin. His confidence came from achievement, and his identity depended on maintaining that image. The moment it shattered, he had nothing left to hold on to. When pride cannot maintain control, it often turns its weapons inward and attacks the very vessel it once sought to glorify.

This is the paradox of the human mind: The same thoughts that elevate can also destroy. The same brilliance that builds empires can build prisons. The same voice that once strategized can become an accuser, whispering that you've failed, that you're finished, that you are no longer worthy of redemption.

In Dante's Hell, Pier's intellect becomes his torment. In our world, the same dynamic plays out in quieter ways—anxiety, perfectionism, burnout, and self-sabotage. We call it "overthinking," but it's really a war of the mind against the heart.

Every time we choose performance over peace, validation over authenticity, or control over surrender, we reenact Pier's tragedy in miniature. We wither in silence, still alive but disconnected from joy, rooted in the fear of not being enough.

But the truth is, failure doesn't define us—it refines us. Shame is not a verdict; it's an invitation. It tells us where grace must enter. The moment we stop trying to earn our worth and instead begin to receive it, the cycle of self-destruction begins to break.

Pier della Vigna could not forgive himself, but his story still teaches us how to begin. The way out of despair is not perfection—it's permission. Permission to be human, to be unfinished, to be loved anyway.

When Dante encounters him, Pier does not merely recite his fate; he reveals the psychology of self-destruction. He shows how pride can turn inward and how ambition combined with fear of dishonor can lead the mind to betray the body it inhabits. The story is tragic because Pier was brilliant, capable, and respected, yet his inability to endure judgment—real or imagined—led to an act that sealed him in a torment worse than any earthly punishment.

Pier della Vigna's tale is a warning: Hatred of self, even when subtle or internalized, can become as violent as hatred directed outward. In life, it may be expressed through despair, self-sabotage, or extreme measures taken to preserve a fragile sense of pride. In Dante's vision, it is eternalized, a constant reminder that the mind can be both creator and destroyer of its own prison.

A Mirror for the Modern Soul

Pier della Vigna's story may seem like ancient tragedy, but his voice still echoes in the hallways of our modern minds. His despair lives on in different forms—anxiety, burnout, perfectionism, silent depression. His branches reach into boardrooms, classrooms, churches, and quiet bedrooms. The scenery has changed, but the sickness hasn't: the belief that our value depends on our victories.

We call it "ambition." We call it "drive." Sometimes we even call it "success." But beneath it the same old fear often hides—*If I'm not impressive, I'm nothing*. So we chase applause. We curate perfection. We fill every silence with motion because stillness might expose the emptiness inside.

And when life eventually interrupts our illusion, when the job is lost or the marriage fails or the recognition fades, we panic. The same mind that once cheered us on now turns against us. It says, "You should have done more. You should have been more." That's the whisper of Pier della Vigna. That's the sound of the branch cracking.

In truth, most of us live somewhere between his brilliance and his despair. We crave to be seen, but we fear being known. We measure our worth by productivity, by likes, by titles—by anything but peace. And so, like Pier, we mistake exhaustion for purpose and pressure for identity.

Yet there's another way. When the branches of pride finally break, something sacred can grow from the wound. The pain that once felt like punishment can become the soil for humility, compassion, and grace. The moment we admit, "I can't do this alone," the roots begin to heal.

Self-awareness is not self-condemnation; it's the first breath after suffocation. When you see your own reflection in Pier's sorrow, don't turn away. Look closer. Beneath the guilt, there's a deeper truth waiting to be found: You were never meant to prove your worth—you were meant to live from it.

The modern soul doesn't need more accomplishment. It needs acceptance. It needs space to rest, to forgive, to grow in the light instead of burning in it. The heretic trusted intellect; the violent trusted power; but healing begins when we learn to trust grace.

Pier della Vigna's story is a mirror for us all. His torment may seem distant, a figure lost in an old poem, but the forces that destroyed him are not. Pride, shame, despair, and self-hatred—these are not just ancient sins; they are modern prisons.

Have you ever felt yourself turning inward with a kind of quiet self-hatred?

Have you ever wondered if your life was too broken to be repaired?

Have you ever been trapped inside your own thoughts, as if your mind had become a cage you couldn't escape?

If you have, know this: You are not broken. You are not alone. Those thoughts are not the truth of who you are; they are a storm passing through the mind, not your essence. Beneath the noise, beneath the shame and the pain, there is a self within you that is loving, capable, and resilient—a self that has always been there, waiting to be met.

Meeting the Stranger Within

Pier della Vigna's story is more than a warning—it's an invitation. Every branch that bleeds in Dante's wood whispers a question: "When will you stop wounding yourself?"

Most people spend their lives trying to outrun their own reflection. They silence the voice that trembles, they bury the dream that failed, they armor themselves with noise and distraction so that they never have to hear what the quiet is saying. But sooner or later, the silence catches up. And when it does, you meet a stranger—the part of you that you've ignored, misunderstood, or even despised.

That moment can feel terrifying, but it's holy. Because the stranger isn't your enemy. It's the unhealed part of yourself that still remembers who you were before the world taught you fear. It's the child who wanted to create, to love, to trust. It's the self that still believes life can be beautiful, even after all the storms.

To meet that stranger is to begin reconciliation with your own soul. It means sitting in the quiet and asking, "What have I been running from?" It means listening when the answer comes.

At first, the voice might sound like pain—like regret, guilt, or grief. But if you stay long enough, you'll hear something deeper: truth wrapped in tenderness. The voice will tell you that you were never meant to be perfect; you were meant to be present. That your scars don't make you unworthy; they make you real.

This meeting doesn't happen in one sitting. It unfolds over time through forgiveness, reflection, and small acts of courage—every moment you choose awareness instead of avoidance, compassion instead of criticism, love instead of pride. Each choice loosens the chains that self-hatred forged.

And when you finally learn to see the stranger not as a threat but as a teacher, transformation begins. The stranger becomes an ally. The wounded part of yourself becomes the wise part. And the quiet you once feared becomes home.

When that happens, you realize the truth Dante hinted at in every circle: that the journey through darkness is not about escaping Hell—it's about recovering the self that was lost in it.

By the end of this book, if you walk with me honestly and openly, you will begin to meet that self. You will learn to see the stranger within you not as an enemy to be feared or destroyed but as a wounded part of yourself longing for healing. And as you do, you will discover that self-love is not an empty phrase but a quiet revolution—the key that opens the gate of the city within.

Imagine meeting yourself fully, without judgment. Imagine sitting with that part of yourself that has been hidden, listening to its fears, its sorrows, its quiet longing. Over time, that stranger transforms. The self you once feared becomes a companion, a guide, a teacher. You will discover that self-love is not a fragile, fleeting feeling; it is the foundation for the rest of your life. It is the key that unlocks the gates of your inner city where curiosity, courage, and compassion await.

This is not a promise of instant change nor a cure for the storms of the mind. It is an invitation to notice, to confront, and to embrace. Pier della Vigna's tragedy shows the cost of self-hatred and despair, but your story does not have to end there. You can choose to meet yourself differently. You can choose to step forward into awareness and love, to cultivate a relationship with the stranger inside, and, in doing so, to discover a person you have always carried but never truly known.

Pride, Hatred, and the Journey of the Self

The link between the two circles is clear: Pride births hatred. Pride that refuses humility becomes self-hatred when confronted with weakness or injustice, and that same pride becomes hatred of others when it seeks to assert control, punish, or destroy. The journey through Hell, then, is a journey through the layers of the self: first inward, in thought and intellect, then outward, in action and consequence.

Understanding this is the first step toward reconciliation. Hatred, whether of self or others, is a mirror revealing where the ego has overstepped and where impulse and intellect have been misapplied. Anger, pride, despair, and violence are not merely external phenomena; they are signposts along the path of the self, pointing to the parts of us we do not want to acknowledge. Confronting them is terrifying because it means facing the parts of ourselves we call "stranger"—the mind that rebels, the heart that envies, the hands that hurt. Yet only by seeing these forces clearly can one begin to disentangle them, to move from reaction to awareness and from hatred to understanding.

In this way, heresy and violence are two sides of the same coin. The Sixth Circle teaches that pride can blind the mind, while the Seventh Circle teaches that pride can wound the world. Together, they reveal the continuum of human alienation: from self to others to existence itself. And the journey, for both Dante and the reader, is about learning to recognize these strangers within, to confront them without fear, and ultimately to reclaim the self from the shadows of hatred.

Every journey through darkness reveals the same pattern: Pride gives birth to hatred, and hatred—when left unattended—gives birth to destruction. Pride blinds the mind; hatred breaks the heart. Together they fracture the self, turning life into a war between who we are and who we pretend to be.

The Sixth Circle showed us the mind gone astray and intellect divorced from humility. The Seventh Circle shows us the will gone wild and action divorced from empathy. Between them lies the most human battlefield of all: the space where thought becomes choice. Pride whispers, "I can handle this alone." Hatred answers, "Then destroy whatever stands in your way."

When pride turns inward, it becomes self-hatred—resentment of our own weakness, shame, or failure. When it turns outward, it becomes violence—an attempt to control what we fear or cannot forgive. Both are symptoms of the same sickness: separation from love, from humility, from truth.

But here's the paradox Dante wants us to see: Even in these depths, redemption begins with recognition. The same fire that burns can purify when faced with honesty. The same mind that rebels can reason its way back to faith. The same will that wounds can also heal.

The journey through Hell is, in truth, the journey through the self. Each circle strips away another illusion, another mask, another excuse. The wrathful learn that fury enslaves them. The heretics learn that intellect without humility imprisons them. And the violent learn that power without compassion destroys them. Step by step, the soul confronts its own handiwork until it can finally say, "This is what I built—and this is what I must rebuild."

This is where I Am My Biggest Stranger comes alive. The stranger you fear—the one capable of anger, pride, envy, or despair—isn't here to shame you; it's here to show you where you've stopped loving yourself and, by extension, others. When you meet that stranger, you begin the ascent. The same energy that once fueled destruction becomes the force that fuels creation.

The path forward isn't about perfection—it's about presence. To walk upward from the circles of pride and hatred is to walk toward awareness, humility, and love. It's to recognize that every act of cruelty—whether toward yourself or another—is just love gone unanswered.

And so, as we leave the burning forests and rivers of blood behind, the question changes. It's no longer "What have I done?" but "Who am I becoming?" Because every step toward humility is a step toward freedom, and every moment of awareness is a spark of light in the dark wood of the soul.

Do not be overcome by evil, but overcome evil with good.

Romans 12:21 (ESV)

Chapter 13

The River in Our Time: Healing the Violence Within

Modern-Day Violence

As Dante and Virgil step deeper into Hell, the noise changes. The arguments and wailing of the heretics fade, replaced by screams that sound less like pain and more like war. The air thickens, the light disappears, and before them stretches the River of Blood—a boiling current where the violent are submerged according to the measure of their cruelty. Some are buried to their throats, others to their eyes. The more blood they spilled in life, the deeper they sink.

It's one of the most haunting images in the *Inferno*, not because it's fantastical, but because it feels familiar. The river hasn't vanished. It's just changed form. Today, we see it every time we turn on the news: another shooting, another act of rage, another moment where someone's pain becomes everyone's tragedy. Our modern river doesn't flow through Hell—it runs through our cities, our schools, our homes, and sometimes through our own hearts.

Violence is no longer just physical. It's emotional, psychological, and digital. It hides behind comment sections, ideologies, and lonely screens. It's what happens when people lose the ability to feel seen, heard, or loved and instead choose control, dominance, or destruction. The same pride that blinded the heretics and the same hatred that boiled in the wrathful now lives on disguised as self-righteousness, resentment, or despair.

We keep asking, "*Why?* Why would someone walk into a school and destroy innocent lives? Why would a person kill strangers or even themselves?"

These are not only questions of morality—they are questions of meaning. Because at the root of violence, we never find strength. We find emptiness.

The violent soul is not born monstrous; it is born human—wounded, unseen, disconnected. Over time, pain ferments into rage, and rage begins to look like identity. Violence becomes a voice—a desperate cry to be noticed in a world that has gone deaf.

And so the river overflows. It floods our timelines and neighborhoods, our conversations and relationships. We condemn it, fear it, and debate it, but we rarely look at what created it. Violence doesn't appear out of nowhere. It is cultivated. It grows in silence, in loneliness, in humiliation. It grows wherever empathy dies.

The lesson Dante teaches through the Seventh Circle is the same lesson the modern world refuses to learn: You cannot stop violence by force alone. You can only stop it by healing what causes it.

Because every act of violence begins long before the act itself—in the fracture between self and soul, between one's humanity and one's pain. Once empathy dies, anything becomes possible.

The Roots of Violence

Every act of violence begins long before the act itself. It starts quietly with a fracture. A small separation between who we are and who we believe we must be. Between our pain and our ability to express it. Between our humanity and our need for control.

When that separation grows wide enough, empathy begins to die. And when empathy dies, everything else follows.

Many of those who commit acts of violence describe the same haunting pattern: lives marked by isolation, humiliation, and neglect. They feel unseen, unheard, unwanted—ghosts walking among the living. Over time, that pain festers until rage becomes the only language they can speak. Violence becomes their translation of despair.

For some, it's not hatred that drives them—it's invisibility. For others, it's ideology or delusion—a warped attempt to reclaim meaning in a meaningless world. And for many, it's trauma—a wound that was never healed, only redirected outward.

When the pain inside a person grows louder than the love around them, destruction becomes the only form of expression left. That's why Dante's river of blood feels so timeless. It's not just punishment—it's a reflection. Every person submerged in that boiling current once believed they were taking back power. But all they really did was lose their humanity piece by piece.

Violence is never born from strength. It is born from disconnection—the slow decay of empathy until the soul no longer recognizes itself in another.

And that is the tragedy of the Seventh Circle: It doesn't just expose the cruelty of man; it reveals the emptiness that fuels it.

The Illusion of the Monster

We like to believe that violence belongs to "other people." That the ones who kill, who destroy, and who harm are monsters. It's comforting, in a way. If they're monsters, then we're safe. If they're nothing like us, then we could never become them.

But that illusion is the very thing that blinds us. Violence doesn't come from some separate species of humanity—it comes from the same soil we all stand on. The same capacity for pain, for pride, for disconnection lives in every one of us. The difference is only what we do with it.

History and psychology echo this truth over and over. The Columbine shooters—one driven by control and superiority, the other by despair and self-hatred. The Parkland shooter, drowning in loss and resentment, seeking control through destruction. John Hinckley Jr., confusing obsession for love. Lee Harvey Oswald, isolated and invisible, trying to carve meaning into history with a bullet. Different names, different motives, but beneath them all, the same fracture: a loss of belonging.

Violence is not born in an instant. It's cultivated. It begins in the small corners of the heart in the moments when compassion dies and pride takes its place. When we start mocking weakness instead of helping it. When we choose dominance over understanding. When pain becomes easier to spread than to heal.

And here's the quiet horror Dante understood: The river of blood isn't filled with monsters. It's filled with people who once thought they were right. People who justified harm in the name of pride, power, justice, or survival.

Violence always begins with a story—one that says, "I was wronged" or "I had no choice" or "They deserved it." It's the story we tell ourselves when we stop recognizing the humanity on the other side. And by the time the story ends, we've forgotten that the monster we feared was never real—it was just the part of ourselves we refused to face.

The Death of Empathy

Empathy doesn't die in one moment—it fades quietly. It begins when we stop listening. When we scroll past suffering because it's inconvenient. When we tell ourselves, "That's not my problem." Over time, the heart hardens and the line between apathy and cruelty begins to blur.

That's how anger becomes wrath. Pain becomes cruelty. Fear becomes domination. Violence isn't born from strength—it's born from disconnection. It's what happens when the soul forgets it belongs to something greater than itself.

Dante's river of blood wasn't just punishment—it was prophecy. He saw what happens when humanity forgets how to feel. When the voice of compassion grows faint and is replaced by the roar of pride and resentment. Those submerged in that river aren't merely sinners—they're reminders of what happens when empathy is stripped away, drop by drop, until all that remains is instinct.

In our world, the same river flows invisibly through everyday life. You see it in the driver who rages over a mistake. In the parent who lashes out from exhaustion. In the friend who ghosts you instead of being honest. In yourself, when bitterness feels easier than forgiveness.

The death of empathy is not a headline. It's a slow erosion; one that begins the moment we stop imagining what it feels like to be someone else. And when that imagination dies, we stop being fully human.

The cure isn't found in sermons or systems. It begins in small resurrections—one kind word, one moment of understanding, one decision to stay soft when the world tells you to harden. Because empathy, like any muscle, atrophies when neglected but strengthens when practiced.

And here's the truth Dante knew: Hell is not just fire—it's the absence of warmth. The absence of empathy is Hell.

The River Overflows

We keep asking why. Why the violence, the rage, the cruelty? Why the endless stream of headlines, of lives cut short, of moments that stain entire generations? But the truth is, we already know why. We just don't want to look that deep.

Violence doesn't appear out of nowhere—it's cultivated in silence. It begins long before the breaking point, in the invisible spaces where people feel unseen, unheard, and unloved. That's where the river starts—a trickle of loneliness that grows into a flood of despair.

We tell ourselves these are isolated events—"bad apples," "mental illness," "evil people"—but that's a comfortable lie. The real cause is spiritual starvation. We live in a culture that rewards dominance, mocks vulnerability, and confuses attention for love. We glorify those who take and forget those who give. Then we act surprised when the river overflows.

Every time we turn away from compassion, every time we choose indifference over involvement, we feed that current. Every unhealed wound, every neglected soul, every moment of silent despair adds another drop to the flood.

We've mistaken silence for peace, control for strength, and isolation for safety, but those are illusions. Silence festers. Control cracks. Isolation suffocates. And when enough hearts harden, the river breaks its banks.

Dante saw this centuries ago: the violent trapped in their own boiling blood, patrolled by centaurs to keep them submerged. But here's what he couldn't have imagined—the river has risen. It's no longer confined to Hell. It's flowing through our cities, our homes, our hearts.

And here's the hard truth: We're all standing in it. Every time we dehumanize, dismiss, or disconnect, we step a little deeper into that blood-red tide.

But the same current that destroys can also cleanse if we're willing to wade back toward empathy. When we choose to see, to listen, to care, the river begins to cool. It doesn't happen all at once. Redemption never does. But the moment we remember that connection is sacred—that every life is bound to every other—the water starts to clear.

The river overflows because we forget how to love. It will calm the moment we remember.

The Way Back

The way back isn't paved with judgment—it's built with compassion. It doesn't begin in politics, protests, or policies. It begins quietly in the hidden space between your heart and someone else's.

To heal the violence around us, we must first heal the violence within us. Because no matter how civilized we seem, every person carries the same fire and the same capacity to wound or to heal. The question isn't whether the fire exists. It's whether we've learned to tend it or let it burn.

Anger left unexamined becomes bitterness. Bitterness left unchecked becomes cruelty. Cruelty left unhealed becomes history repeating itself.

The way back is remembering what the world forgot—that connection is not weakness and empathy is not a luxury. It's strength. It's the very architecture of a soul that's alive.

Every person who lashes out has, in some way, already been broken inside. That doesn't excuse the act, but it does explain the sickness. Violence is a symptom of separation. Healing begins when we restore belonging.

You can't stop every tragedy in the world, but you can stop the one that begins in your own heart. You can choose to see the humanity in others—even those who've forgotten theirs. You can forgive yourself for the moments when you were the one who hurt and decide that your story doesn't end there.

This is how redemption works. Not through grand gestures or dramatic revelations but through one quiet decision at a time—to listen instead of accuse, to reach instead of retreat, to love instead of fear.

Dante's centaurs patrolled the riverbanks to restrain the violent, but your centaur lives within you—the part that must keep your instincts from overrunning your soul. The beast is not the enemy; it's the reminder that you have a choice. Every day, you decide which part of yourself you will obey.

Power without compassion is savagery. But power guided by love—that's transformation.

And that's the way back.

Healing the Violence Within

So where do we begin? How do we heal the silent epidemic of anger, disconnection, and fear that's eating away at the world around us?

It starts where every real transformation begins—in the heart. Not the heart that beats but the heart that feels.

The cure for violence isn't control; it's connection. It's remembering who you are beneath the armor—not the version shaped by pain, pride, or survival, but the one born before the world taught you to hide. The open self. The loving self. The self that knows we were created not just to exist but to give, to serve, to contribute.

When you return to that self, something shifts. You begin to live from abundance instead of fear. You stop guarding love like it's fragile and start offering it like it's infinite. That's when healing begins—not just for you, but for everyone your life touches.

We weren't designed to live divided. We were made for communion with God, with others, and with ourselves. But modern life has made isolation a virtue. We call distance "peace." We call apathy "strength." We build walls and call them boundaries, forgetting that walls don't just keep others out—they keep love out too.

And in that quiet isolation, hatred festers—first toward others, then toward ourselves. Because deep down, the soul knows when it's been cut off from its purpose. It knows it was meant to give, to forgive, to connect. This is the quiet Hell of our age: not fire, but separation. Not punishment but paralysis. Not damnation but disconnection.

The way back is not about fixing the world; it's about reawakening the parts of yourself that still remember love. Every act of kindness, every honest word, every moment of grace is a bridge back to that truth. When you choose compassion, you are performing rebellion against Hell itself.

Dante walked through the darkness to understand what happens when love is forgotten. You walk through yours to remember.

Because when you heal the violence within, the world around you begins to heal too. And when love moves through you—quietly, freely, without expectation—it ripples farther than you'll ever see.

Breaking the Cycle of Self-Hatred: Finding Worth Within

In the chapter on violence, especially the violence we turn inward, we need to address how self-hatred often grows in the shadows of unrequited love and unmet validation. When someone doesn't return our feelings, it can make us question our own value. This is a common human experience, but it can lead to a cycle where we start to see ourselves through the lens of that rejection. We begin to believe that we're not enough, and we might lash out at ourselves internally, wondering why we're not worthy of that love.

But here's the truth: When we rely on others to define our worth, we give away our power. Self-hatred is a form of internal violence that can pull us into a deep depression, making us believe that we're unlovable. But the journey out of that darkness begins with recognizing that your worth isn't determined by someone else's inability to see it.

In this section, we'll explore how to break that cycle by turning inward with compassion. Instead of using rejection as a reason to harm ourselves, we can use it as a stepping stone to build a stronger sense of self-worth that comes from within. We'll talk about practical steps to nurture self-acceptance, replace negative self-talk with kindness, and find validation in our own eyes rather than in the eyes of others.

Let Them Go

I think it's important to point this out: When people walk out of your life, *let them go*. They were never meant to stay. When people do not match your efforts, let them go. Don't keep fighting for someone who will not fight for you. And even if they were meant for you, sometimes God still requires distance, a season apart so both hearts can grow into who they must become.

I'll be honest, when things didn't go my way with Linda, I got depressed at first, but just for a brief moment. But in that moment, we all face a choice; how we will respond, how we will think, how we will process what's happened. We can either create from our pain and make something beautiful, or we can sink deeper into it.

I chose to write from my pain. And that pain became purpose. What once broke me now fuels me. I began asking people how they were really doing—not out of curiosity, but compassion. I started listening, not to reply, but to understand.

The situation with Linda didn't destroy me; it redirected me. It reignited something in me and made me realize I had a calling to reach those who are silently hurting, the ones smiling through storms, pretending everything's fine while fighting battles no one sees. My healing became my message. My pain became my ministry.

I reminded myself what I believe—things don't happen *to* me, they happen *for* me. Everything. The good and the bad.

I believe the Bible when it says, "All things work together for the good of those who love God and are the called according to His purpose" (Romans 8:28). You are also called according to His purpose. So when someone leaves, stop chasing them.

Everything that happens—even the heartbreaks—is for you. It's designed to build you, stretch you, and awaken what comfort kept asleep.

It's easy to fall into a depression, but remember this: I've walked through Hell, and so have many of you. We have to keep reminding ourselves of the pitfalls and the monsters that try to drag us back down. Because even in loss, God is still working. Even in absence, Heaven still moves.

And that's when I realized something deeper—the pain I felt with Linda wasn't just my pain. It was the same quiet ache millions of people carry in silence, the same loneliness that turns hearts hard and keeps us from the connection we were designed for. That's where the real danger begins—not in heartbreak itself, but in the isolation that follows.

The Quiet Hell of Isolation

But too often, especially in modern America, we live as if the opposite were true.

We isolate. We protect. We "mind our business." We say, "I've got enough of my own problems." And slowly, without realizing it, we build invisible walls around our hearts. We convince ourselves that privacy is peace, but really it's a quiet suffocation.

In this isolation, hatred begins to grow—not only toward others, but toward ourselves. Because the soul knows when it's being held back from its purpose. It knows it was made for contribution, not competition. It knows love is its native language.

When we deny that nature, society begins to rot from the inside. We start seeing other people as burdens—something to "deal with" on the way to our goals. The world becomes a series of obstacles instead of connections. That's when we fall into the modern Hell: a place not of fire but of separation.

And just like in Dante's *Inferno*, this Hell is of our own making. Every act of cruelty, every moment of apathy, every refusal to love—it all adds another stone to the wall between us and the divine.

The way back isn't found through laws, politics, or punishment. It's found through becoming real again. Through remembering that the cure for violence isn't control—it's connection. When we heal the violence within, we heal the world without.

Because when a person lives in love, the ripples never stop.

Thought Exercises: Healing the Violence Within

1. **The Stranger Within**

Sit quietly and ask yourself: "What parts of me have I abandoned?"

Write down one quality, passion, or belief you've buried to "fit in" or protect yourself.

Then ask: "What would my life look like if I welcomed that part back home?"

2. **The Mirror of Blame**

Think about someone you've judged harshly or distanced yourself from.

Ask: "What pain might they be carrying that I don't see?"

This isn't about excusing harm—it's about seeing humanity where your anger once built walls.

3. **The Abundance Test**

Recall the last time you gave something—your time, attention, or kindness—without expecting anything in return. How did it make you feel? Compare that feeling to the last time you withheld love out of fear or resentment. Notice which one felt more natural to your soul.

4. **The Quiet America**

Reflect on how often you truly connect with the people around you—your neighbors, co-workers, even strangers. Are you part of your community or merely existing beside it? Write one way you can contribute to the lives around you this week, no matter how small.

5. **The River Within**

In Dante's Inferno, the violent are submerged in a river of boiling blood—symbolic of being consumed by their own rage.

Ask: "Where in my life do I still boil?

What old resentment or grief still burns inside me?"

Imagine cooling that river through compassion—not for the world, but for yourself first.

6. **The Sacred Trade**

Every day we trade something—time, energy, attention.

Ask: "What am I trading my soul's peace for?

Is it worth it?"

Then decide on one small trade to reverse tomorrow—give something loving where you'd normally give indifference.

7. **The Ripple**

Do one quiet act of service this week that no one will ever know about. Don't post it. Don't talk about it. Just let it ripple. That's how you learn that real love doesn't need applause, it just needs expression.

Closing: The Descent into Deception

As the echoes of violence fade, the air in Dante's world grows heavier—not with rage, but with reason gone wrong. The fire of anger burns hot and brief, but deceit is colder, quieter, more patient. It smiles where wrath shouts. It calculates where pride charges forward.

The Seventh Circle revealed what happens when pain explodes outward—when hatred wounds the body and the world around it. But in the Eighth Circle, we'll witness a subtler corruption: What happens when the same pride learns to disguise itself. Here, evil no longer needs to shout or strike; it only needs to whisper convincingly enough to be believed.

Fraud is the mind weaponized. It's the moment the soul

learns to wear masks—to manipulate truth for gain, to twist sincerity into strategy, and to turn trust into a tool. If violence is the hand that kills, fraud is the smile that lies.

And this is where Hell becomes complicated—because now sin looks civilized. It dresses in respectability. It preaches morality. It promises progress. But beneath the polish is poison, and beneath the charm is control.

This next descent isn't about brute force—it's about intention. We're entering the realm where betrayal begins in thought long before it ever becomes action. Where the corruption of truth destroys not only others but also the self that once believed in honesty.

As we step into the Eighth Circle, remember: The greatest deceptions are never told—they are lived. And every mask we wear to protect ourselves from pain eventually becomes the prison that keeps us from love.

The worst kind of fraud is self-deception—
when the liar believes his own lie.

Unknown

Chapter 14

The Mask of Deception: The Eighth Circle—Fraud

The Descent into Deceit

After the rivers of blood and the tombs of fire, Dante and Virgil descend again—this time into a vast, stony pit spiraling downward in ten great ditches. The air is no longer thick with rage or the smell of burning flesh; it's quieter here, eerily calculated. The silence itself feels suspicious, as if even the wind is pretending to be still.

Here dwells the sin of fraud—truth twisted on purpose. These souls didn't lose control like the wrathful or crave without limit like the gluttonous. They knew what they were doing. They planned their deception, rehearsed it, refined it. Every lie was an act of intellect turned against integrity, and every manipulation was a deliberate performance.

And their punishments are fitting. Those who led others astray are whipped by demons—the same way they once drove people with words. Those who filled the world with filth now wade in it, submerged in the very sludge they spread. Those who shined too brightly for their own advantage are wrapped in flames—their false brilliance now their torment.

Here, the light of reason has curdled into arrogance and wisdom has become a weapon. Fraud is colder than anger and quieter than pride. It doesn't scream or strike—it smiles. It shakes your hand while hiding the knife.

Each soul in this circle is chained not by force but by the weight of its own performance. Every deception it once mastered now mirrors back the truth it tried to avoid. The deeper Dante travels, the clearer the pattern becomes: The further the soul drifts from sincerity, the heavier it becomes.

In this place, illusion is currency, masks are identity, and every lie whispered in life echoes forever in the dark.

Fraud As the Corruption of Covenant

Fraud is more than dishonesty—it's betrayal dressed in logic. It's the corruption of covenant and the breaking of the invisible thread that binds trust, truth, and relationship together. Where violence destroys the body, fraud poisons the bond between souls. It's a sin of intellect, not impulse—the mind choosing manipulation over meaning.

In Dante's vision, this makes fraud far more chilling than the bloodshed of the previous circle. Violence can come from passion, desperation, or even ignorance. But fraud? Fraud is premeditated. It studies its victim, mimics sincerity, and turns trust into a tool. It doesn't act out of chaos—it acts out of calculation.

This is the sin of the serpent—deceit disguised as wisdom. In Eden, the first lie didn't shout; it reasoned. It asked a question. It sounded intelligent. And that's what makes this circle so dangerous. Fraud wears the tone of enlightenment. It sounds educated, strategic, justified. But underneath its sophistication lies rebellion against truth itself.

Fraud is the mind's rebellion against covenant. It takes what was sacred—honesty, loyalty, communion—and treats it as leverage. It is intellect without compassion and reason without reverence. Once truth becomes negotiable, everything holy begins to crumble.

That's why Dante considered this circle worse than the violent ones above. Because when the world loses truth, everything that depends on it—trust, justice, love, faith—collapses with it. Fraud is not just a crime of deceit; it's a dismantling of creation's order, one lie at a time.

The Intellect Without Heart

Fraud is not stupidity; it's brilliance without conscience. It's the mind stripped of mercy and the intellect severed from empathy. It's the moment knowledge becomes a weapon instead of a light.

That's why the Eighth Circle feels so chilling. These souls aren't here because they were ignorant; they're here because they knew better and still chose deceit. Their sin wasn't confusion; it was calculation. They used truth not to heal but to harm.

You can see it everywhere today. In politics, where spin replaces sincerity. In business, where profit outweighs integrity. In relationships, where manipulation hides behind charm. Even in faith, where people twist scripture to justify ego.

This is intellect gone cold and cleverness divorced from compassion. And when that happens, even truth itself becomes dangerous.

Because truth without love isn't wisdom—it's warfare.

That's the hidden lesson of Dante's Eighth Circle: You can be right and still be wrong. You can know the facts but miss the heart. You can win the argument and lose your soul.

Fraud happens every time intelligence outpaces humility. When we use knowledge to elevate ourselves instead of enlighten others, we start building our own little circles of Hell—boardrooms of greed, pulpits of pride, and conversations where empathy dies in the name of being "right."

And yet, this circle isn't hopeless. Even here, Dante shows us something redemptive: awareness. The same mind that deceived can learn discernment. The same intellect that once schemed can learn to serve.

Because wisdom, when reunited with love, becomes light again. It stops manipulating and starts mending. It stops performing and starts transforming.

That's how intellect finds its heart again—by remembering that its purpose was never to dominate but to understand.

The Return to Truth

The way out of deception isn't perfection—it's confession. Not to a crowd, not to a confessional booth, but to your own soul.

It begins the moment you stop rehearsing and start revealing. When you stop performing strength and admit, "I'm tired." When you stop pretending control and whisper, "I'm scared." When you stop curating your life and start actually living it.

That's not weakness—that's resurrection.

Truth burns, yes, but it also purifies. It melts the mask. It exposes what's real and reveals what was always beautiful underneath. Once you've tasted the peace that comes from living honestly, deception feels like poison.

And maybe that's the real message of Dante's Eighth Circle: Hell isn't filled with liars because they fooled others—it's filled with liars because they fooled themselves. They forgot who they were beneath the illusion.

The journey back is simple but not easy. It's one act of truth at a time. One honest word. One unfiltered prayer. One vulnerable conversation.

Each one brings you closer to the surface, closer to light, closer to freedom.

Because truth isn't the end of the journey—it's the beginning of becoming real again.

Reflection

Fraud, at its core, is the rejection of sincerity. It's what happens when we value how things look over how they are. The fraudsters in Dante's pit aren't just liars—they're actors who forgot they were acting.

We all do it sometimes—play roles, hide truths, protect images. But every mask we shed brings us closer to peace. Every truth we tell brings light into the pit.

Because the Eighth Circle isn't just Dante's—it's ours. We walk through it every day in the world around us. And every moment we choose truth over illusion, we climb one step closer to the light.

Thought Exercises: The Authentic You

1. **Identify the Mask**

   Take a quiet moment and ask yourself: Where am I pretending? Write down situations where you feel you're performing instead of being real—at work, on social media, with friends, or even with family.

   For each, ask: "Why am I pretending? What fear or expectation is driving this mask?"

2. **Reconnect with Your Voice**

   Think of a passion, belief, or truth you've hidden from the world out of fear of judgment.

   How could you express this truth in a small, safe way this week?

   Example: Share your opinion in a meeting, create art, volunteer, or simply tell someone honestly how you feel.

3. **The Contribution Check**

   Ask yourself: "How am I contributing to others' lives?"

   Make a list of one small thing you can give this week—your time, energy, attention, or knowledge—without expecting anything in return.

   Notice how it makes you feel. Authentic contribution feeds the soul.

4. **Mirror Reflection**

   Look in the mirror and say aloud: "I am enough. I don't need to perform for approval."

   Repeat this daily for a week.

   Reflect on any resistance you feel—that resistance often points to where your fraud lives.

5. **Compare, Don't Copy**

   When you feel envy or comparison, pause and ask:

"What part of this person's life inspires me? And how can I achieve that without pretending to be them?"

Focus on modeling values, not imitation. Authenticity grows when you honor your path.

6. **The Honest Journal**

Spend five minutes a day writing what's true for you—no filters, no justification.

Write about feelings, mistakes, desires, or dreams. Don't edit. Don't perform. Let your raw self speak.

7. **Acts of Love over Image**

Do one act this week that expresses love or kindness—not for praise, recognition, or social clout, but simply because it's who you are.

Observe the difference between giving from your real self versus giving for performance.

False friends are worse than open enemies.

Proverbial wisdom

Chapter 15

The World of Illusion: Modern Fraud and the Search for Authenticity

The Brunch That Wasn't Real

I remember once complimenting someone on a beautiful brunch photo they posted—the kind that looked straight out of a lifestyle magazine. The lighting was perfect, the food arranged like art, the caption heartfelt: "Grateful for slow mornings and simple things."

When I saw them later, I said, "That lunch looked amazing."

They laughed—not the embarrassed kind, but the exhausted kind—and said, "Oh, that? The food was cold. We spent ten minutes taking pictures, and my friend was on their phone the whole time. I just posted it because it looked happy."

That moment stuck with me. Not because of the photo but because of the honesty that followed. They didn't post to deceive; they posted to *feel* okay. To look like they were living the life they wished they had.

And that's the quiet danger of modern fraud—it doesn't always come from malice. Sometimes it's born from longing. We curate peace when we don't feel it, post connection when we feel alone, and edit joy when it's missing. The lie isn't in the photo—it's in the belief that our worth depends on how convincing the picture looks.

We've all done it, haven't we? Smiled for the camera when our heart was breaking. Posted words of gratitude while quietly battling anxiety. Presented a version of ourselves that looked strong because admitting weakness felt unsafe. The world rewards appearances, not authenticity, and the temptation to perform is everywhere.

That brunch photo wasn't a lie in the traditional sense; it was a mirror of what so many of us do every day. We don't lie to harm; we lie to belong. We edit reality not out of pride but out of pain—hoping someone, somewhere, will see the image and think, *They're doing great*.

But here's the truth: Pretending to be whole keeps you from ever becoming whole. The moment you start curating your truth for approval, you begin to lose your peace.

And that's where we find ourselves now—in an age where illusion has been industrialized.

The Modern Fraud

Fraud didn't die in Dante's pit—it just changed its wardrobe. It no longer hides in cloaks and contracts; now it scrolls your feed, smiles through screens, and sells you "authenticity" in carefully edited doses.

Today, deceit isn't whispered in alleys—it's marketed in high-definition. Politicians twist truth into branding. Corporations build entire campaigns on empathy they don't feel. Influencers peddle "realness" that's anything but real. We call it content, strategy, and optics, but at its core, it's still the ancient lie: illusion over integrity.

Fraud has gone digital, but its motive hasn't changed. It promises belonging while deepening loneliness. It offers connection while rewarding performance. We build personas instead of character and followers instead of friendships. The algorithm becomes our confessor, and likes become our sacraments.

The saddest part? Most of this fraud isn't born from malice—it's born from fear. Fear of rejection. Fear of being unseen. Fear that the real self won't be enough. So we create masks to survive, forgetting that masks, once worn too long, begin to suffocate their wearer.

This is the quiet tragedy of modern life: people living convincing lies, scrolling through illusions of intimacy, and calling it community. We've mistaken attention for love and exposure for purpose.

Dante's sinners used words to deceive others; we use images to deceive ourselves. But the cost is the same. Every falsehood erodes the soul. Every performance distances us from peace.

The truth is, fraud today doesn't just fill prisons—it fills timelines. It's not measured in money lost but in authenticity abandoned. And somewhere between filters and followers, humanity has forgotten that the truth—raw, unpolished, inconvenient truth—is the only thing that can still set us free.

The Masks We Wear

Everyone wears a mask. Some are painted with charm, others with confidence, some with humor so convincing that we even start believing it. We learn early how to perform: how to say what keeps the peace, how to smile through pain, how to look "fine" when we're breaking inside. And after a while, we forget we're acting.

I've watched people build entire identities out of defense mechanisms—ambition to hide insecurity, humor to hide fear, control to hide chaos. The mask becomes armor, but armor is heavy. You start confusing the weight you carry with the person you are.

The danger of masks isn't just deception; it's disconnection. Every time you hide behind one, you trade authenticity for approval. You silence your real voice in exchange for applause that never satisfies. It's like living in a costume so long that your own reflection starts to feel like a stranger.

I've been there. I've played the part of the one who "has it together," who never needs help, who's always "good." But beneath that performance was exhaustion—the quiet kind that doesn't show on your face but steals your peace. The longer you wear the mask, the more you begin to fear what might happen if someone sees you without it.

But here's the truth: The people meant for you—the ones who truly love you—don't need the mask. They need the real you, scars and all. They need your laughter that isn't rehearsed, your honesty that isn't filtered, your presence that isn't performing.

The world doesn't need another flawless image; it needs the courage of someone who's willing to be seen.

So, if you've been pretending—if you've been smiling through storms, performing peace, or carrying an image that doesn't match your heart—it's time to lay it down. Remove the armor. Take off the mask. Let your soul breathe again.

Because authenticity isn't weakness. It's the return of strength.

A World of Illusion

We live in a world that prizes appearance over authenticity. Where truth has to compete with filters, and depth loses to distraction.

Everywhere you look, illusion sells. People don't build lives anymore—they build brands. We measure worth in engagement, not integrity, and in likes, not love. We scroll through curated perfection, then call it reality. And the saddest part? We know it's not real but we keep chasing it anyway.

Illusion is the new oxygen. We inhale other people's highlight reels and exhale our own, trying to convince the world—and ourselves—that everything is fine. But beneath the digital gloss, souls are starving. People don't want more content; they want connection. They don't want to be impressed; they want to be understood.

We've mistaken visibility for value. Fame for fulfillment. Recognition for purpose. But attention is not affection. And being seen is not the same as being known.

That's the quiet tragedy of this modern fraud: We're so busy performing that we forget how to live. We're surrounded by noise but aching for meaning. We're constantly "connected" but deeply alone.

Dante's fraudsters used words to deceive others; today, we use images to deceive ourselves. We don't forge documents—we forge identities. The city of Dis has gone digital, and its glow fits neatly in our palms.

But truth still calls to us—a whisper cutting through the static. It says: "Be real." Drop the pose. You are enough without the performance. Because every illusion, no matter how dazzling, eventually fades. But authenticity—that lasts forever.

The Wake-Up Call

Sometimes it takes a shock to remind us what's real. For me, that moment came with the passing of Charlie Kirk. I didn't follow every word he said. But I respected his conviction—his willingness to stand for what he believed, to show up, to give, to speak light into dark places.

When news of his assassination broke, it didn't just sadden me; it sobered me. It was as if the noise of the world went silent for a second, and I heard a single question echo inside me: *What am I doing with the time I've been given?*

Because life is fragile. We pretend it isn't, we fill our days with deadlines, devices, and distractions, but every breath is a borrowed miracle. And when someone who dared to live with purpose is suddenly gone, the illusion of "someday" shatters. There is no "later." There is only now.

That realization became the fuel for this book. I wanted to help people remember what actually matters—not applause, not perfection, but contribution. To give what's inside you before the clock runs out. To live in such a way that when you're gone, your love and your courage keep echoing.

Charlie's death reminded me that authenticity isn't optional; it's sacred. We are here to give, to lift, to serve, to leave behind something that outlasts us. That's how you defeat the fraud of this world: by refusing to perform and daring to contribute.

The truth is, legacy isn't built by fame. It's built by faithfulness. It's built every time you choose honesty over image, compassion over comfort, and courage over fear.

So the wake-up call isn't just about death, it's about life. It's a reminder to stop hiding, stop waiting, and stop pretending. To live fully, love deeply, and speak truth while you still can.

Because one day, the curtain falls, and all that will remain is what was real.

The Trap of Performance

The greatest lie of modern life is that success can substitute for peace. We live in a culture that teaches us to perform, not to live. Everything becomes a stage: work, relationships, even faith. We learn to measure our worth by applause, not alignment. We build our lives for visibility instead of vitality.

At first, performance feels harmless. You post, you smile, you hustle—you play the part. But over time, the act consumes the actor. You start living for optics instead of purpose. Every move becomes a strategy, every smile a disguise. And slowly, you lose the ability to tell where the mask ends and you begin.

That's the quiet prison of performance: It feels like control, but it's actually captivity.

You start comparing your behind-the-scenes to everyone else's highlight reel. You scroll through their vacations, their houses, their filtered joy, and something inside you starts whispering, "I'm behind." So you push harder. Work more. Pretend more. Smile wider.

And the world claps. But your soul stays tired.

Dante's fraudsters lied to others; we lie to ourselves. We convince ourselves that if we just achieve a little more, post a little better, look a little stronger, we'll finally feel whole. But you can't "fake it till you make it" with the soul. It knows the difference.

Wholeness doesn't come from performing for love. It comes from being loved while unmasked.

The trap of performance is that it never ends. The spotlight always shifts, the audience always changes, and the applause always fades. But when you live from authenticity, you no longer need the stage. You live from truth—steady, grounded, unshakable.

So yes, chase excellence. Dream boldly. Build something meaningful. But let your success be an overflow of your authenticity, not a substitute for it.

Because the world doesn't need another performance. It needs your presence—the real, unpolished, unfiltered you.

Closing: From Illusion to Betrayal

Every circle so far has revealed a deeper fracture in the soul. But none wound the heart like this next one.

Fraud was the lie, but treachery is the betrayal. Fraud bends truth; treachery breaks trust. Fraud hides behind a mask; treachery smiles while holding the knife.

When Dante leaves the Eighth Circle, he enters a place where even deceit freezes. The warmth of manipulation gives way to the cold silence of betrayal—the point where love itself turns against love.

If fraud is intellect without empathy, then treachery is intimacy without loyalty.

It is the final corruption: not of mind, not of will, but of the heart. And in its frozen pit, Dante shows us the cost of living without love: a soul so numb that even the fires of Hell can't melt it. That's where we go next, into the Ninth Circle, where every broken promise and every betrayed heart waits to be seen for what it is—not just evil, but absence, and not just sin, but the end of relationship itself.

The hottest places in Hell are reserved for those who, in times of great moral crisis, maintain their neutrality.

attributed to Dante Alighieri

Chapter 16

The Frozen Heart: Treachery and the Ninth Circle

The Descent into the Frozen Pit

After the tombs of flame, the rivers of blood, and the fires of fraud, Dante and Virgil descend into a silence more terrifying than any scream—the Ninth Circle of Hell, where treachery reigns. Here, the air itself is frozen. The world is still, not with peace, but with the suffocating quiet of souls locked in eternal ice. Bodies are twisted and bound, stripped of warmth, light, and motion. Their punishment reflects their crime: the betrayal of trust and the cold severing of love.

Where fraud was cunning and deceitful, treachery is deliberate and final. It is not a moment of weakness but a calculated act—the death of loyalty itself.

In this final circle, Dante maps the hierarchy of betrayal with chilling precision. Those who betrayed family lie in Caina, frozen up to their necks, their faces bowed in silent shame. Deeper still, in Antenora, lie those who betrayed country and community—their frozen faces turned upward, defiant yet helpless. Ptolomea holds those who betrayed the sacred bond of hospitality—the trust between guest and host. And in the deepest abyss, Judecca, lie the ultimate traitors—those who turned against their benefactors, their leaders, and even God. Here, even tears freeze before they can fall.

Dante's frozen *Inferno* reveals something profound: that the absence of love is colder than the presence of hate. Fire may destroy, but ice isolates—it hardens, numbs, and suffocates the human heart.

We'll now explore each realm—not merely as ancient poetry, but as a reflection of modern life. For treachery is not confined to the pages of the *Divine Comedy*; it walks among us still, in broken trust, silent betrayal, and the slow freeze of human connection.

Caina: Betrayers of Family

Caina is the first layer of the Ninth Circle, where betrayal begins at its most intimate level—the family. It is named after Cain, who struck down his own brother, marking humanity's first recorded act of treachery. Here, those who betrayed blood and kin are trapped neck-deep in ice, unable to move, their faces bowed in shame. Their crime wasn't political or strategic—it was personal. They destroyed the bonds meant to be sacred: love, trust, and belonging.

The punishment mirrors the sin. The cold immobilizes them just as betrayal freezes relationships in life. They can see each other, but they cannot touch. They can cry, but they cannot feel warmth. They are locked in eternal isolation—a mirror of what happens when love is violated from within one's own home.

Family is meant to be the first refuge, the first source of identity and safety. When that refuge becomes a battlefield, something inside the soul fractures. Whether it is physical abuse, emotional neglect, manipulation, or abandonment, betrayal from family wounds deeper than any external enemy could. It doesn't just break trust—it reshapes how we see love itself.

Caina is not a distant myth. It's the story of every child who was never believed, every parent who abandoned their role, every sibling who betrayed loyalty for envy. It's the chilling silence that fills households where forgiveness has been replaced by pride.

But Dante's vision also carries a warning for us—one that extends beyond the literal punishment. When we turn our hearts cold toward family, we don't just betray them; we betray the divine order of love itself.

Forgiveness becomes the act that thaws the ice. It doesn't mean forgetting or reconciling with danger. It means refusing to remain frozen. Forgiveness is reclaiming the warmth of your own heart, even when others have turned theirs to stone.

A Personal Story: The Fracture of Family

Betrayal from strangers cuts, but betrayal from blood reshapes the soul. There was a time when I believed family meant protection—that no matter what storms raged outside, there would always be warmth within. But warmth can vanish fast when trust breaks. Sometimes, the people who should hold you the closest are the ones who wound you the deepest.

When my own mother wrestled with addiction, it wasn't just her body that became consumed—it was her love. One moment she was there, tender and alive; the next, her eyes were distant, her voice sharp, her affection unpredictable. Home became a place of both love and fear. I learned to read moods like weather, always anticipating when the next storm might come.

That kind of betrayal doesn't always announce itself loudly. Sometimes it happens in quiet neglect—in the moments when you realize that the person who should love you most is no longer capable of showing it. The pain isn't just emotional; it's existential. It makes you question your worth, your safety, and even your ability to trust.

Years later, I came to understand something I couldn't see back then—she wasn't just lost in her addiction. She was enslaved by it. Her betrayal wasn't born of hatred but of bondage. And that realization changed everything. It didn't excuse the pain, but it reframed it. Addiction had stolen from both of us.

That's the nature of betrayal in Caina—it's never clean. It entangles love, loyalty, and pain until you can't tell where one ends and the other begins. But even there, in the coldest moments, something greater whispers—the call to forgive, not for them, but for your own freedom.

Forgiveness and Caina: The Thawing of the Soul

The betrayal of family is unlike any other pain. It's intimate, personal, and unforgettable. The wounds don't just scar the surface—they seep into the bones of your identity. Betrayal from a stranger hurts your pride. Betrayal from blood fractures your soul.

Caina represents that fracture—the coldness that follows when love is violated by those who were meant to protect it. Some betrayals come through abuse. Some through neglect. Others through addiction, manipulation, or abandonment. No matter the form, the result is the same—the ice forms slowly, hardening around the heart until you can no longer feel warmth.

But here is the paradox of healing: The only way to thaw the ice is to release what froze it—and that release is forgiveness.

Forgiveness is not forgetting. It is not denying the pain. It is not reconciliation when reconciliation would reopen wounds. Forgiveness is the act of reclaiming your own temperature. It is saying, "I will no longer let this pain define the climate of my soul."

When I began to forgive my mother, it wasn't because she earned it. It was because I couldn't keep living numb. I realized that every ounce of resentment kept me chained to the same storm she was drowning in. Unforgiveness is its own addiction—a slow poison that convinces you that holding it makes you strong, when all it does is keep you small.

Forgiveness is not weakness; it is warfare. It is steering the boat in a storm you didn't create. It's grabbing the oars of your own life and saying, "The waves don't get to decide who I become."

When you forgive, you reclaim authorship. The person who hurt you no longer writes the next chapter of your life—you do.

This doesn't mean you must trust again. Boundaries are wisdom, not bitterness. Some people belong in your prayers, not your presence. Forgiveness releases the weight of hate, but boundaries protect the light that remains.

Caina reminds us that betrayal is the coldest fire, but forgiveness is the only warmth that survives it. Every act of grace, every refusal to repeat the harm, every quiet decision to love anyway is a rebellion against the ice.

Forgiveness is not a single act; it is a practice. Some days you'll feel peace. Other days, the frost will creep back. That's okay. Healing isn't linear—it's cyclical. But every time you choose to thaw instead of freeze, you rise above the Ninth Circle.

Reflections on Caina: Family Betrayal and Forgiveness

1. **Where has betrayal touched my life?**

   Consider your family relationships. Have there been moments of neglect, abuse, or manipulation? Write them down without judgment. Naming them is the first step to understanding their impact.

2. **What emotions am I carrying?**

   Anger, fear, shame, sadness—these are natural responses to betrayal. Acknowledge them. Which of these emotions are frozen inside you like the souls in Caina? Which ones are guiding your actions today?

3. **Can I separate the person from their actions?**

   Think about the person who hurt you. What might have been their struggles, fears, or limitations? Understanding does not excuse the harm, but it can soften the grip of resentment on your heart.

4. **What part of myself am I hiding?**

   Betrayal often teaches us to protect ourselves by hiding, avoiding intimacy, or withholding trust. Which parts of your authentic self have been frozen or silenced because of past pain?

5. **Where can forgiveness free me?**

   Forgiveness is not about excusing the betrayal. It's about reclaiming your own heart. Who or what do you need to forgive—even if only internally—to thaw the ice and regain freedom?

6. **How can I protect without hardening?**

   Setting boundaries is essential, especially when betrayal comes from family. What boundaries do you need to establish to protect yourself while staying open to love and connection?

7. **What steps can I take toward reclaiming my boat?**

   Imagine your life as a boat navigating a stormy ocean. What actions today—journaling, therapy, conversation, or self-reflection—can help you regain control and move forward?

The Ice Within: When I Betrayed My Own Vows

Some of us can both be betrayed and the betrayer. I was both. When I look back at my marriage, I can admit now that I wasn't ready. I was in turmoil—broke, uncertain, and still trying to figure out who I was as a man. You need more than love to make a marriage work; you need stability, direction, and a sense of identity. We went to a pastor once for advice, and he told us, "No one is ever really ready for marriage." But that's not true. You need to have some things in order—emotionally, spiritually, and financially—or you end up building a covenant on sand.

Inside, I was scared. I wanted to be the provider, the leader, the husband my wife and son could depend on. But when I couldn't live up to that image, I sought validation somewhere else. That's when I started hosting those adult parties I spoke earlier about. This was something I justified as harmless fun, business networking, even empowerment. In reality, it was the ultimate betrayal.

At those parties, I felt alive. Important. Desired. I had thirty or forty models around me every week. Gorgeous women all fighting for my attention, and for a few hours, I could pretend I was on top of the world. Meanwhile my wife and child were home while I was chasing a feeling—not of love, but of worthiness. It was a false confidence, a temporary high wrapped in the illusion of control. But after every event, I came home more empty than the night before.

I hid it all—from my wife, from my friends, even from myself. But eventually, the distance grew. My wife and I stopped sleeping together. I'd spend nights on the couch, convincing myself she wasn't the right one for me, that she didn't believe in me, that she nagged too much. But those were excuses. Deep down, I knew the truth: I was betraying not just her but also my son—the boy who deserved to see a man of integrity leading his home.

When the marriage fell apart, I wanted to point fingers, but every time I looked closer, the finger pointed back at me. I wasn't ready for the responsibility of love. I didn't understand that leadership wasn't about control—it was about accountability. I ran when things got hard instead of standing firm.

In time, my faith was shaken. When the excitement of those parties faded, I realized I had nothing to run to. The validation, the models, the money—none of it could fix what was broken inside me. The truth hit me one night like cold water: *I traded a marriage for a moment of feeling important*. I had become the man in Proverbs 6:26— "The prostitute will reduce you to a loaf of bread." Even though these models weren't technically "prostitutes," they might as well have been. The people around me didn't care about me. They cared about what I provided. It was transactional, not transformational.

That realization broke me open. It forced me to face the real enemy: not my wife, not my circumstances, but the emptiness inside me. I began to pray again, to read scripture, and to sit in silence with my guilt. I started asking harder questions: Why did I need so much attention? Why did I run from love that demanded maturity? Why did I equate worthiness with being wanted?

Forgiveness didn't come overnight. It began with forgiving myself—not to excuse what I did, but to stop reliving it. I had to accept that redemption is not about rewriting the past but reclaiming your future. And as I learned to forgive myself, I found a strange peace—one that comes only when you stop hiding behind your own excuses and start living with truth.

People betray when they're trying to fill a void. They seek what they've lost inside themselves, hoping someone or something else can replace it. But nothing external can heal an internal wound. That healing comes only through confrontation, confession, and grace.

I betrayed my marriage. But that betrayal became my awakening—the beginning of the man I was meant to become.

Today, I'm divorced, but I have a son who's grown up surrounded by love. He has two parents who care deeply for him, a stepfather who loves him, and an incredible support system around him. What once looked like the end of a family became a different kind of beginning—one built on respect, forgiveness, and growth.

We'll discuss more about this in later chapters because it is so vital that you grasp the power of forgiveness. But for now, we will move on.

Redemption Beyond the Ice

No matter how far you've fallen, your story can be redeemed. What defines you is not the betrayal itself but what you choose to do afterward. Guilt may have its place—it wakes us up—but it was never meant to be a home. You don't have to live frozen in regret.

I tell you this not to brag that I was horrible before and now I'm not. I tell you this to reassure you—as someone who went through Hell and came back knowing myself and who I truly am. I came back as a conqueror. I don't glorify my past; I expose it so you can see that redemption is possible. You can fall, lose everything, and still rise stronger, wiser, and freer than before.

The truth is, there will always be people who want you to stay in your guilt. Some will remind you of what you did, not because they care about your growth, but because your redemption confronts their comfort. It forces them to see their own reflection in your forgiveness. But you don't owe anyone your continued suffering.

Freedom begins the moment you release

bitterness—toward yourself, toward others, toward the past. Forgiveness is not a sign of weakness; it is the most radical act of power you can perform. It says, "I am not bound by what broke me."

When you let go, you reclaim the authority over your own story. The weight lifts, not because the past changes, but because its grip does. You begin to see that your failure was not final—it was formative. God can use even the ashes of betrayal to build something beautiful.

You don't have to live in the cold. You don't have to keep punishing yourself for what's already been surrendered to grace. When you forgive yourself and others, you become free. And that freedom is what allows you to move forward with courage, integrity, and peace.

The ice doesn't melt all at once. Beneath every act of personal redemption lies another layer—the betrayals that shape nations, cultures, and even faith itself. What begins in the home spreads through the world, and every cold heart eventually chills the air around it.

For what is a man profited, if he shall gain the whole world, and lose his own soul?

Matthew 16:26 (KJV)

Chapter 17

The Silence of Ice: The Final Depths of Treachery

Transitioning from Caina to Antenora

Redemption begins in the personal—in the healing of our own hearts and the forgiveness of our own failures. But betrayal doesn't stop at the family table. Once the heart learns to turn cold, the chill spreads. What begins as private pain can become public corruption. The same ice that freezes love at home can extend into society, politics, and leadership—chilling entire communities.

The next layer of treachery that Dante describes, Antenora, is where loyalty to country, cause, or collective trust is shattered. Here, betrayal is no longer intimate; it is institutional. It's the kind of deceit that poisons nations, divides people, and turns communities against each other.

If Caina shows us the fracture of family, Antenora reveals the fracture of civilization. And both remind us that when the human heart grows cold, it doesn't just destroy relationships, it freezes the very world we live in.

Antenora: Betrayers of Country or Political Allegiance

In Antenora, the souls of those who betrayed their nation, their political allies, or their leaders lie deeper in the ice. Their punishment is harsher than Caina because their betrayal affects the wider community. It is the freezing of conscience in service to ambition and the severing of loyalty not just to people but to principle.

In Dante's *Inferno*, the souls of Antenora lie deeper in the ice, their bodies contorted and stiff, their very breath frozen. These are the betrayers of country, comrades, or cause—those who turned on their people for gain, power, or survival. The air itself is sharp and unfeeling; the silence here is political, not personal. It is the quiet that follows when truth itself has been silenced.

In Antenora, betrayal is no longer born from passion—it is calculated. It wears the face of leadership but carries the heart of deceit. It is the politician who sells out the people he swore to protect. The leader who prioritizes personal gain over public good. The insider who leaks, manipulates, or lies—not to survive, but to profit.

This level of treachery is devastating because it infects entire systems. When a single individual betrays another, the wound is personal. But when leaders betray those they lead, the wound becomes cultural—it spreads like frost through the veins of a nation. Trust collapses. Hope freezes. Communities fracture under the weight of disillusionment.

Modern Antenora

You don't have to look to medieval Italy to find Antenora. It's visible in every society that has chosen greed over justice, corruption over service, comfort over conviction. It's in the workplace where truth is silenced to protect image. It's in communities where loyalty to power outweighs loyalty to people. It's in nations where leaders abandon integrity and citizens turn on each other for ideology.

This is modern treachery—a slow cultural freeze.

And yet, the message of Dante—and the lesson of life—is this: *Integrity begins where compromise ends.* Every time you choose truth in a world that rewards deceit, you are defying Antenora. Every time you stand for justice when it costs you comfort, you are melting the ice.

Reflection: Personal Responsibility in a Frozen Culture

It's easy to condemn the politicians, the executives, or the elites. But betrayal doesn't always happen on stages of power. It happens in the small spaces too—when we abandon principle for approval, when we gossip instead of protect, when we stay silent when truth demands a voice. Every small act of integrity in your life—every honest word and every courageous stand—keeps you from becoming part of the freeze.

To remain warm in a cold world is an act of rebellion. To remain honest in a dishonest culture is an act of faith. And to remain loyal to truth when deception is easier—that is how you stay human.

Ptolomea: Betrayers of Guests and Hosts

If Antenora represents the betrayal of country and community, then Ptolomea is more intimate and more insidious. Here, Dante places those who betrayed the sacred trust of hospitality. These are the ones who smiled across a table and shared bread and warmth, only to strike when trust was at its most vulnerable.

In this frozen realm, the punishment fits the crime: Souls lie face-up in the ice, their eyes open, their tears freezing before they fall. It's as if they are forced to watch forever the very trust they destroyed. Even before their bodies die, their souls descend into Ptolomea—a haunting image of what happens when deceit and intimacy coexist.

The Betrayal of Safety

Hospitality is more than food or shelter—it's the offering of safety. When you welcome someone into your home, your life, or your heart, you make an unspoken vow: *You are safe here*. Those who betray this promise don't just wound the body—they violate the soul. They weaponize vulnerability. They turn comfort into a trap.

Modern Ptolomea lives in homes where kindness is used to control, in friendships that manipulate trust, in relationships that begin with warmth and end with deceit. It's the business partner who smiles while plotting your downfall. The friend who listens, only to use your words against you. The person who offers refuge but harbors resentment. This form of betrayal cuts deeply because it hides behind love, care, and belonging.

The Cold Mask of Pretended Warmth

Ptolomea shows us the danger of counterfeit compassion—of people who offer warmth not out of love but out of strategy. These are the betrayers who disguise manipulation as mercy. Their hearts remain cold even while their words sound kind. And the hardest part? Sometimes, we're guilty of it too—when we offer kindness to gain something in return, or when we pretend to forgive but still secretly resent. The lesson of Ptolomea is not only to beware of others' deceit but to confront our own hidden motives.

Healing After Betrayal of Trust

If you've ever been betrayed by someone who once made you feel safe, you know the pain that follows—confusion, disbelief, self-blame. You replay conversations, meals, and shared laughter, wondering how long the lie was alive. But there is freedom beyond that ice. Healing begins when you stop blaming yourself for believing in goodness. Trusting others is not your flaw; it's your humanity. The betrayer's deceit does not define your worth—their actions define theirs.

Forgiveness here is about reclaiming trust in yourself. You may not invite everyone in again, but you can open the door to peace. The lesson of Ptolomea is to protect your heart without turning it to stone—to keep loving, even after being deceived.

Reflection: Guarding Warmth Without Losing It

1. Have I ever been betrayed by someone I once trusted completely?
2. How did that experience shape the way I trust others today?
3. Do I use emotional distance as protection or as avoidance?
4. What does healthy trust look like for me now?
5. How can I offer kindness without compromising discernment?

Judecca: Betrayers of Benefactors and God

At the deepest point of the Ninth Circle lies Judecca—the final, most silent region of Hell. Here, the souls are fully encased in ice, twisted beneath its surface, unable to move, speak, or even weep. No sound, no flame, no motion—only stillness. For Dante, this is the bottom of the human condition: the point where love is completely extinguished and the soul is frozen in isolation.

These are the betrayers of benefactors, mentors, leaders, and of God Himself—those who turned against the very source of their good. It is named for Judas Iscariot, the disciple who betrayed Christ for silver. In Dante's vision, Judas is chewed eternally in the jaws of Lucifer along with Brutus and Cassius, the betrayers of Julius Caesar. Together, they represent the destruction of divine, personal, and political order.

The Death of Reverence

Judecca is where gratitude dies. To betray someone who trusted you is one thing, but to betray the very hand that lifted you up is another. This form of treachery is not merely disloyal; it is a rejection of grace itself. It's the student who undermines the teacher who believed in him. The disciple who denies the truth for comfort. The person who, blessed by opportunity, turns their back on the very source that gave them hope.

In life, these betrayals appear subtle—a slow decay of appreciation, a shift from humility to entitlement. But beneath it lies the root of all spiritual ruin: pride. The belief that we no longer owe gratitude, accountability, or devotion to anyone, not even God.

The Coldest Truth

What makes Judecca terrifying isn't punishment—it's the absence of warmth. No fire, no torment, no noise. Just stillness. Because ultimate betrayal isolates you from the Source of Love itself. You don't burn; you freeze. This is what happens when the heart becomes numb to grace. When ego replaces reverence and selfishness replaces submission. The result isn't chaos; it's silence. Because even hate has passion, but indifference has none.

The absence of love is colder than the presence of hate.

Modern Judecca

Judecca still exists—not beneath the earth, but in the hearts of those who forget gratitude. It's the culture that mocks faith while benefiting from its moral framework. It's the mentor betrayed by those he raised. It's the friend who turns on the one who once carried them. It's every moment we choose self-worship over reverence, choosing the throne over humility.

And yet, Dante's descent wasn't meant to end in despair—it was meant to remind us that even at the bottom, *there is a way out*. Because when Dante and Virgil reach this final depth, they do not perish—they climb. They ascend through the frozen core, emerging on the other side of the world, where light breaks through again. It is Dante's way of saying: Even from the deepest betrayal, redemption is possible.

The Way Back Up

No one is beyond redemption. The coldest heart can still thaw when it remembers grace. You may have betrayed someone who trusted you. You may have turned away from God, your purpose, or your truth. But the same way Dante emerged from the ice, you can rise. How? By remembering gratitude. By confessing honestly. By realigning with love, humility, and truth.

God's forgiveness doesn't melt the ice for you—it gives you the strength to break through it.

Reflection: Climbing Out of the Ice

1. Who have I turned my back on—mentors, supporters, or loved ones—that I need to make peace with?
2. Have I taken blessings in my life for granted, mistaking grace for entitlement?
3. Do I still recognize the people and moments that shaped my growth?
4. Where have I placed myself above accountability or gratitude?
5. What would it look like to climb out—to reconnect, to repent, to return to grace?

Treachery As the Death of Connection

Treachery is the death of connection. It is the ultimate inversion of love. Anger consumes. Fraud deceives. But treachery destroys trust itself. It freezes the heart, extinguishes empathy, and leaves nothing but isolation.

Modern Betrayal

We see echoes of this frozen landscape in our world today. Betrayal doesn't always come with grand gestures or dramatic headlines. Often, it hides in the quiet moments—a friend who uses your vulnerability against you, a colleague who takes credit for your work, a family member who turns away when you need support. Each act of treachery may seem small in isolation, but like Dante's ice it hardens the heart, chills relationships, and spreads coldness far beyond the initial act.

Treachery is the ultimate loneliness. Those who betray do not just harm others; they isolate themselves from humanity. Even when surrounded by people, their hearts remain frozen. They cannot truly connect and cannot give or receive love because trust—the lifeblood of human connection—has been shattered. This is the modern Ninth Circle: the emotional isolation, the alienation, the endless feeling of being cut off from genuine human warmth.

The Human Cost

I've experienced the ripples of this freeze—both as the betrayed and as someone who has faltered in loyalty. The sting of broken trust lingers far longer than anger or shame. While fury burns hot and passes, and deception twists but eventually unravels, betrayal leaves a frost that can take years to thaw. Relationships strain, communities fracture, and the betrayed are left to navigate a world that suddenly feels cold and hostile.

Yet, even in this deepest circle, there is a lesson. Treachery is a mirror showing us the stakes of connection. To honor trust, to act with loyalty, to speak and live with integrity—these are defiance against the ice. Every act of honesty, every commitment kept, every word spoken with sincerity is a spark of warmth in a frozen world.

The Ninth Circle reminds us that love and loyalty are not abstract virtues. They are survival tools—bridges that keep the human spirit from fracturing. Every betrayal is a warning: The more we put selfish desire over connection, the colder our world becomes and the colder we become ourselves.

Treachery also exposes a painful truth: Every connection we hold is sacred. Family, friends, colleagues, even casual bonds of respect and honor—these are threads that weave the fabric of society. Cut them, and the fabric tears. The world doesn't recover from betrayal the way it does from anger or dishonesty. The wound is colder, slower, and deeper.

And yet, the Ninth Circle is not just a warning about others. It is a mirror for ourselves. Every small betrayal—a lie to a friend, a deception to gain advantage, a moment of disloyalty—plants a shard of ice in our own heart. Every act that severs trust, no matter how small, leaves us colder, less human, and less capable of genuine love.

The Path to Warmth

Treachery is a reminder of the power of fidelity and honesty. To honor trust is to fight against this frozen fate. To be loyal, to speak truth, and to act with integrity—these are acts of defiance against the ice.

The path isn't easy. Rebuilding trust after betrayal requires courage, vulnerability, and consistency. But the alternative is the slow freeze of the heart, a chilling isolation from the world and from ourselves.

In the Ninth Circle, the ultimate crime is choosing self-interest over love, power over loyalty, and ambition over connection. The ultimate punishment is not fire, not drowning, but a frozen soul—aware, immobile, and alone.

Reflection Questions

1. Where in my life have I betrayed trust—in words, actions, or silence?
2. Who have I hurt by putting self-interest above connection?
3. What small act of integrity can I commit today to rebuild warmth in my relationships?
4. Where am I allowing coldness—fear, resentment, ego—to freeze my heart?
5. How can I honor trust and loyalty, even in small, everyday ways?

Treachery is the ultimate test of humanity. It strips away pretense, cunning, and anger, leaving only the cold truth of isolation. But it also offers a lesson: connection, loyalty, and honesty are more powerful than ambition, cleverness, or fleeting desire. They are the fire that thaws the ice.

Because even in the deepest freeze, warmth is possible when we choose love, integrity, and fidelity over selfishness.

Closing the Ninth Circle: Lessons from the Frozen Depths

The Ninth Circle of Hell is the ultimate mirror of human betrayal. From Caina's frozen necks of family betrayal, to Antenora's rigid ice of political and national treachery, to Ptolomea's exposure of broken trust in hospitality, and finally to Judecca, where the ultimate betrayal freezes even the soul's deepest loyalty, the message is clear: Betrayal destroys connection. It isolates, immobilizes, and chills the human spirit.

But Dante's frozen Hell is more than punishment—it is a warning. The deeper the betrayal, the colder and more immobilizing the consequences, not only for the victim, but also for the betrayer. Every act of treachery diminishes the heart, stifles growth, and erodes the capacity for love.

Modern life mirrors this frozen depth. Broken family ties, political corruption, intimate betrayals, and the moral failures of leaders or benefactors leave their own mark. Each act of treachery chills relationships, fosters mistrust, and makes society a colder place. Yet the Ninth Circle also illuminates a path forward: awareness, integrity, and forgiveness.

- **Awareness:** Recognize where betrayal has touched your life and how it may have shaped your responses or blocked your growth.
- **Integrity:** Guard against committing betrayal yourself, even in small ways, by aligning actions with values.
- **Forgiveness:** Release resentment, not as a gift to others, but as liberation for yourself. Freeing your heart is the first step to thawing the ice and regaining movement, warmth, and connection.

The Ninth Circle reminds us that the ultimate act of living is not avoidance, hiding, or bitterness. It is choosing love, loyalty, and contribution even when life has taught us betrayal. It is reclaiming the boat in the storm, steering with intention, and refusing to be immobilized by past wounds.

Treachery is the coldest fire, but every act of courage, every choice to forgive, and every effort to rebuild trust brings warmth back into our lives. To navigate the Ninth Circle is to face the deepest betrayal, reflect on its impact, and rise from it with purpose, compassion, and authenticity.

The frozen souls of Caina, Antenora, Ptolomea, and Judecca are not just allegorical punishments—they are warnings and mirrors. Their lesson is simple yet profound: Betrayal isolates, forgiveness liberates, and love restores.

Climbing Out of the Ice: The Redemption Beyond Treachery

Dante's journey through the Ninth Circle does not end in despair—it ends with ascent. After witnessing the frozen souls of betrayal, he and Virgil climb down Lucifer's body, through the core of the earth, and emerge into a new hemisphere beneath the stars. What begins as descent becomes rebirth.

This is not just poetry—it's a map of the human soul. Every descent into darkness carries within it the possibility of awakening. Every betrayal, every wound, every frozen place within you can become a doorway back to grace *if you choose to climb.*

Each region of the Ninth Circle reveals a truth about healing:

- **Caina** taught that betrayal within family breaks the closest bonds, but it also teaches that forgiveness—even if private—frees the soul from endless winter.
- **Antenora** exposed the cost of abandoning truth for power, showing that integrity is the last defense against cultural decay.
- **Ptolomea** revealed that deceit cloaked in intimacy is the cruelest kind, but it also revealed that trusting again without losing wisdom restores the warmth of humanity.

- **Judecca** showed that even the deepest betrayal—the betrayal of grace—can be redeemed through gratitude, humility, and return.

Together, they teach this: Hell is not punishment. Hell is revelation. It reveals the parts of us still frozen—the pride, fear, or bitterness we refuse to let melt. But once we face it, we rise.

From Ice to Light

To climb out of the Ninth Circle is to choose warmth again. It is to say: "I will not let betrayal define me. I will not stay frozen in what hurt me. I will rise, even if I must crawl through the cold." It's the moment you realize that grace doesn't erase the past—it transforms it. The very ice that once trapped you becomes the ladder that lifts you higher.

Reflection: Emerging into Light

1. What part of my heart still feels frozen from betrayal or guilt?
2. What "ice"—fear, resentment, or shame—am I ready to break through?
3. How has my descent taught me to love, forgive, and live with deeper integrity?
4. What does redemption look like for me—not in theory, but in practice?

Closing: The Warmth of Becoming

When Dante emerged from Hell, he did not come out unchanged. Neither will you. Your descent into pain, betrayal, or loss has reshaped you. It has stripped away illusion and revealed truth. You are no longer who you were when you entered the darkness. You are wiser, humbler, stronger, and capable of compassion that only those who've walked through Hell can truly give.

Because redemption is not forgetting what happened. It's remembering it differently—through the lens of growth, not guilt. It's seeing that even in the coldest depths, grace was waiting for you to rise.

I am the vine; you are the branches. Whoever abides in Me and I in him bears much fruit, for apart from Me you can do nothing.

John 15:5 (ESV)

Chapter 18

Abiding in Christ Through the Dark Wood

The Nonnegotiable Path to Renewal

By now, you've seen what the dark wood reveals. You've walked through the circles of lust, gluttony, greed, anger, etc. and seen how each one mirrors the restless, broken patterns of the human heart. You've seen how desire can turn to obsession, how comfort can turn to captivity, and how pride can disguise itself as progress.

But before you move forward, before you learn how to master the mind and rebuild your inner world, there's one truth you have to settle deep within you: You must abide in Jesus.

He's not someone to call on when things fall apart; He's the only way to stay whole. He's not the light at the end of the tunnel; He's the light that walks with you through it.

Every circle showed what happens when the soul disconnects from its Source. Every struggle was a reflection of life apart from the Vine. Abiding is the only way to restore what was lost—to move from chaos to clarity and from striving to stillness.

As John 15:5 says, "Abide in Me, and I in you... for apart from Me, you can do nothing." Those words aren't a suggestion—they're survival.

Knowing God vs. Just Saying You Trust Him

It's easy to say, "I trust God," but trust isn't built on words, it's built on relationship. You can't truly trust someone you don't know. And you don't get to know God by visiting Him once a week or whispering His name only when life falls apart. You get to know Him by dwelling with Him and by inviting Him into every corner of your chaos.

To abide in the dark wood means you stop managing God and start surrendering to Him. You talk to Him honestly, worship when it hurts, and keep showing up even when the answers don't come quickly. You don't wait for the light to return before you pray—you pray until the light returns. You cry out to Him in your pain, through your trials, or you just sit in silence, listening for His voice.

You don't say you trust Him and then take back control the moment things feel uncertain. That's not trust—that's convenience. Real trust stands firm when everything else shakes. It doesn't negotiate; it anchors.

For Those Who Don't Yet Know Him

Maybe you're reading this and thinking, *I don't even know God like that*. Maybe you've heard His name but never felt His presence. Maybe religion hurt you, people misrepresented Him, or life made you doubt He was real.

If that's you, you're not disqualified. *You're invited.*

God isn't looking for perfect people; He's looking for honest ones. He's not waiting for you to fix your life before you approach Him—He's waiting for you to approach Him *so He can help you fix your life.*

Knowing God doesn't start with rules. It starts with a relationship. It's as simple as being real with Him. You don't need fancy prayers or church language. You can start with one sentence: "God, if You're real—show me who You are."

That's all it takes. A genuine heart, an open door. And He will. Not through thunder or lightning, but in quiet moments when you least expect it: a peace that doesn't make sense, a word that lands differently, a comfort that feels personal.

God already knows your story. He's seen every mistake, every regret, every time you tried to fix things on your own. And still, He's saying, "Come home." The door back to Him isn't locked; it's been open the whole time.

If you've never known Him, start there, with honesty. If you've known *about* Him but never truly met Him, start there, with humility. And if you've walked away, start again, with grace.

Because knowing God is not about religion; it's about relationship. It's not about perfection; it's about connection. And the moment you decide to reach for Him, you'll find He's already reaching for you.

Abiding After the Fire

You've faced your giants. You've walked through your storms. Now, abiding is how you rest from the battle—how you rebuild your roots before climbing higher.

When you've been through fire, you don't rush out of it; you sit with God in the ashes until something sacred begins to grow. That's what abiding does. It turns wounds into wisdom and struggle into strength.

To abide means to dwell, not visit. It's when prayer becomes an atmosphere, not an appointment. It's when scripture becomes oxygen, not obligation. It's when worship becomes your default response, not your Sunday routine.

Abiding doesn't mean the storms stop, it means they lose the power to shake what's been rooted in Him. This isn't spiritual nonsense. It's a fact. If you do this, you will have peace. I'm living proof.

The Peace That Surpasses Understanding

When you abide in Christ, something miraculous happens—the Holy Spirit begins to produce peace within you that no circumstance can touch. It's not denial; it's divine design.

This peace isn't the absence of trouble; it's the presence of assurance. You can be standing in the middle of a storm and somehow your spirit feels settled, like there's an unseen hand steadying you.

That's the secret strength of abiding—you start to experience what Paul called "the peace of God, which surpasses all understanding" (Philippians 4:7, ESV). It's almost like a spiritual cheat code—not to escape pain, but to move through it unshaken.

The Holy Spirit becomes your translator when words fail, your comfort when life cuts deep, and your calm when everything else screams chaos.

This is how you know you're truly abiding; when the storm outside no longer dictates the stillness inside.

The Practice of Abiding

If you want to prepare your mind for renewal, you must first anchor your spirit.

Here's how that looks in real life:

1. **Talk to Him honestly.**

    No filters. No pretending. Tell Him what you feel, even if it's ugly. The moment you stop performing for God, you start experiencing Him.

2. **Sit with His Word and let it read you.**

    Don't just study scripture; let it study you. Let it search your motives, expose your fears, and fill your emptiness. His Word doesn't just inform—it transforms.

3. **Worship through fatigue.**

    When you worship in weakness, you declare that your faith isn't conditional. Worship isn't an escape from pain, it's an invitation for God to meet you in it.

4. **Protect your silence.**

    Stillness is where your soul remembers who it belongs to. Turn off the noise. Let the quiet convict you, calm you, and cleanse you. The world will always offer distraction, but God meets you in the pause.

The Fruit of Abiding

Abiding produces what striving never can: peace, patience, strength, and clarity. The same storms that once broke you now serve as the soil where your faith grows. The same places that once tempted you now remind you how far you've come.

You stop reacting out of fear and start responding out of faith. You stop chasing the next "fix" and start resting in a steady presence that never leaves.

Because abiding is what turns revelation into transformation. It bridges the gap between understanding truth and living it.

You've walked through Hell—now it's time to learn how to live in peace.

The Fruit and the Pruning

Abiding produces what striving never can: peace, patience, strength, and clarity. But fruit never comes without pruning.

When Jesus said, "Every branch that does bear fruit he prunes, that it may bear more fruit" (John 15:2, ESV), He wasn't describing punishment, He was describing preparation. God doesn't prune the dead branches first; He starts with the ones that are already alive.

That means you can be doing well—producing, growing, building—and still feel His hand cutting things away. It's not rejection. It's refinement.

He removes what drains your strength, even if it once looked like success. He trims what distracts you from purpose. He makes space for new growth by clearing what's overgrown.

The same pain that once felt like loss becomes proof of His love. Because pruning is never about taking, it's about making room.

The same rain that once drowned you now nourishes your roots. The same storms that broke you now strengthen you. That's the fruit of abiding: transformation through every season.

Reflection Questions

*Reminder: You most likely will want to record these questions and answers in a notebook.

1. What does abiding in Christ look like in your daily life?
2. Where in your journey do you struggle to remain connected to Him?
3. What has God pruned from your life recently? Did you cling tighter or let go? What fruit followed?
4. How can you make your time with God less of an appointment and more of an atmosphere?
5. When was the last time you truly felt connected to God—when you didn't just believe in Him, you felt His presence shaping your decisions? What changed when you drifted away?
6. What distractions, relationships, or ambitions keep you from abiding consistently—and are they worth the peace you're losing?
7. Think of a time when you were in chaos but felt a calm that made no sense—the peace of the Holy Spirit. What did that moment reveal about the Holy Spirit's role in your life? What did it teach you about trust?
8. If abiding became your atmosphere—not a routine—what would have to change about your mornings, your thoughts, and your priorities?

Transition: Preparing the Mind

The next battle you'll face isn't external—it's internal. The battlefield moves from the world around you to the world within you.

To master your mind, you must first learn to still it—to root it in something greater than your emotions, your habits, or your past. That's why abiding comes first. Without it, all other growth collapses.

Abiding is where transformation begins. The mind is where it's sustained. So take a breath. You've walked through the fire, and you're still here. Now it's time to renew your thoughts, rebuild your focus, and rise into who you were created to be.

You have power over your mind—not outside events. Realize this, and you will find strength.

Marcus Aurelius

Chapter 19

The Battle Within: Mastering Your Mind

The War No One Sees

The greatest battles are not fought on open fields, in boardrooms, or in the noise of the crowd. The fiercest wars rage in silence, in the space between your thoughts.

Your mind is the true battlefield. It's where your giants rise, where fear multiplies, and where every victory or defeat in life begins. This is where hesitation takes root, where faith is tested, and where purpose is either born or buried. Before you can conquer the world around you, you must first conquer the world within you.

Your thoughts, emotions, and beliefs are the armies of your mind. They march under your command, shaping how you see yourself, how you respond to challenge, and what you believe is possible. When left untamed, they turn against you—loyal soldiers turned mutineers. They whisper lies of fear and doubt, fortify the walls of limitation, and sabotage your pursuit of purpose. They make you fight invisible wars against yourself.

But when disciplined, those same forces become your greatest allies. A trained mind can turn fear into focus, doubt into discernment, and pain into power. When you command your inner world, your outer world follows.

Mastery of the mind does not mean silencing every storm—it means learning to stand firm in its center. It is the process of transforming chaos into clarity, impulse into intention, and emotion into energy.

The mind can be your prison or your kingdom. The difference lies in who holds the throne.

Dante understood this better than most. His journey didn't begin in Hell; it began lost in *the selva oscura*, the dark wood of his own confusion. The monsters he met—the leopard of self-deception, the lion of pride, and the she-wolf of never-enough—were not creatures of the forest. They were the shadows of his inner world. His external journey was only a mirror of the war inside him.

In the next sections—and throughout this book—we explore how faith and science meet in the renewal of the mind. These pages are offered for insight and reflection, not clinical advice. Healing is both a divine and human process. Sometimes God works through prayer, sometimes through professionals, and often through both.

This chapter offers spiritual and educational insights and is not a substitute for professional medical, psychological, or therapeutic care.

I believe the greatest battlefield we face is within our own minds. If therapy, medication, or a combination of both help you win that battle, embrace it. Just never forget the God who created the wisdom behind it.

The Nature of the Inner Battle

Your mind is both the prison and the key.

- **Prison:** When dominated by anxiety, guilt, or self-doubt, it chains your potential. Thoughts become repeating loops of limitation. Decisions are frozen, energy is drained, and life feels heavy with invisible weights.
- **Key:** When disciplined, your mind clarifies purpose, amplifies courage, and channels energy into meaningful action. Focused thought becomes power. Emotional regulation becomes freedom.

The giants you've faced—fear, anger, resentment, shame—all find fertile ground here. They whisper, distort, and manipulate perception. Every unexamined belief, unresolved emotion, or habitual thought strengthens them.

Identifying Mental Giants

The first step to mastering your mind is identifying its enemies. Common mental giants include:

1. **Self-Doubt:** That voice telling you you're not enough, not capable, or undeserving. It thrives on hesitation and inaction.
2. **Fear of Failure:** Imagined consequences that paralyze your decisions and prevent bold action.
3. **Regret and Guilt:** Past mistakes replayed endlessly, keeping you anchored in what cannot be changed.
4. **Comparison:** Measuring your life against others, cultivating envy, and eroding self-worth.
5. **Procrastination:** The silent giant that convinces you to delay until conditions are "perfect," which they rarely are.

Dante's beasts were symbolic, but so are ours. The leopard was distraction and deception. The lion was arrogance and false strength. The she-wolf was insatiable desire. Every one of us meets versions of these same creatures in our minds. They block the path upward until we confront them directly.

Each of these giants is a subtle manipulator. They never shout; they whisper. They rarely announce themselves, instead they seep into our daily thoughts, actions, and choices.

Mental Discipline: Training the Army Within

Mastery begins with training. You cannot command an army that acts on autopilot. You must drill, exercise, and condition your mind.

Practices for Mastering Your Mind

1. **Awareness:** Observe your thoughts without judgment. Notice patterns, triggers, and recurring fears. Awareness is the foundation of control.
2. **Journaling:** Write down intrusive thoughts, recurring doubts, and moments of mental sabotage. Seeing them on paper gives perspective and power.
3. **Affirmation & Truth:** Replace lies whispered by giants with reality. "I am capable." "I am resilient." "I am enough."
4. **Visualization:** Imagine yourself confronting challenges, succeeding, and navigating life with clarity. Your mind rehearses reality through imagination.
5. **Mindful Pause:** When fear or anger arises, pause. Breathe. Name the emotion. Decide your response instead of reacting impulsively.

6. **Decision Discipline:** Practice making small, deliberate choices quickly. Each victory over indecision strengthens your mental authority.

Confronting Cognitive Distortions

Giants of the mind often disguise themselves as truth. Cognitive distortions are the weapons of these giants. Examples include:

- **All-or-Nothing Thinking:** "I must succeed completely, or I am a failure."
- **Catastrophizing:** "If this goes wrong, everything is ruined."
- **Mind Reading:** "They think poorly of me; I know it."
- **Overgeneralization:** "I failed once; I will always fail."

Your sword of courage must strike here. Question assumptions. Test reality. Replace distortion with evidence. Discipline is not denial; it is clarity.

The Role of Emotion in the Inner Battle

The mind cannot be mastered without the heart. Thoughts are intertwined with emotion. Unprocessed feelings—anger, grief, resentment, fear—cloud judgment and fuel mental giants.

- Naming emotions reduces their unconscious power.
- Feeling fully without acting impulsively strengthens resilience.
- Integrating lessons from past pain turns that pain into a resource instead of a prison.

Courage, integrity, and clarity are useless if the heart remains tethered to unresolved trauma or emotional chains. Emotional mastery is mental mastery.

Understanding the Landscape of the Mind

Before you can master your mind, you must first understand the terrain you're standing on. The mind is not a simple battlefield; it's an entire landscape made of valleys of emotion, mountains of memory, and rivers of thought that carve the shape of your life.

Every thought you have leaves an imprint. Every emotion builds a pattern. Over time, those patterns create the mental "maps" that determine how you respond to the world. When those maps are drawn in pain—through abuse, loss, or betrayal—they can mislead you. You begin to navigate life as if danger is always near, even when the battlefield is long gone.

The mind is both a weapon and a wound. It holds every word spoken over you, every secret fear, and every unhealed memory. It remembers not just events but how those events *felt*. That's why someone who's been physically safe for years can still feel trapped. The mind hasn't caught up to the body yet.

But the same mind that remembers trauma also holds the power to rebuild. It can be retrained, rewired, and retaught how to see the world through clarity instead of fear. Every time you challenge a negative thought, you redraw your map. Every time you choose peace instead of panic, you reclaim lost territory.

Your thoughts, emotions, and memories are like the armies stationed within this inner world:

- **Thoughts** are the commanders, giving direction and strategy.
- **Emotions** are the soldiers, reacting to every perceived threat or opportunity.

- **Beliefs** are the laws of the land, shaping what those soldiers think is worth fighting for.

When you live unconsciously, these armies fight among themselves—thoughts contradict feelings and beliefs clash with purpose. But when you become aware, when you start to observe instead of react, you become the general who commands them with intention.

This is the beginning of mental mastery: learning that your mind is not your enemy. It's your greatest ally, but only when you learn its language.

The path forward requires curiosity, not condemnation. You don't heal the mind by declaring war on it; you heal it by understanding it.

Because once you understand the landscape, you can begin to shape it.

A Mind Reclaimed: The Story of Elizabeth Smart

At just fourteen years old, Elizabeth Smart was kidnapped from her bedroom in Salt Lake City by a man who claimed to be sent by God. For nine long months, she was held captive—abused, starved, and psychologically manipulated by her abductors.

In those months, her world shrank to survival. Her captors tried to erase her identity, forcing her to live in constant fear. The trauma wasn't just physical—it was also psychological. They didn't only chain her body; they tried to chain her mind.

When Elizabeth was finally rescued, her greatest battle was not over. She had to face the war that followed her home—the whispers of shame, the nightmares that revisited her, and the public's endless questions. Many wondered how a young girl could survive something so dark and not be consumed by it.

Elizabeth later said, "I realized the only way I would ever feel free again was to forgive."[4]

Just like Dante emerging from the depths of Hell, she stepped out of a mental prison stronger than when she entered. Her ascent wasn't instant—it was step by painful step, truth by truth, choice by choice. The same path Dante climbed, she climbed in her own way.

That sentence carries the essence of a healed mind. Forgiveness didn't mean forgetting what happened. It meant releasing the power it had over her. It meant refusing to live in the same mental prison her captors once controlled.

Through therapy, faith, and unshakable resolve, she began to rebuild her inner world. She chose to speak publicly about her trauma—not for sympathy, but to shine a light for others still trapped in their silence. Her courage transformed her pain into purpose.

Today, Elizabeth Smart is an author, advocate, and voice for survivors. But more than that, she is living proof that even when the body has been violated, the mind can be reclaimed.

She turned her story into a declaration that I heard or read once and has stuck with me: "They took nine months of my life. But they don't get the rest."

Her healing reminds us that the mind is not destroyed by what happens to it—it is destroyed only when we stop believing it can heal.

---

4 Elizabeth Smart, *My Story* (St. Martin's Press, 2013).

The landscape of her mind was once scorched by trauma, but she rebuilt it—one choice, one truth, one moment of courage at a time.

The Science of Healing the Mind

Healing isn't just a spiritual or emotional process—it's biological. Every thought, emotion, and belief has a physical footprint in the brain. Trauma literally reshapes neural pathways, altering how you think, feel, and respond to life. But here's the hope: The brain is not fixed. It can change, adapt, and rebuild itself—a phenomenon known as neuroplasticity.

Neuroplasticity means your mind is capable of rewiring—of replacing fear with peace, doubt with confidence, and pain with purpose. The same brain that once learned to survive can learn to thrive.

Neuroplasticity Is in the Bible

"Do not be conformed to this world, but be transformed by the renewing of your mind" (Romans 12:2, NKJV).

This verse is the cornerstone of biblical neuroplasticity. Paul is literally describing a mental rewiring process—a renewal (Greek: *anakainosis*).

This implies a continuous transformation, not a one-time event. It's the same concept neuroscientists describe: Consistent thought patterns create new neural pathways. The Bible calls it transformation through truth; science calls it neuroplastic adaptation.

"We take captive every thought to make it obedient to Christ" (2 Corinthians 10:5, NIV).

This verse speaks to cognitive discipline: consciously intercepting and redirecting negative or destructive thoughts. In neuroscience, this parallels *cognitive restructuring*, where we interrupt automatic negative thought patterns and replace them with healthier ones.

Guarding the Mind (Philippians 4:6–8)

"And the peace of God, which surpasses all understanding, will guard your hearts and your minds in Christ Jesus." (ESV)

"Whatever is true, whatever is noble, whatever is right, whatever is pure... think about such things." (NIV)

This is a direct instruction to retrain focus—to intentionally dwell on truth, beauty, and goodness. Modern brain studies show that focusing on gratitude and positive thought reshapes the brain's default mode network, increasing resilience and emotional stability. Paul was giving a divine prescription for mental rewiring centuries ago.

Be Renewed in the Spirit of Your Mind (Ephesians 4:22–23, NKJV)

"Put off... the old man... and be renewed in the spirit of your mind."

Here, the Bible describes the shedding of old mental habits and the adoption of new identity-based thinking—the essence of transformation. It's the spiritual equivalent of pruning old neural connections and forming new ones.

The Power of Meditation (Psalm 1:2–3, Joshua 1:8, ESV)

"But his delight is in the law of the Lord, and on his law he meditates day and night."

Meditation—focusing on truth and repeating it—creates long-term mental conditioning. In neuroscience, meditation strengthens the prefrontal cortex, enhancing self-control and calm. Biblically, it anchors the believer in God's Word, producing fruit "in season"—a stable, flourishing mind.

As a Man Thinketh (Proverbs 23:7, KJV)

"For as he thinketh in his heart, so is he."

This ancient proverb captures the heart of cognitive science: Our thoughts shape our identity and behavior. Repeated thinking patterns (beliefs) literally sculpt neural architecture and influence emotional health.

Dante understood that transformation doesn't happen in an instant. His ascent symbolized a slow, deliberate unlearning of old patterns and the practice of new ones until virtue became natural. That is neuroplasticity. That is Romans 12:2. Healing is the refining process that reshapes the mind until the old self falls away and the new self rises in its place.

How Trauma Rewires the Brain

When you experience trauma, your brain's alarm system—the amygdala—goes into overdrive. It becomes hypersensitive, always scanning for danger. Meanwhile, the prefrontal cortex, the part of your brain that makes rational decisions, becomes underactive. You might know logically that you're safe, but your body and emotions disagree.

The hippocampus, which organizes memory, can also shrink under chronic stress, making it harder to distinguish between past and present danger. This is why a sound, smell, or tone of voice can feel like a direct threat—even when you're safe.

In other words, trauma hijacks your brain's natural rhythm. You're not "broken"—your brain is simply doing what it was designed to do: protect you. The goal of healing isn't to erase that instinct but to retrain it.

The Healing Brain: Rebuilding Through Practice

The same neuroplasticity that once helped your brain adapt to trauma is the very thing that can undo it. Through consistent, mindful practice, new neural pathways form, teaching your brain that peace and safety are now possible.

1. **Mindfulness and Breathing:** Deep breathing and mindfulness calm the amygdala and strengthen the prefrontal cortex. Each moment you pause before reacting, you're reprogramming your response to stress.
2. **Therapy and Reprocessing:** Approaches like EMDR (Eye Movement Desensitization and Reprocessing) and CBT (Cognitive Behavioral Therapy) help the brain reprocess traumatic memories safely. These methods teach the brain to file old pain where it belongs: in the past. These are evidence-based therapeutic methods administered by licensed clinicians.
3. **Faith and Meditation:** Prayer, scripture reflection, and spiritual meditation activate the brain's "default mode network," associated with self-awareness and inner peace. Faith-based focus produces measurable changes in brain chemistry, increasing dopamine (motivation) and serotonin (stability).
4. **Movement and Physical Health:** Exercise releases endorphins and increases blood flow to the brain, promoting new neural growth. Trauma is stored not only in the mind but in the body, and movement helps release it.

5. **Community and Connection:** The brain thrives in connection. Sharing your story and allowing safe relationships rewires isolation into belonging. When others see you and understand you, your nervous system relaxes and safety becomes relational again.

If you want to explore any treatments that require a therapist, it's best to get with a licensed therapist and obtain information about the different methods available. Pray about it. God put these things in place because they work.

Faith Meets Neuroscience

Science explains *how* the brain heals. Faith gives you the reason to believe it can.

Scripture tells us to "be transformed by the renewing of your mind." Modern neuroscience confirms it: Renewal is not poetic—it's physiological. When you choose forgiveness over bitterness, gratitude over despair, or hope over fear, you're physically reshaping your brain.

Every prayer, every journal entry, every boundary kept is a neural exercise. Healing becomes not just belief but biology.

The Discipline of Rewiring

Healing isn't instantaneous. The brain learns through repetition. You cannot think your way into peace once; you must practice it daily.

- **Morning Reset:** Begin each day by grounding yourself—breathe, pray, or journal before consuming the noise of the world.

- **Midday Awareness:** Notice your emotional temperature. When tension rises, stop and reframe your thoughts: I'm safe. I'm present. I'm in control.
- **Evening Reflection:** End your day with gratitude. Gratitude rewires the brain faster than almost any other emotion because it reinforces safety, sufficiency, and connection.

  Consistency, not intensity, heals the mind.

When the Mind and Spirit Align

When the mind is trained and the spirit is anchored, healing deepens. The voice of fear grows quieter and the nervous system learns to trust again. You no longer react—you respond. You no longer survive—you create.

This is what mastery of the mind looks like:

- A steady heart under pressure.
- A clear mind under confusion.
- A peace that no storm can shake.

It is the harmony of faith and focus—the soul and the science working as one.

The Weapons of Thought: Replacing Lies with Truth

The battle within is not won by silence; it is won by strategy. Every thought is either a sword or a chain. Each one you allow to linger shapes how you see, feel, and live. Left unguarded, thoughts become tyrants, but trained, they become warriors that serve your freedom. The mind follows the direction of repetition. What you tell yourself daily, it begins to believe. What you believe, it begins to create.

These are the same weapons Dante used on his journey: truth against deception, clarity against confusion, intention against impulse.

The Power of Repetition

Science calls it *neuroplasticity*. Scripture calls it renewal. Both describe the same divine design: The brain rewires itself according to what it hears most often. If fear is what you rehearse, fear becomes familiar. If faith is what you feed, faith becomes natural. The battlefield is not about what you know; it's about what you repeat.

Exposing the Lies

Before truth can rebuild your mind, you must expose the lies that have built false foundations. These lies are often quiet, inherited, or learned through pain:

- "I'm not good enough."
- "It's too late for me."
- "If people knew the real me, they'd walk away."
- "I'll always be broken."
- "I can't change."

Each one is a whisper that pretends to protect you but only keeps you small. The longer a lie remains unchallenged, the more it feels like truth.

Exercise: Truth Mapping

Write down the lie that shows up most often. Beneath it, write the truth that dismantles it.

Example:

Lie: "I'm not enough."

Truth: "I was created intentionally and completely. My worth isn't earned; it's inherited."

Repeat your truth every time the lie resurfaces. Over time, your brain will stop defaulting to fear and start defaulting to freedom.

Reframing Reality

The mind heals when you reframe meaning. You can't change what happened, but you can change what it means.

- **Old Frame:** "That failure ruined me."
- **New Frame:** "That failure revealed what I still needed to learn."

Reframing transforms wounds into wisdom. It tells your brain that pain was not punishment—it was preparation.

Faith Connection: "All things work together for good" (Romans 8:28, NKJV). That doesn't mean all things are good; it means they can be used for good. Your mind begins to heal when you start assigning purpose to pain.

Building Your Arsenal

You don't need hundreds of strategies; you just need a few weapons sharpened by use.

1. **Gratitude:** The discipline of noticing what is working trains your brain to see possibility instead of loss.
2. **Affirmation:** Speak identity over insecurity. Words shape wiring.
3. **Visualization:** Picture yourself succeeding, forgiving, or standing firm before you do it. The brain can't distinguish between rehearsal and reality.

4. **Faith Statements:** Anchor yourself in divine truth. Scripture is both shield and sword.
5. **Silence:** A still mind is a strong mind. Quiet moments reset emotional chaos.

Use these weapons daily. Your giants depend on your passivity; they lose power when you fight with intention.

The Daily Battle Plan

Morning: Set the Tone

Before your phone, your news, or your schedule, train your thoughts. Say aloud: "Today I lead my mind, my mind does not lead me."

Midday: Intercept the Lie

When discouragement or comparison hits, replace it instantly.

"I'm overwhelmed" → "I'm being stretched, not broken."

"I can't do this" → "I can do hard things; I've done them before."

Evening: Renew and Record

Reflect before sleep. Ask: "Which thoughts served my purpose today, and which ones sabotaged it?" Write one truth to carry into tomorrow. Repetition carves new mental roads.

When the Mind Feels Too Loud

Some days, silence feels impossible. That's when simplicity is your ally. Breathe. Pray. Speak one sentence of truth, even if it feels forced.

"I am still here." "This moment will pass." "I am stronger than this thought."

You don't have to conquer every lie in one day—you just have to refuse to let them all speak at once. Each time you replace fear with truth, your brain changes. Each small victory is rewiring.

Faith, Focus & Freedom

As discussed earlier in this chapter, Paul's ancient word for renewal—*anakainosis*—meant a total renovation of the mind. That's what this practice is: tearing down the walls of lies and rebuilding them with truth, one thought at a time. This is not positive thinking; it is spiritual reconstruction. It is the divine and the neurological working together to make you whole again.

Your thoughts are not your enemies when they are trained. They are your soldiers. Teach them to serve your purpose, not sabotage it. Because when your thoughts align with truth, your life will follow.

Victory in the Inner Battle

When you master your mind, you unlock freedom.

- You move without hesitation.
- Fear becomes a signal, not a jailor.
- Doubt becomes a tool for discernment, not paralysis.
- Resentment becomes awareness, not a leash.

Mastery of your inner battle allows your courage to be precise, your integrity to be consistent, and your contribution to flow without obstruction.

Reflection Questions

1. Which mental giants influence my daily decisions most?
2. Where do I allow fear, doubt, or regret to dictate my actions?
3. What daily practices can strengthen my mind and discipline my thoughts?
4. How can I transform recurring negative patterns into clarity and purpose?
5. What victories over the inner battle have I achieved that I can celebrate?

Reflection Exercises: Mastering Your Mind

1. **Identify Your Mental Giants**

Take ten quiet minutes to write down the recurring thoughts that challenge your peace or purpose. Ask yourself:

- What thoughts keep me up at night or cause me to hesitate during the day?
- Which thoughts replay most often when I feel anxious, ashamed, or inadequate?

Once written, circle the three that have the strongest emotional grip on you. These are your mental giants—the ones that demand your focused attention and courage.

Reflection Prompt:

"This thought has controlled me long enough. What truth could take its place?"

2. **Journal of Awareness**

For one week, practice mental awareness by journaling moments when your thoughts drift toward negativity or fear. Note:

- The situation that triggered it.
- The emotion that followed.
- The decision or behavior it led to.

At the end of each day, reread your entries and highlight moments where you could have chosen a different thought. This exercise isn't about perfection—it's about recognition. Awareness precedes transformation.

3. **Rewrite the Story**

Pick one memory that still holds emotional power over you—a failure, betrayal, or wound. Write it down from two perspectives:

- **The old frame:** How you've always remembered or interpreted it.
- **The new frame:** What that experience taught you, how it revealed strength, or how it prepared you for where you are now.

This practice retrains your mind to assign purpose to pain. What was once a chain becomes part of your armor.

Faith Connection: "All things work together for good to those who love God" (Romans 8:28, NKJV). Every painful chapter can become part of the story that shapes your strength.

4. **Confront the Cognitive Distortion**

Choose one recurring lie you've believed about yourself—something like:

"I always mess things up." "No one really cares about me." "It's too late for me to change."

Now, apply truth and evidence:

- Is this absolutely true?
- What evidence exists to the contrary?
- What would I tell someone else who said this about themselves?

End by rewriting that thought in truth-based language.

"I've made mistakes, but I've also grown. I am capable of learning, rebuilding, and thriving."

Every time that lie resurfaces, confront it with your new truth until your brain accepts it as the new normal.

5. **Emotional Integration Practice**

When you feel anger, grief, fear, or shame, don't run—instead, reflect.

Take a few deep breaths and ask yourself:

- What emotion am I really feeling beneath the surface?
- When was the first time I felt this way?
- What does this emotion want me to understand, not suppress?

Then write a simple release statement in your journal:

"I acknowledge this feeling, I release it with grace, and I choose to move forward in peace."

Emotional honesty breaks the chain of suppression. As scripture reminds us, "Be angry, and do not sin" (Ephesians 4:26, NKJV). Feel, but do not be ruled.

6. **Mind Renewal Declaration**

Every morning for the next seven days, speak this declaration aloud:

"My mind is not my enemy. It is my ally. I train it to align with truth, courage, and purpose. I have the mind of Christ. I am being renewed day by day."

Repeat it daily, especially when self-doubt or anxiety appears. Neural pathways are carved through repetition; faith grows through confession.

7. **End-of-Day Reflection**

Before bed, write brief answers to the following:

- Where did I win the inner battle today?
- Where did my giants gain ground?
- What thought or truth strengthened me most?
- What lesson can I carry into tomorrow?

Keep this nightly log for at least fourteen days. You'll begin to see patterns of progress—evidence of a mind being renewed through awareness, discipline, and divine partnership.

Closing

Your mind is a battlefield. Every day presents skirmishes and tests. Every decision is a move in the war between limitation and potential, fear and courage, paralysis and action.

Mastering your mind is not optional—it is essential for living fully, for contributing meaningfully, and for defeating giants both internal and external. The sword of courage in your hand is only as effective as the mind guiding it.

Train your thoughts. Discipline your emotions. Master your inner battle. The giants are formidable, but your mind is a stronger ally than you realize.

Stand vigilant. Act deliberately. Command your inner army. Your life, your purpose, and your contribution depend on it.

At the end of *Inferno*, Dante writes, "And then we came forth to see again the stars."

That is the promise of mastering your mind—that no matter how dark the inner battle becomes, there is always a way back to the light. Your stars are waiting.

Important Note:

The battles of the mind can be fierce, layered, and deeply personal. While this chapter offers spiritual, emotional, and educational insight, it is not a substitute for professional mental health care. If you are navigating trauma, persistent anxiety, depression, or overwhelming thoughts, please seek guidance from a licensed therapist, counselor, or medical professional. Healing the mind is both a spiritual and sometimes a clinical journey, and there is strength, not shame, in asking for help. God often heals through prayer, through people, and through professionals. Use every resource available to you.

This day the Lord will deliver you into my hand, and I will strike you down and cut off your head. This very day I will give the carcasses of the Philistine army to the birds of the air and the beasts of the field, so that all the earth may know that there is a God in Israel.

1 Samuel 17:46 (ESV)

Chapter 20

Facing the Giants: The Call To Battle

The Roar Before the Battle

The wind is heavy. The ground beneath you trembles as if the earth itself remembers every battle fought before this one. The air tastes of dust and memory. The shadow in front of you isn't just a threat; it's everything you've run from, rising up at once. Every failure, every wound, every lie that said you weren't enough has taken shape and now stands before you, daring you to flinch.

The giant's presence is suffocating. Its voice echoes through your mind, reminding you of every time you almost gave up. It mocks your prayers, questions your progress, and sneers at your faith. Its armor gleams with the reflections of your past, as if it wears the memories of who you used to be.

Every story has a breaking point. This is yours. The air thickens with choice: retreat or rise. This is where belief becomes muscle and faith becomes motion. You've walked through darkness, stripped away your masks, endured betrayal, silence, and surrender. You've been refined in the fire long enough to know that pain doesn't mean defeat; it means preparation.

Now the lessons you've gathered are no longer words on a page. They've become weapons in your hands. Every quiet night of honesty, every confession that broke your pride, every tear that watered the soil of your courage—all of it was rehearsal for this moment.

Your giant won't always look like Goliath, but you'll feel its breath the same way: close, loud, and real. Sometimes it wears a familiar face. Sometimes it looks like your own reflection. But whatever form it takes, the battle is the same—truth against deception, courage against fear, faith against the familiar.

Dante understood this moment long before we did. When he stood in the dark wood, three beasts blocked his path—the leopard, the lion, and the she-wolf. They weren't animals; they were manifestations of his internal giants: deception, pride, and the hunger that is never satisfied. Before he could rise toward the light, he had to face the shadows that rose within him. Every giant you face now is a reflection of the same truth: Before elevation comes confrontation.

Here you stand. Your heart is steady, the sling is in your hand, and purpose burns in your chest. You don't face this giant to prove your strength. You face it to reveal it, to let the world see what God has been building in silence.

The Real Test

Giants don't only come at the end of the journey. They wait for you at every threshold—some at the start, others near the summit. The first giants you meet are often the hardest because they stand between who you are and who you're called to become. They whisper every reason you shouldn't begin. They question your worth, your readiness, your purpose.

For many, these are the giants that keep the dream locked inside. They convince you that healing can wait, that preparation isn't enough, that the risk is too great. These early giants guard the gate to the path itself. You defeat them the moment you take your first step.

But later, when you've grown stronger and wiser, new giants appear. They're quieter, subtler, but just as dangerous. They don't test your potential, they test your maturity. They rise to see if what you've learned will hold under pressure—if your faith, discipline, and integrity can stand when no one is watching.

So yes, giants can meet you at the beginning, but they never stop appearing. They change form as you do. They meet you at every level of growth, each time demanding a deeper kind of courage.

In the *Divine Comedy*, Dante meets giants twice—once near the beginning, and again as he ascends beyond the deepest circles. The message is the same in your life: Giants don't only guard the gate; they guard the next level. The early ones test your willingness to begin, the later ones test your readiness to rise. Every advancement requires a deeper surrender, a sharper clarity, and a more courageous step.

The battlefield isn't out there; it's within. The roar of the giant is the sound of your own fear colliding with your destiny. And every time you face one—whether at the start or the summit—you are being refined, not ruined.

When the giant roars, don't shrink. Remember who you've become. Remember the storms that didn't break you, the nights you almost gave up, the tears that watered the ground of your faith. Remember the promises whispered in your wilderness, the prayers that lifted you when you couldn't stand, and the discipline that shaped you when no one was watching.

This moment isn't about proving strength. It's about living from it. You fight not for recognition but for release—release from the weight of what once defined you, from the cycles that tried to claim you, from the lies that told you you'd never change.

You fight so the world can see what faith looks like when it stands tall and doesn't back down. You fight because freedom demands confrontation. You fight because somewhere behind this giant is the next version of your life, the one God has been preparing you for all along.

Why Confronting Giants Is Essential

The giants you face are not just obstacles to your happiness; they are barriers to your purpose. Every moment you carry unresolved anger, fear, or deception, you divert energy from your calling. Every unhealed wound diminishes your ability to love, to serve, and to contribute. Every mask you wear, every lie you tell yourself, every compromise of integrity becomes a chain that holds your power hostage.

Conquering these giants is essential because your purpose cannot flourish in fear or compromise. Your potential cannot emerge while you are still hiding from yourself. True contribution—the kind that changes lives—can only come from a place of authenticity, power, clarity, and presence.

Think of it this way: Your life is a vessel. If it is cracked, clogged, or filled with debris from unresolved pain and unprocessed emotion, what flows from it cannot nourish anyone.

Only when the vessel is whole—clear, strong, and open—can it pour out life, love, and grace for others.

When You Don't Face Your Giants

Not everyone faces their giants. Some run. Some freeze. Some rationalize their fear until the opportunity is gone.

The Israelites did this once. God promised them the land of Canaan, a place overflowing with abundance and peace. But when they reached its borders, they sent out spies to survey the land. Ten of the twelve came back trembling. They said, "We saw giants there, the descendants of Anak. We seemed like grasshoppers in our own eyes" (Numbers 13:33).

That single sentence defined their destiny. They didn't lose the land because the giants were too big; they lost it because their faith was too small.

Fear magnifies the problem and minimizes the promise. The giants were real, but so was God's word. Still, fear won the day, and that generation wandered the desert for forty years, never stepping into what was already theirs.

That's what happens when you don't face your giants. You stay busy. You stay moving. But you don't progress. You talk about potential but never walk in it. You live in the desert of delay, circling the same fears, the same habits, the same excuses.

God didn't remove the giants from the land; He left them there to reveal who had faith and who didn't. The Promised Land isn't handed to the fearful. It's inherited by the faithful.

That's why facing your giants isn't optional. Avoidance isn't safety—it's slow spiritual death. The desert may feel familiar, but it's not home. You can't heal what you won't face.

You can't conquer what you keep running from. And you can't step into your promised land while still bowing to your giants.

Dante didn't descend into Hell to admire the darkness—he went there to expose it. Every soul he encountered revealed a truth he once ignored about himself. That's what happens when you face your giants. You descend into the places you've avoided, not to stay there, but to understand what must be released so you can rise. There is no ascent without honesty and no transformation without truth.

The Nature of Giants

Giants are not meant to scare you away. They are meant to teach you your limits and then show you how to rise above them.

A giant is a mirror. It reflects what is unresolved, unclaimed, and denied. It is uncomfortable and relentless. But every encounter with a giant is also an opportunity. Every confrontation, no matter how terrifying, reveals your strength, your resilience, and your capacity for love.

When Dante finally encounters the actual giants in *Inferno*, they are chained—towering in size but powerless to move. That's how your own giants truly are. They look intimidating, but once you confront them, you realize they have less power than you imagined. Avoidance magnifies them; exposure diminishes them. They're only free when you keep them unchallenged.

Some giants are obvious—a person who betrayed you, a toxic relationship, a life circumstance that seems impossible to overcome. Others are subtle: the fear of failure, the shame carried from childhood, or the voice that says you are not enough.

You cannot bypass them, negotiate with them, or hide behind distraction, busyness, or performance. Giants demand your attention. They demand honesty, and they demand confrontation.

Courage and the Role of Preparation

Facing giants requires preparation. You have already done much of this work:

- You have reflected on anger and resentment.
- You have named the masks you wear and confronted self-deception.
- You have acknowledged betrayal and begun to unfreeze your heart.
- You have wrestled with greed, fraud, and manipulation—in yourself and others.

These exercises are the training ground for your courage. Courage is not the absence of fear; it is action in spite of fear. And to act in the face of giants, you need awareness, clarity, and alignment with your truth.

Without this preparation, you risk being paralyzed. The giants will intimidate you. They will manipulate your emotions. They will convince you that you are powerless. But because you have done the work, you now have tools: insight, self-compassion, discernment, and discipline.

The Consequence of Avoidance

Avoiding giants comes at a cost.

- Your heart stays frozen.
- Your relationships remain shallow or fractured.
- Your purpose stays dormant.
- Your life becomes smaller, quieter, less impactful.

Avoidance is a slow suffocation. It is subtle. It is seductive. It whispers that comfort is better than confrontation, that safety is better than growth, and that illusion is easier than truth.

But the cost is far greater than the temporary relief of avoidance. Giants left unconfronted grow. Fear becomes habit. Resentment calcifies. Unhealed pain becomes a blueprint for the next betrayal, the next disappointment, the next cycle of self-sabotage.

The Victory of Confrontation

Confronting giants is transformative. Every act of courage unblocks energy. Every moment of honesty frees your heart. Every step toward the truth strengthens your soul.

When you face your giants:

- You reclaim your life.
- You reclaim your time, your energy, your choices.
- You regain your heart, your clarity, your purpose.

And more importantly, you become a source of victory for others. Your confrontation with your own giants allows others to see possibility. It allows others to believe that they too can rise.

You do not conquer giants for glory, for recognition, or for applause. You conquer them to live fully. You conquer them to give fully. You conquer them so your life, love, and grace can be poured into the world, helping others stand tall in their own storms.

Dante had Virgil. David had God and his sling. And you have the lessons you've gained in your field seasons—the hidden years of preparation where courage is forged, faith is tested, and character is built long before anyone is watching. Every hero is prepared before the world ever sees them. Before Dante could enter Paradise, he had to face the giants, the temptations, the shadows, and the lies that tried to claim him. Before David could enter the throne, he had to face the giant that embodied every doubt spoken over his life. These moments aren't punishments; they are promotions disguised as threats.

The Shepherd and the Giant

Before David ever stood in front of Goliath, he was a shepherd—quiet, unseen, and often forgotten. While his brothers were trained soldiers, David spent his days in the fields tending sheep, fighting off lions and bears, playing music, and praying under the open sky. To others, his work looked ordinary, even insignificant. But in those lonely hills, God was training his hands for battle and his heart for purpose.

David wasn't chosen because he looked the part. When the prophet Samuel came to anoint the next king, every brother was brought before him except David. His own father didn't even think to call him in from the field.

That's how overlooked he was. Yet that moment of dismissal was divine preparation. The world saw a shepherd; God saw a warrior. The quiet seasons of being unseen are often the seasons when you're being shaped for your Goliath.

Those long days with the flock were not wasted time. Each sling stone David threw, each moment he spent guarding sheep from predators, and each prayer whispered under the stars was practice. He was building discipline, precision, and faith in the dark so that when the light of battle came, he was already ready. The fight with Goliath wasn't luck; it was the culmination of unseen faithfulness.

When David stood before the giant, he wasn't intimidated by Goliath's size. He had already faced giants in the wild—they just looked different. He had learned to protect what was entrusted to him. He had built courage through repetition. He had trusted God when no one was watching. What happened in public was simply the revelation of what had already been forged in private.

That's what facing giants is really about. The battle isn't won when the giant falls; it's won in the quiet field when you choose to stay faithful even when no one applauds. It's won when you practice courage in the small things, when you protect what's yours with integrity, and when you believe in your purpose even while others overlook you.

We all have our shepherd seasons—the quiet places where no one sees our effort, our growth, or our faith. But those seasons matter. They are the soil of greatness. They are where your hands learn skill and your heart learns strength. When your Goliath finally appears, it won't be the first time you've fought; it will simply be the first time the world notices.

Preparation Before the Battle

This story isn't just about David; it's about all of us. Every one of us will face giants. But the truth is, you don't defeat your giants by hitting them once. You defeat them through preparation.

David didn't win the battle the day he stood before Goliath. He won it years earlier when he was alone in the field. Every sling stone he practiced with, every predator he faced, every night he prayed while watching over sheep—those were the moments of training. That was discipline. That was faith being built one quiet day at a time.

When the giant appeared, David wasn't scrambling to figure out who he was or where his strength came from. He had already learned that in solitude. He had already proven to himself that courage wasn't a performance; it was a habit. The same sling that killed lions in the shadows brought down a giant in the light.

And this is exactly why your reflection, journaling, and self-examination matter.

The field is where the unseen work happens. It's the place where God refines your heart, sharpens your discernment, and builds your endurance. If you skip the field, you won't survive the fight. You can't conquer what you refuse to prepare for.

When you did the reflection questions, when you faced your anger, greed, fraud, or betrayal, that was your field. That was where you learned to aim, to listen, to trust. Every time you chose truth over illusion, forgiveness over resentment, and courage over avoidance, you were learning to sling your stone.

Preparation isn't glamorous. It's repetitive, quiet, and often lonely. No one applauds you for choosing integrity when no one's watching. No one sees you wrestle with doubt in private or pray through your pain. But that's where the real victories are born. By the time your giant stands before you, you'll realize you've already fought this battle a hundred times in smaller forms, and you've already won.

The field shapes warriors. It doesn't just teach you how to fight; it teaches you who you are. The solitude of preparation builds confidence that can't be shaken by size, fear, or noise. That's why David could look at Goliath and say, "The same God who delivered me from the paw of the lion and the bear will deliver me from this Philistine" (1 Samuel 17:37). He wasn't guessing; he was remembering.

Preparation is remembering. It's the daily practice of faith that builds muscle memory for the moment fear shows up. It's why your spiritual work, your self-reflection, and your commitment to honesty and healing all matter.

You can't hit your giant once and expect it to fall. You must train your mind to believe, your heart to endure, and your spirit to stay aligned when the pressure comes. The battle is not won in the moment of confrontation; it's won in the hours, days, and years of consistency leading up to it.

So when your Goliath appears—whether it's fear, addiction, betrayal, or self-doubt—remember this: The sling is already in your hand. You've been training for this. You've done the work. You are ready.

Dante ended the journey through Hell with one of the most powerful lines ever written: "And then we came forth to see again the stars."

That's what happens when you face your giants. The darkness breaks. The fear subsides. The path opens. And the stars—the very promises God hung above your life—come back into view.

The giant is not the end of your story. It is the gateway to the next chapter of your life.

For the weapons of our warfare are not carnal, but mighty through God to the pulling down of strongholds.

2 Corinthians 10:4 (KJV)

Chapter 21

Slaying the Giants: The Practice of Victory

Identifying Your Giants

Not every giant stands before you with a sword. Some have no faces. They live inside your mind—in fear, in shame, in memories that still echo when the world goes quiet.

These faceless giants are harder to fight because you can't see where they stand. They don't roar—they whisper. They convince you that you're not ready, not strong enough, not worthy. They live in hesitation, in comparison, in every unfinished dream and every unspoken truth.

You can't throw a stone at these giants. You have to face them differently—with truth, consistency, and faith. These are the enemies that fall only when you stop running and start remembering who you are.

Like David, you don't fight them because you feel powerful. You fight them because you remember what you've already survived. You fight them because you refuse to let them write the ending to your story.

Some giants wear faces. Some don't. But all of them fall the same way—when faith steps forward and fear finally stands still.

Before you can conquer your giants, you must name them. You can't defeat what you refuse to define. Giants thrive in vagueness—they hide behind words like "I'm fine," "It's not that bad," or "I'll deal with it later." Naming them breaks their power. Clarity exposes them to light.

Start with awareness. Look at your life honestly—your habits, your thoughts, your relationships, your cycles of avoidance. Giants often disguise themselves as normal behavior. They blend into your routine until they feel invisible.

Here are some of the most common giants we face—though you may recognize others unique to your own story:

1. **The Giant of Fear:** Fear of failure. Fear of rejection. Fear of success. Fear of being seen. Fear is the great paralyzer of purpose. It convinces you that comfort is safety, but all it really gives you is stagnation. You defeat this giant not by becoming fearless but by moving forward *while afraid*.
2. **The Giant of Shame:** Shame hides behind silence. It tells you that your story is too messy to be redeemed, that your mistakes disqualify your calling. But shame cannot survive in truth. When you expose it to honesty and grace, it begins to crumble. You defeat shame when you realize that your scars are not your identity—they're your testimony.
3. **The Giant of Pride:** This giant can be subtle—sometimes it's arrogance, other times it's the fear of appearing weak. It makes you compete instead of connect. You conquer it by practicing humility and by realizing you don't lose anything when you admit your humanity. You gain peace.

4. **The Giant of Validation:** Validation becomes toxic when you depend on others to tell you who you are. It convinces you that approval equals identity, that attention equals love, that being noticed equals being needed. But the moment you make someone else the source of your worth, you give them the power to take it away. You defeat this giant by rooting your identity in truth, not attention, and by knowing that you are already chosen, already worthy, already loved.
5. **The Giant of Regret:** Regret traps you in a past that can't be changed. It tells you "If only..." until you lose the present entirely. You defeat it by transforming regret into wisdom. Every mistake becomes a teacher when you decide to learn instead of linger.
6. **The Giant of Control:** Control pretends to be order, but it's really fear in disguise. It says, "If I can just manage everything, nothing will go wrong." But life doesn't bend to your grip—it breaks under it. You defeat this giant when you surrender—not to chaos, but to faith. When you trust that what's meant for you doesn't need to be forced.
7. **The Giant of Comparison:** This giant thrives in the age of social media. It tells you that someone else's success is proof of your failure. It drains joy and replaces it with envy. You defeat it by focusing on your own lane and by remembering that your story isn't late, it's unique. God's timeline for you was never supposed to look like theirs.
8. **The Giant of Procrastination:** This one doesn't roar—it whispers, "Tomorrow." It convinces you that delay is harmless. But days become weeks, and weeks become

years. You defeat it with discipline. Momentum is built one small act of obedience at a time.

9. **The Giant of Unforgiveness:** This giant holds your soul hostage. It feeds you the illusion of control while keeping you bound to pain. You defeat it by releasing your grip. Forgiveness doesn't free them—it frees *you*.
10. **The Giant of Bitterness:** Bitterness grows where pain was never processed. It starts as hurt, then hardens into cynicism. You conquer it by confronting the wound—not by pretending it doesn't exist, but by letting love and truth touch what anger has guarded.
11. **The Giant of Distraction:** This is one of the most dangerous giants of modern life. It doesn't destroy you with violence; it numbs you with noise. It keeps you scrolling, busy, and entertained but never fulfilled. You defeat it through focus—by learning to be still, to listen, to choose depth over distraction.
12. **The Giant of Unbelief:** This giant makes you doubt your worth, your calling, even your faith. It's not that you stop believing in God—you stop believing that He can use you. You defeat it by remembering every time you were carried when you didn't think you could stand. Faith grows when you look back and see His fingerprints on your past.
13. **The Giant of Comfort:** It whispers that you've done enough—that growth is optional and discipline is overrated. It lulls you to sleep in mediocrity. You defeat it by choosing discomfort on purpose—by stepping into challenges that stretch you, knowing that purpose always lives on the other side of pain.

Dante understood the power of naming what hunts you. In the dark wood, he couldn't escape until he recognized the beasts blocking his path for what they truly were—not animals, but manifestations of the fears, compulsions, and temptations that had ruled his life. Each creature symbolized a giant within him. And nothing changed for Dante until he stopped running and finally faced what had been stalking his soul. Naming the giant is always the first act of freedom.

These are just some of the giants that walk beside us—some loud, some quiet, some hidden under years of habit or hurt. But now that you've named them, they've lost their camouflage.

Because giants only thrive in the dark. Once seen, they can be faced. Once faced, they can be conquered.

My Giant of Validation: The Wound That Followed Me into Manhood

I didn't understand it for most of my life. I didn't see how deeply the Giant of Validation had woven itself into my identity. But the truth is this: I learned to chase emotionally unavailable women because I grew up with an emotionally unavailable mother.

My mother wasn't always that way. In the beginning, she was loving. Present. Warm. But as drugs and alcohol consumed her, everything changed.

The house grew quieter. The laughter stopped. Her bedroom door became a wall that never opened.

She began spending her days locked away, lost in addiction and broken relationships. She prostituted herself. She grew numb, distant, unreachable. And as a boy, I learned something that shaped my entire emotional life:

Love is something you earn.
Love is something you wait for.
Love is something that hides behind a closed door.

Her approval was unpredictable.
Her attention was inconsistent.
Her presence was fading more and more each day.

I remember her coming out of her room only to eat something and then disappear again. I remember my sister and I entertaining ourselves. Trying to make noise sometimes just to see if she'd notice. Trying to be good enough, loud enough, interesting enough—anything to pull her out of that room.

I didn't realize it then, but something was forming inside me: A belief that love had to be chased. That affection had to be earned. That connection belonged to people who were always slipping away.

That wound followed me into adulthood like a shadow I couldn't see.

And that's how I ended up drawn to emotionally unavailable women—not because they were right for me, but because they felt familiar.

They felt like home.

One woman had a boyfriend, yet I found myself trying to "win" her anyway. Trying to prove I was the better choice. Trying to earn what was never mine to earn.

Another woman pulled me into a storm of promises, mixed messages, and soul-deep confusion. We crossed lines we shouldn't have crossed. And still, I stayed, thinking if I just loved harder, maybe she'd finally choose me.

But the truth is, I wasn't trying to win *her*. I was trying to win my mother's love through her.

And then there was Linda.

She wasn't the cause—she was the mirror.

She awakened something in me I didn't even know was still alive: the ache to be chosen by someone who couldn't choose me back.

She told me it was normal for her to disappear for months or speak once a year. She had a boyfriend. She was struggling with her own battles. She didn't have anything to give emotionally.

And yet... her distance made me cling harder.

When she pulled away, it triggered something ancient—that boy inside me waiting for his mother to come out of her room. That longing. That ache. That hope.

I wasn't in love with her. I was in love with the possibility of finally being chosen.

But she couldn't give me what I hoped for—not because she was cruel, but because she wasn't capable of giving it.

Just like my mother.

And here's the part that broke me: After my accident, during the stillness of recovery, I was forced to see all of this.

I was lying in bed, barely able to move, dealing with nightmares, pain, fear, and trauma, and she didn't reach out. Not even once.

My father did.

My son did.

People who *actually* love me did.

But emotionally, I was more affected by the silence of someone who was never mine in the first place.

That was the moment I realized that this was never about her. It was about the wound I carried from childhood. It was about the boy who learned to earn love from his mother instead of receiving it.

If I could talk to that boy today, I'd tell him: "She cannot give you what you need—not because she doesn't want to, but because she can't. Her wounds are bigger than you. Her addictions swallowed her long before you ever tried to reach her. But listen to me: You are loved. You are valued. You have people—real people—who care about you deeply. Focus on them. Cherish them. Because their love is yours without you having to earn it."

The Giant of Validation wasn't born in adulthood. It started in childhood. And the women I chose weren't mistakes—they were mirrors revealing a wound I finally had to face.

And once I named it, once I saw the pattern clearly, the giant lost its power.

This is where healing begins.

Reflection: How I Broke the Cycle

You might be asking yourself how I broke the cycle. The truth is, it didn't happen overnight, and it didn't happen by accident. The first step was simply seeing it. I had to look in the mirror and start asking myself the hard questions: "Why am I drawn to people who cannot choose me back? Why does emotional distance feel familiar? Why do I feel like I have to earn love?"

It took soul-searching. It took long walks. It took silence—the kind of silence I never gave myself until life forced me into it. And it took prayer. Real prayer. Not the quick Sunday prayers that disappear by Monday but the kind of prayer where you're on your face before God, asking Him to reveal what's broken, what's buried, and what's been running your life without your permission.

Just like what we talked about in chapter 18 regarding abiding in Christ, this wasn't theory. It wasn't inspiration. This was survival. Transformation. It was God opening my eyes and showing me exactly why I kept choosing the same kind of pain disguised in different people. And when I finally got the answer, everything shifted. I stopped trying to earn what God had already spoken about me. I stopped letting the behavior of someone else define my value. I began affirming who I was in Christ instead of who I was to my past, my mother, or any emotionally unavailable person.

Even today, that giant tries to rise from time to time. Those old whispers still come back. But now I recognize them for what they are: patterns, not identity; wounds, not destiny; echoes, not truth. And when they show up, I stop, breathe, and remind myself that I am enough, I am chosen, and I deserve the kind of love I freely give.

As for Linda, I cut her off completely. Not out of anger, not out of hatred, but out of clarity. She played her purpose in my story. She revealed the wound I didn't want to admit was still there. If our paths ever cross again, I will wish her well. I hold no bitterness. She taught me what she was meant to teach me. And the message was simple but life-changing: Stop accepting breadcrumbs, stop confusing inconsistency with connection, and stop settling for fragments. You deserve love in the same fullness you give it.

All of you reading this deserve that. I may not know your story or your wounds, but I know this: You deserve more than the cycles you've been repeating. You deserve wholeness, peace, and love that does not make you perform. You deserve to break your cycle—and you can. This is the work. This is the healing. This is the freedom. And this is where your story begins to change.

The Deep Giants: The Ones That Wound the Soul

Some giants are louder than others, and some are buried deep. They don't roar; they whisper. They hide in memory, in the body, and in silence. These are the giants born from trauma—being hurt in ways no one should ever experience.

Maybe you were molested as a child. Maybe you were raped. Maybe someone you trusted took something sacred from you and left you to carry the weight of their sin. These are the hardest giants to face because they don't just threaten your confidence; they threaten your sense of safety. They make you question whether you'll ever be whole again.

You can't fight these giants with the same weapons you use for fear or pride. They require tenderness, healing, patience, and often help from God, from therapy, from community, and from truth.

You can't pretend these wounds didn't happen, and you can't pray them away overnight. Healing isn't denial; it's daily surrender. It's saying, "What happened to me was real, but it does not define me."

When pain this deep is ignored, it doesn't disappear—it multiplies. It bleeds into relationships, into self-worth, and into faith. The person you were meant to become gets trapped behind the walls you built to survive. But survival isn't the same as living.

You were never meant to live permanently guarded. You were never meant to stay small, silent, or afraid of your own reflection. You are not what happened to you. You are what you do with what happened to you.

Facing these giants isn't about forgetting; it's about reclaiming. It's not about pretending the wound didn't change you. It's about choosing how it will shape you. The moment you decide that what broke you won't define you, the healing begins.

And like David, you don't face these giants because you feel strong. You face them because you've decided to stop letting them win. You face them with courage, with tears, with trembling if you must, but you face them. Every time you do, you reclaim one more piece of your soul.

Dante discovered that the deepest circles of his journey were not filled with monsters but with the frozen, silent pain of souls trapped in the consequences of what had been done to them and what they could not let go of. Trauma is like that—frozen places of the heart. The way out was not denial or speed but understanding, naming, and reclaiming meaning. Like Dante, you rise not by pretending the darkness never happened but by walking through it with truth as your guide.

How This Connects to Contribution

This book is not about self-improvement for its own sake. It is about authentic contribution. Your purpose is realized when your victory serves others.

Every giant you conquer gives you

- **Perspective**—you understand pain, struggle, and fear.
- **Empathy**—you can guide, teach, or console because you have walked through the fire.
- **Presence**—you can show up fully, without masks or distractions.
- **Love**—you have reclaimed the energy that fear or resentment once stole.

By facing your giants, you become a conduit of victory for others. Your healed, present, authentic self is the spark that can ignite transformation in someone else. This is the essence of contribution: helping others live in victory by allowing the life, love, and grace you've given yourself to flow outward.

The Practice of Giant-Facing

Before any battle, a wise warrior studies their enemy. The battlefield is prepared, the terrain mapped, the weaknesses understood. The same is true for the giants that live within us.

They are not mythical creatures; they are real forces that shape our decisions, reactions, and relationships. And they are cunning. They hide in plain sight, disguise themselves as reason, or whisper lies that make us doubt our own hearts.

To defeat a giant, you must first know it intimately. You must observe, analyze, and anticipate its moves.

Facing giants is not a single act. It is a daily discipline. Here are practices to make it real.

1. **Identify Your Giants:** Write down every fear, limitation, unresolved pain, or toxic influence in your life. Name them. Look them in the eye.
2. **Journal the Truth:** Record how each giant manifests. How does it influence your behavior, thoughts, relationships, and choices?
3. **Take One Action Against Each Giant:** Break the patterns. Confront the fear. Speak the truth. Set boundaries. Ask for help. Seek therapy or counsel.
4. **Reflect on the Growth:** Each encounter with a giant strengthens your capacity to love, serve, and contribute. Celebrate small victories. Document the progress.
5. **Share Your Light:** Use your experience to help others. A healed heart, a reclaimed life, and a courageous soul are contagious.

Reflection Questions (Journal)

- Which giants have I been avoiding and why?
- How do these giants influence my relationships, choices, and purpose?
- What preparation have I done through reflection, honesty, and forgiveness that equips me to confront them?
- What is one action I can take today to face a giant in my life?

- How can conquering this giant allow me to give more fully to the world?
- Who can I inspire or help by standing in victory?

Closing: Stepping into Victory

The giants are real. They are terrifying. They are relentless. But so is your courage, your insight, and your heart.

You have done the work to see yourself clearly. You have confronted shadow, betrayal, fraud, and frozen hearts. You have faced the truths that most people avoid. Now it is time to face the giants, to claim your life, and to unleash your contribution upon the world.

Every giant you defeat is a victory not just for you but for the people who will feel your light, love, and grace. Every battle strengthens your soul and expands your ability to serve.

When Dante completed his ascent, he did not return to the darkness. He stepped into light so brilliant it reshaped his very being. And that same promise is yours. The work you're doing—the naming, confronting, grieving, and rebuilding—is your ascent. It is the climb toward clarity, toward purpose, and toward the life you were always meant to live. Giants don't guard your failures; they guard your future. And every one you slay moves you higher.

Your life is not for hiding, performing, or pretending. It is for facing giants, living fully, loving courageously, and giving relentlessly.

Stand tall. Step forward. Confront the giants. Live your purpose.

When God wants to make a man great, He breaks him first.

attributed to A. W. Tozer

Chapter 22

Rising from the Ashes: Transforming Pain into Power

The Shift After the Giants

You have faced your giants. You've stared into the frozen depths of betrayal, walked through the fires of anger, and witnessed the chains of greed, fraud, and deception. You've peeled back every mask and confronted the truth of who you are with raw honesty.

But now the work shifts. Confrontation alone does not complete the journey. Awareness, no matter how clear, cannot transform your life. The next step is alchemy—taking every wound, every betrayal, every shadow, and forging them into strength. This is what it means to rise from the ashes.

Transformation begins when pain becomes purpose. The fire that once burned you now becomes the very energy that propels you forward. Every scar is a reminder that the flames did not win. You did. Pain was never meant to destroy you; it was meant to reveal what could not be broken. The fire was not punishment—it was preparation.

You have spent time in the depths, learning to identify the monsters within you. Now it's time to learn what to do with what you've found. The ashes of your old self—the parts that burned away in shame, regret, and fear—are not waste; they are the soil of rebirth. From them, new strength can rise, new purpose can emerge, and new identity can form.

You are not returning to who you were before the storm. That version of you no longer exists. You are becoming someone new—someone forged in fire and made resilient through trial. The shift after the giants is the movement from fighting to forging, from surviving to creating. The descent taught you awareness; now the ascent demands transformation.

Dante understood this exact moment. After confronting the beasts, the frauds, the betrayers, and the frozen souls of the Inferno, he reached the darkest point—the center of Hell, where everything seemed lost. But then came the shift.

In a single, stunning reversal, Dante and his guide turned their bodies upward and began to climb. The moment they chose ascent, the entire world changed. They were no longer descending; they were rising. And for the first time, Dante saw the stars again. This is the moment you're in now. The turn. The upward motion. The beginning of your ascent.

The journey from pain to power begins here.

My Own Ashes: The Accident That Changed Everything

About a year ago, I survived a car accident that should have paralyzed me. I shouldn't be walking, but by the grace of God, I am.

For weeks, I couldn't do anything. I was stuck in bed, barely able to move, waking up from nightmares of the impact—not just from that crash, but from others before it. The memories hit like aftershocks. The fear, the helplessness, the replaying of what could have happened... it was all fire. And this time, I couldn't run from it.

My life stopped.
My body stopped.
My plans stopped.

But my mind—for the first time in years—grew quiet enough for God to speak.

And in that stillness, where my strength ended, something new began.

I picked this book back up and started writing again. It was already halfway done, but one day while I was lying in bed, I watched *Patch Adams* with Robin Williams. He quoted the first line of *The Divine Comedy*, and something in me snapped awake. It was like Dante calling out across centuries: "Midway upon the journey of our life..." In that moment, I felt it—the spark, the calling, the push to finish what God had already begun in me.

I didn't start writing this book because life was peaceful or convenient. I started writing because I literally couldn't do anything else. My body was broken, but my spirit was being rebuilt. The accident forced me into stillness, and in that stillness, God birthed purpose.

What I thought was a breaking became a becoming. What I thought was loss became direction. What I thought was the end became the beginning of the book you are holding now.

I rose from those ashes one page at a time.

The Nature of Transformation

Transformation is not easy. It is not quick. It is not comfortable. It demands intensity, honesty, and unflinching courage. It asks you to stand inside the very fire that once threatened to consume you and trust that what burns away was never meant to remain. Growth is never accidental—it is always intentional. And transformation, real transformation, requires three sacred ingredients: acknowledgment, responsibility, and focus.

1. **Acknowledgment**

You cannot rise from ashes you refuse to see. The pain you carry—the guilt, the resentment, the fear—must be faced before it can be released. Pretending it isn't there only buries it deeper, where it continues to control you from the shadows. Acknowledgment is not self-pity; it's sacred honesty. It's looking at your reflection and saying, "Yes, this hurts. Yes, I failed. Yes, I fell, but I'm still here." When you allow yourself to see what burns inside without judgment, you stop running from it. The moment you stop running, you gain the power to reshape it. Awareness is the first act of freedom.

2. **Responsibility**

The fire cannot refine you if you keep handing it over to others. Growth doesn't happen because someone rescues you—it happens because you choose it. Responsibility means reclaiming authority over your life. You cannot control what others have done, but you can control how you respond, how you rebuild, and who you become. It's easy to blame circumstances, people, or the past. But every time you do, you surrender your power. Responsibility is not about guilt—it's about taking back authorship of your story. It's saying, "I may not have chosen the fire, but I will choose what comes from it."

3. **Focus**

Transformation requires direction. You cannot rebuild while you are distracted by noise, fear, or constant escape. True change demands focus—deep, deliberate attention to what matters most: healing, clarity, and purpose. When you focus, you stop scattering your strength across worry, doubt, and regret. You start channeling it into growth. Focus turns chaos into progress; it aligns your heart and your mind toward what lasts. Every act of focus—every prayer, every small victory, every honest effort—adds weight to the foundation of your new life.

Together, acknowledgment, responsibility, and focus form the foundation of transformation. Dante understood this shift as well. After walking through the depths of darkness, he began the long upward journey toward renewal—a climb that required discipline, humility, and the willingness to let go of everything that weighed his soul down. His rise wasn't instant; it was intentional. Every step demanded clarity, honesty, and surrender.

This is your upward path now—not a place of punishment, but a place of purification. It is the deliberate, daily shaping of your character as you rise toward the life you were created to live. These disciplines turn fire into refinement and pain into purpose. Practiced consistently, they don't just change what you do—they change who you are.

The descent revealed your brokenness. The ascent now demands your wholeness.

From Ashes to Strength

When Dante emerged from the darkness of the *Inferno*, he found himself beneath a sky washed in soft light—a dawn he had not seen for what felt like ages.

The ground was unfamiliar, but hope was real again. He was surrounded not by flames or ice but by open air and the possibility of becoming someone new. That is what rising from the ashes feels like. A dawn after years of night. A breath after years of suffocation. A beginning built from what survived the fire.

Imagine the ashes of your old self scattered before you—fragments of pain, guilt, disappointment, and fear. They are the remnants of every moment that broke you open. But within those ashes lies everything you need to rebuild. Transformation begins when you stop seeing them as evidence of failure and start recognizing them as the materials of creation.

Every act of courage, every honest choice, every moment you forgive instead of retaliate becomes a brick in the foundation of your new life. Each decision to rise above what once defined you is a declaration that the past no longer has authority over your future.

Rising from the ashes is not about forgetting who you were; it's about transforming the meaning of what happened. The things that once brought shame can become sacred markers of growth. The memories that once held you hostage can become testimonies of survival. The pain that once silenced you can become your most powerful voice.

When you choose integrity over convenience, compassion over resentment, and consistency over comfort, you turn the fire that once burned you into light that guides you. Pain no longer dictates your path; purpose does. The ashes no longer weigh you down; they become the soil where your strength grows.

This is the essence of rising: not running from your past, but reclaiming it; not erasing your story, but rewriting its ending. What once destroyed you now refines you. What once silenced you now empowers you. What once held you captive now prepares you to lead others out of their own fire.

Your scars are not signs of defeat—they are symbols of resurrection. Each one whispers the same truth: *You didn't just survive. You transformed.*

Biblical Parallels: Beauty for Ashes

Dante knew something about sacred fire. On the terrace of the final purification, he passed through flames that did not destroy him but instead refined him. The fire burned away only what could not enter the higher realms. It was painful, even terrifying, but on the other side was vision, clarity, and the freedom to rise. Scripture and Dante agree on this truth: Fire is not only a symbol of judgment; it is also a symbol of restoration. It reveals what is eternal in you.

In scripture, ashes were never the end—they were the beginning of transformation. God has always used ashes as symbols of surrender, repentance, and rebirth. When everything seems lost and when the fire has taken what you loved or who you were, that's where renewal begins.

Job sat in ashes after losing everything, yet it was in that place of ruin that God restored him twice over. David fasted in ashes when his spirit was crushed, but from that place of humility, his heart was renewed. And Isaiah declared a promise that still stands today: "He gives beauty for ashes, the oil of joy for mourning, and the garment of praise for the spirit of heaviness" (Isaiah 61:3).

Ashes represent what once was—your past failures, losses, and wounds. But in God's hands, ashes become the soil for new life. What burned away becomes what grounds you. The destruction that once defined you becomes the evidence of divine renewal.

The exchange is not instant, but it is certain. When you surrender your pain—truly surrender it—you allow God to transform it. You don't erase your story; you let Him rewrite it with redemption. The beauty that emerges is not about perfection or performance; it's about peace. It's about living in alignment with who you were created to be, no longer defined by what you've lost but by what you've become through the fire.

The miracle of beauty for ashes is not that the pain disappears—it's that you no longer see it the same way. What once symbolized defeat now represents grace. What once spoke of failure now testifies to faith. You stop asking, "Why did this happen to me?" and start declaring, "Look what God built through me."

Transformation becomes sacred when you realize the ashes were never meant to bury you—they were meant to plant you. And from that soil, your purpose begins to bloom.

Studying the Ashes: Learning from What Burned

When Dante descended through the circles of the Inferno, he learned one truth again and again: Every wound has a history, every deformity has a cause, and every soul is shaped by the choices it made and the pain it carried.

Dante didn't witness these scenes to judge them; he witnessed them to understand them. The same is true for you. Studying your ashes is not about condemnation; it is about revelation. It is the wisdom that comes from looking honestly at what the fire exposed.

Before you rise, you must first study what remains. The ashes of your life tell a story—not of defeat, but of refinement. Every wound, every mistake, every loss holds a lesson. When you pause to examine what the fire left behind, you begin to see patterns, insights, and truths that were once hidden beneath the chaos.

1. **Identify the Origin**

   Ask yourself: "When did the fire start?" Every emotional burn, every betrayal, every breakdown has a root. Maybe it began with childhood pain, family dysfunction, unhealed trauma, or a broken promise you never forgave. Naming the source gives clarity. It takes the vague fog of suffering and turns it into something you can understand and therefore heal.

2. **Recognize the Manifestation**

   How does that old fire show up in your life today? Does it appear as anger, fear, people-pleasing, emotional detachment, or self-sabotage? These are the ashes of unresolved pain—signs that something still smolders beneath the surface. When you identify how the past still moves through you, you stop being its prisoner.

3. **Extract the Lessons**

   Every hardship contains revelation. The betrayal that shattered your trust taught you to discern. The failure that broke your pride taught you humility. The loneliness that tested your patience taught you self-compassion. Every ember has wisdom in it if you're willing to sift through the ashes with grace instead of resentment.

4. **Reclaim the Useful Coals**

   Not all remnants are meant to be discarded. Some pain refines you. Some memories, once purified, become the fire that fuels purpose. Take the strength, the empathy, and the resilience and leave the bitterness behind. Carry forward only what will serve your ascent.

5. **Build the Blueprint**

   The ashes are not rubble—they're the blueprint of your rebirth. When you look closely, you see the outline of who you were always meant to become. Every scar marks where the foundation of your new life will be laid.

Transformation doesn't ignore the ashes; it studies them. It learns from them. It uses them. Because the past is not your prison—it's your preparation. The same fire that tried to consume you has now refined you, and what remains is stronger, clearer, and unshakably grounded in truth.

This is how you rise—not by erasing the fire, but by mastering it.

The true test of a man's life is not what he achieves, but what he gives.

attributed to Oswald Chambers

Chapter 23

From Power to Purpose: Turning Transformation into Legacy

The Role of Pain in Contribution

The transformation you've undergone was never meant to end with you. Rising from the ashes is not only about healing yourself—it's about awakening your ability to heal others. Pain, once transformed, becomes the most powerful instrument of purpose.

A person who has never suffered may offer comfort, but a person who has walked through the fire brings authority. You have seen darkness up close. You have wrestled with shame, fear, and regret. Now you carry something that cannot be taught—depth. Your empathy has been earned, your wisdom forged, and your compassion refined in the furnace of experience.

When you turn your pain into purpose:

- You model **courage**, showing others that healing is possible.
- You embody **truth**, refusing to wear masks that hide your scars.

- You extend **grace**, because you know what it's like to fall and rise again.
- You give **permission**, showing others that transformation is not only real; it's available to them too.

Your scars are no longer signs of weakness; they are credentials. They prove that you've endured, learned, and overcome. You become a bridge for others still trapped in their fire.

Each story of suffering you've redeemed becomes a spark for someone else's awakening. When you share what you've learned—through words, actions, or even quiet presence—you create ripples that reach further than you'll ever know.

That is contribution in its purest form: turning your personal resurrection into collective hope.

The same ashes that once symbolized death now become the soil of life—not just for you, but for others. In this way, the fire that once burned you becomes the light that guides the world.

From Power to Purpose: Rising for Others

Transformation reaches its highest form when it moves beyond personal healing into purposeful living. The fire that once refined you now fuels your contribution. The strength you've cultivated is no longer just for survival, it's for service.

Pain without purpose is suffering. Pain with purpose is strength. And strength shared becomes legacy.

You are no longer defined by what you've endured; instead you are defined by what you create from it. Every scar is now a story of redemption. Every lesson is a tool for impact. When your transformation turns outward, your life becomes a testimony—not just that healing is possible, but that it's powerful enough to change others too.

1. **Serve from Experience:** Your past has equipped you with empathy and discernment that theory can't teach. You now carry the language of the wounded and the wisdom of the healed. Use it. Mentor someone. Volunteer. Speak truth. Write. Create. Wherever there is darkness, your light has a place.
2. **Teach What You've Lived:** The greatest teachers are not those who have studied suffering but those who have survived it. You don't need perfection to teach—you need perspective. Share what you've learned: how to endure, how to rebuild, how to rise again. Your story can become a roadmap for someone else's return to hope.
3. **Model Wholeness:** You don't inspire by pretending to be flawless. You inspire by being real—by showing that peace is possible after chaos, forgiveness after betrayal, strength after breaking. You are living proof that resurrection isn't a myth.
4. **Expand the Ripples:** Every act of service, honesty, and love sends ripples far beyond your sight. You may never know who you reach—the person who overhears your story, reads your words, or watches your quiet faithfulness. But the ripples continue, multiplying through lives you'll never meet.

This is how power becomes purpose: by flowing outward. And this is how purpose becomes legacy: by lighting torches in others.

Your ashes have now become seeds, planted in the hearts of those who still wander in darkness. Let your life remind them: The fire doesn't have to end them. It can awaken them.

A Story of Transformation: The Man Who Refused to Stay Broken

I had a friend, a man named Anthony who had been through more in thirty years than most people face in a lifetime. His childhood was marked by violence and addiction. His father drank to forget his own pain; his mother disappeared for weeks at a time, caught in her battle with drugs.

Anthony learned early how to survive—not by trusting, but by hiding. He became a professional at pretending. At school, he smiled. At home, he endured. And as he grew older, he carried that same quiet pain into adulthood, trying to outrun the ghosts that followed him.

He worked two jobs, started a family, and promised himself he'd never become like his parents. But when the pressures of life closed in, the very same darkness crept back—just wearing different clothes. He found himself angry, exhausted, distant.

He loved his wife and children, but he couldn't stop replaying the voice that told him he'd never be enough. The more he tried to bury the past, the more it rose up inside him. He didn't realize it then, but he wasn't running from life—he was running from healing.

Everything changed one night when he sat alone in his car outside his house, engine off, hands shaking on the steering wheel. He was tired of fighting everyone—tired of fighting himself. He whispered into the silence, "God, if You're real, I can't do this anymore. Please make something out of this mess." He didn't hear a voice, but he felt something shift—not outside, but inside. It wasn't peace. Not yet. It was surrender. And for the first time, surrender didn't feel like defeat. It felt like release.

In the months that followed, Anthony started therapy. He got honest about his anger. He began journaling, praying, and learning how to forgive—not just his parents, but himself. He started seeing pain as a teacher instead of a sentence. When his old memories surfaced, instead of running, he sat with them. When guilt whispered, he spoke truth back: "That was me then. It's not me now."

Slowly, the man who used to break everything he touched began to rebuild. He learned how to talk to his kids instead of yelling. He apologized to his wife and showed her with action, not words, that he was changing. He joined a men's group at his church, helping others who carried silent burdens. He discovered that his scars were not signs of shame—they were evidence of survival.

Years later, Anthony stood in front of a group of recovering addicts and told his story. He said, "I used to think the fire came to punish me. But it came to purify me. The things I thought would kill me actually set me free."

His voice cracked, but he didn't hide it. Because real transformation doesn't look perfect. It looks honest. It looks like a man who has walked through his own fire and come out carrying light for others.

Reflection on Anthony's Story

Anthony's journey is a mirror of what it means to rise from the ashes. He didn't wait for perfect circumstances or instant healing—he started with surrender. He faced his pain, forgave his past, and used what had once destroyed him to help others heal. That is transformation. Not becoming someone new but remembering who you truly are beneath the ashes.

The Formula of Transformation

Anthony's story isn't unique—it's universal. It's the same process woven through every chapter of this book, the same pattern that has echoed through time. First, he had to surrender to the truth that he was in his own dark wood—lost, afraid, surrounded by internal monsters he could no longer ignore.

Through therapy, prayer, reflection, and accountability, he began naming those monsters one by one—anger, shame, guilt, fear, and self-deception.

He faced his giants, not with perfection, but with persistence. He fell, he rose, and he kept walking. And in doing so, he discovered what every soul who enters the fire must eventually learn: *Transformation always begins with confrontation.*

This process works every time. Not because it's easy, but because it's true. You cannot heal what you refuse to face. You cannot conquer what you deny. You cannot rise until you've first acknowledged what has been keeping you down.

Facing the ugly parts of yourself—the shadows, the lies, the unhealed pain—is not weakness. It's the only doorway to strength. The person who avoids the dark never sees the dawn.

Anthony's journey proves that the same formula that guided Dante through Hell, that helped David face Goliath, and that has carried countless others through their own storms still works today. When you stop running, when you meet your giants head-on, when you allow God to use the fire to refine instead of destroy—that's when you rise.

Transformation isn't magic. It's a process—honest, painful, and sacred. It's the decision to face what's broken until it becomes whole.

The Mechanics of Rising

Transformation is intentional. It is structured. It is deliberate. Here are the practical steps to turn ashes into power:

1. **Inventory the Ashes**

Write down every pain, every wound, every source of fear or doubt. Do not filter or rationalize. This is your raw material.

2. **Analyze the Lessons**

Next to each item, write what it has taught you—even the smallest insight. Where did it expose weakness? Where did it reveal strength?

3. **Reclaim Your Power**

For each wound or fear, identify one action that takes your power back:

- Speak your truth.
- Confront a fear.

- Forgive yourself or others.
- Set boundaries.
- Take a bold step in your purpose.

4. **Transform Energy**

Use your physical body, your mind, and your will. Exercise, meditation, journaling, visualization—these are tools to convert past pain into present strength. The fire moves from destruction to creation.

5. **Anchor Your Transformation**

Celebrate the small victories. Record them. Ritualize them. Create habits and structures that reinforce your new identity.

The Daily Battle

Rising from the ashes is not a one-time act; it is a daily practice. Each morning, ask yourself:

- What ashes do I carry today?
- How will I transform them into power?
- Where will I channel my energy to serve others and honor myself?

Each night, reflect:

- Where did I act from fear, avoidance, or anger?
- Where did I act with courage, clarity, and love?
- How will I rise stronger tomorrow?

Transformation is iterative. It compounds. The more consciously you engage, the stronger, more capable, and more radiant you become.

Reflection Questions

1. Which past experiences have left ashes in my soul that I need to examine?
2. How have I been using my pain as a crutch, mask, or excuse?
3. What lessons have I ignored that are begging to be acknowledged?
4. Which actions today can reclaim my power and convert past pain into purpose?
5. How can my transformation inspire or support someone else's journey?

Reflective Exercises: The Practice of Transformation

Transformation is not something you simply think about—it's something you *practice*. These reflections are designed to move your growth from the page into your daily life. Take your time with each one. Write. Pray. Reflect. Let truth rise from the ashes.

1. **Acknowledgment Journal:** Sit quietly and ask yourself, "What pain, memory, or regret have I been avoiding?" Write freely—no editing, no justifying. Let your truth surface unfiltered. Then, next to each entry, write how that experience still shapes your emotions or decisions today. Awareness brings light. Light begins healing.

2. **Ownership Audit:** Draw two columns. In the left column, write the areas of your life where you feel powerless—relationships, habits, emotions, or routines. In the right column, write one action you can take to reclaim responsibility in each area. It might be setting a boundary, having a difficult conversation, or simply saying "no." Responsibility is not about blame; it's about reclaiming authorship of your story.
3. **Focus Mapping:** Distraction is the enemy of transformation. List the three biggest distractions that pull you away from healing or purpose—they could be social media, toxic relationships, fear, or even overcommitment. Now ask yourself: "What deeper emotion am I avoiding through this distraction?" Commit to replacing each distraction with one focused act—prayer, journaling, exercise, or quiet reflection, something that centers you in truth.
4. **The Mirror of Honesty:** Stand before a mirror and look into your own eyes. Say out loud: "I see you. I forgive you. I'm ready to rebuild." Notice what emotions arise—resistance, sadness, peace. Those emotions will reveal where your transformation is still needed. Repeat this practice daily for seven days, watching how your reflection—and your heart—begin to soften.
5. **The Fire Statement:** Write one sentence that defines your current transformation. Start with this phrase: "The fire in me is refining ______." Fill in the blank with the truth of your journey—fear, self-doubt, guilt, resentment, or pain. Keep this statement visible—on your mirror, your phone, your journal. Let it remind you that transformation is not destruction. It's divine refinement.

6. **The Gratitude Ashes List:** Write down three painful experiences from your past. Next to each one, write at least one thing you've gained from it—wisdom, empathy, strength, or purpose. This is how you learn to thank the fire. Gratitude turns suffering into strength and ashes into beauty.
7. **The Daily Reset:** Each evening, reflect.
   - Where did I live in alignment with truth today?
   - Where did I hide behind fear or distraction?
   - What can I release tonight so I wake lighter tomorrow?

End with a simple affirmation: "I am being refined, not destroyed."

These practices will deepen your transformation from awareness into embodiment. When you do them with intention, you'll begin to feel the shift—not just in what you believe, but in how you live, love, and lead.

From Power to Purpose

Rising from the ashes is preparation for the next stage of life. Your power is not meant to remain private. It is meant to flow outward. Every giant you face, every betrayal you heal from, every fear you conquer amplifies your ability to serve.

Your purpose is not simply to survive. Your purpose is to rise, to heal, and to illuminate the path for others. When your pain becomes power, it becomes contribution. When your ashes become energy, they become life, love, and grace extended to the world.

Closing

The fire that once threatened to consume you is now the furnace that refines you. The ashes of betrayal, failure, and fear are now your arsenal. Every scar is a symbol of survival, resilience, and readiness.

Stand in the remains of your past and declare: "I am more than what hurt me. I am stronger than my giants. I am rising."

Rising from the ashes is not optional. It is necessary. It is the crucible in which power, purpose, and contribution are forged.

The giants may still roam, the shadows may linger, and the fire may flare again, but you now carry the armor, the insight, and the courage to face it all.

You rise. You transform. You give.

Your ashes are your power. Your power is your gift.

No man is free who is not master of himself.

Epictetus

Chapter 24

Commanding Your Kingdom: Mastery over Life and Influence

Command and Sovereignty: The Rise of the Inner King

The fires have cooled, and the storms have passed. The giants no longer guard your gates. You have fought through chaos and temptation and through doubt and delay. What once felt like an unending war within has now been won through persistence, humility, and grace. You stand not in survival but in sovereignty.

For the first time, the silence that surrounds you is not emptiness—it is peace. You are no longer reacting to life; you are responding with purpose. The weapons you once carried have become tools of wisdom. The armor you once wore in defense has become a robe of discernment. You are no longer a wanderer lost in the dark wood—you are a ruler standing at the edge of your own restored kingdom.

In the same way, when Dante finally escaped the dark wood, he did not emerge as the same trembling soul who first stood at the foot of the hill. He rose with clarity. His fear had become understanding. His confusion had become direction. The moment he stepped out of the shadows and onto solid ground was the moment he realized he was not just surviving the journey—he was beginning to rule himself. His path forward required sovereignty, not panic.

What lies ahead is no longer an inner war; it is the governance of a life reclaimed. The battlefield expands beyond the self into every word you speak, every space you inhabit, and every life you touch. Mastery is not about conquering new lands; it's about maintaining sacred order within the one you've been entrusted with. It is about living with intention, discipline, and integrity in a world that constantly tempts you toward distraction and division.

This is the chapter of command—where wisdom becomes strategy, influence becomes architecture, and your life becomes a kingdom to be mastered. The lessons that once healed you must now guide others. The strength that once protected you must now build and bless. You are no longer just surviving your story—you are shaping it.

The Quiet Crown: Leading from Within

True sovereignty is not loud or boastful. It is quiet confidence born from obedience to truth. It is the still authority of one who has walked through the storm, faced the giants, and emerged humbled and not hardened. The ruler who leads with love governs a realm that endures. This is the season where the inner warrior becomes the wise king, where the lessons of fire become the laws of peace, and where the heart that once fought to survive now learns to reign with grace.

The Cup of Water: The Measure of a King

There's a story told about Alexander the Great as he led his army across the blistering deserts of Persia. The sun was merciless. Days passed without water, and the men grew faint from thirst. Their lips cracked, their armor scorched their skin, and their steps slowed to a crawl.

At last, a small group of scouts returned with a single helmet filled with water—barely enough for one man. Exhausted, they offered it to Alexander. Every soldier watched, desperate for a sign of relief, believing their king would drink first.

Alexander took the helmet, looked at the faces of his weary soldiers, and without saying a word, lifted it high and then poured every drop into the sand. The water sank into the earth, lost forever.

For a moment, there was silence. Then there was a roar. His men stood taller. Their fatigue lifted. The same soldiers who were near collapse moments before suddenly found strength to continue. They would follow him through the fires of the world if he asked—not because he was their king, but because he was one of them.

That day, Alexander conquered more than territory—he conquered himself. He understood what few rulers ever do: Leadership is not about privilege; it's about presence.

True mastery is not measured by what you take for yourself but by what you're willing to surrender for the sake of others. A ruler's power is not proven in comfort but in restraint.

Alexander's act became legend not because it fed his men's bodies but because it fed their spirits. The man who could command thousands chose instead to serve their hearts.

And that's the essence of sovereignty—the wisdom to know that authority without humility destroys, but authority guided by compassion multiplies.

The greatest kings do not need to shout. Their silence speaks louder than their power ever could.

The Carpenter and the Castle

There was once a carpenter who spent his whole life building homes for other people. He worked hard, rose early, and poured his skill into every board and beam. But as the years passed, he grew tired and restless. His hands still worked, but his heart no longer burned with purpose.

When the time came to retire, his employer asked him to build one final house—a gift to honor his years of service. The carpenter agreed, but his spirit was half gone. He cut corners, used cheaper materials, and hurried through his work. The walls leaned slightly and the wood didn't fit tightly, but he told himself, "It's good enough."

When the house was finished, the employer smiled and handed him the keys. "Congratulations," he said. "This house is yours. It's my gift to you."

The carpenter froze. He realized that the home he had built carelessly would be the one he would live in for the rest of his life. What he had neglected out of fatigue now became his reality.

We are all builders of our own kingdoms. Every thought, every decision, every act of integrity or neglect becomes part of the house we inhabit. Some days, we build carefully. Other days, we rush, unaware that we are shaping the walls we'll one day live within.

When you understand that your choices are bricks in the architecture of your destiny, you begin to rule with intention instead of emotion. That is the heart of mastery.

Your Life As a Kingdom

Imagine your life as a vast kingdom. Every thought, every habit, every relationship, and every decision is a piece of its territory. The mind is your council chamber, the heart your throne, and the body your land. Every emotion is a messenger, every value a law, and every boundary a wall that protects what you've built.

Your time, attention, and energy are your armies—forces that can either defend your purpose or be scattered in meaningless battles. When you lead with discipline, your realm thrives. When you neglect your post, chaos creeps in quietly through unguarded gates.

A weak ruler allows disorder to spread. Boundaries crumble, priorities scatter, and old enemies—fear, pride, and distraction—begin to invade again. But a strong ruler surveys their kingdom daily. They walk their lands, tend to their fields, and listen to the needs of their people. They understand that mastery is not a moment of triumph but a lifetime of stewardship.

Your life works the same way. You can't rule what you don't understand. You can't protect what you don't tend to. Every area—your faith, health, finances, relationships, and purpose—is a province that needs attention, order, and care. The more intentional your governance, the stronger your peace.

This is where wisdom becomes structure and where strategy replaces impulse and clarity replaces confusion. The chaos that once ruled you now becomes your material for creation. Every discipline becomes a brick, and every act of self-control becomes a foundation stone.

But the moment you stop walking your land, neglect takes root. And neglect, when left unattended, becomes rebellion.

True peace never begins outside of us. It begins when we return to the inner work God entrusted to us, when the steward within finally takes the throne again under His authority. Chaos enters when we stop governing our thoughts, our impulses, and the stories we tell ourselves. Order returns when we choose clarity over confusion, discipline over drift, and truth over emotion.

You don't gain control of your life through force or perfection; you gain it through alignment—aligning your desires, your thoughts, and your will with the One who is truly sovereign. When the inner war stops and your soul stops fighting itself, something powerful begins to happen: Healing starts to flow, and the mind takes its rightful place as a servant of God rather than a slave to fear.

Peace is not a gift the world can offer; it is a crown worn by those who walk through their inner kingdom daily, tending it with God's help, refusing to let fear rule where purpose and calling belong.

The Neglected Kingdom (Allegorical Parable)

There was once a ruler who inherited a small but thriving kingdom. The rivers ran clear, the fields bore fruit, and the people lived in quiet contentment. The ruler had fought many battles to earn peace and believed that, with victory secured, the kingdom would govern itself. So he retreated to the palace, resting, indulging, and trusting that the order he had built would sustain itself.

At first, nothing seemed amiss. The markets still bustled, the crops still grew, and the walls still stood. But slowly, things began to shift. The roads cracked and were never repaired. The guards relaxed their watch at the borders. The wells went untended and began to dry. The people grew uncertain, and their hope dimmed like torches in the fog.

Seasons passed, and neighboring lands began to encroach. Not because they were stronger but because neglect had made the once-mighty kingdom soft. When the ruler finally left the palace, he was unrecognizable to his people. The land he once loved was covered in weeds and ruin. The very peace he had fought to secure had become the source of his downfall.

It wasn't invasion that destroyed his kingdom. It was inattention. In that moment, the ruler understood that mastery is not maintained by memory but by mindfulness. A kingdom cannot be ruled by comfort. It requires vigilance—daily presence, steady attention, and care for what seems small before it becomes broken.

So he began again. Each morning, he walked the roads himself. He listened to his people. He repaired the cracks in the walls with his own hands. In time, the kingdom flourished once more—not through conquest, but through consistency. Prosperity returned not because of victory but because of care.

Your life is no different. The fields are your habits, the walls are your boundaries, and the people are your relationships. When you neglect them, disorder spreads quietly until one day you awaken and realize the kingdom has shifted beneath your feet.

Neglect rarely roars; it whispers. It disguises itself as rest, as "taking a break," as "I'll get to it tomorrow." But tomorrow is how empires fall.

To lead your life well, you must walk your land. You must be present with your own mind, tend your disciplines, and nurture what is good before it fades. That is mastery: not control, but care; not dominance, but devotion.

The Mindset of Transformation

Transformation begins long before the world sees the results. It starts in the unseen territory of the mind—in the quiet, personal decision to change long before any evidence appears. The same fires that once burned you now become the forge that shapes you. The same storms that once threatened to drown you now carry you forward.

Growth never begins in comfort. It begins in confrontation, the moment you decide that the life you've settled for is no longer worthy of who you're becoming. The mind must first accept that the familiar is not always safe and that true peace often requires disruption.

The mindset of transformation is rooted in ownership. Nothing changes until you claim responsibility for your life: not with blame, but with authority. You may not have chosen every wound, every loss, or every betrayal, but you are responsible for what you build from them. Transformation begins the instant you stop asking, "Why did this happen to me?" and start asking, "What is this here to teach me?" That question turns pain into power and resistance into refinement.

Transformation is also not a single event—it's a process of steady refinement. Like a sculptor chiseling stone, you shape yourself through every act of discipline, every moment of integrity, every refusal to return to what once enslaved you. Some days, the progress will be visible. Other days, it will feel like silence—only the sound of the hammer striking within. But even in those quiet moments, change is happening beneath the surface.

True mastery requires patience. The strongest rulers don't rush growth—they cultivate it. They understand that wisdom comes in seasons, and each one has a purpose: spring for planting, summer for working, autumn for harvesting, and winter for reflection. The impatient ruler destroys the soil with haste; the wise one allows the land to rest and renew.

But perhaps the greatest transformation of all is the shift in identity. You cannot step into new power while clinging to the identity that created the old patterns. You can't become a new ruler while wearing the crown of your former self. Transformation demands rebirth—a conscious decision to think, speak, and live as the person you are becoming, and not as the one you've been.

When purpose fuels your mindset, every struggle becomes sacred. Pain without purpose breaks you; pain with purpose remakes you. The ruler who learns this truth can withstand any storm. Because the battle no longer happens on the outside—it happens within, where every thought becomes a decree, and every belief becomes law in the kingdom of the self.

To rule your life is to master your mind. To master your mind is to govern your destiny.

Reclaiming Your Worth and Releasing What Wasn't Meant for You

As Dante climbed upward from the circles, one truth became clearer with every step: Not every soul can go with you. Some remain in the shadows because they choose the shadows. Others stay behind because their journey ends where yours begins. The farther he rose, the more he realized that spiritual elevation requires separation—not out of pride, but out of purpose.

The same is true for us.

Sometimes the heart attaches itself to someone who cannot or will not return what you feel. And that pain—even when the relationship was never fully formed—can cut just as deeply as something you once called love. In my own situation with Linda, I'm not saying it was love, but the impact reached a wound that existed long before her. Because unreturned affection doesn't just hurt for what it is; it hurts for what it awakens.

That's the danger of the giants we met earlier on the journey: They collaborate. The Giant of Abandonment stands beside the Giant of Validation, and together they whisper, "If they didn't choose you, maybe you weren't worth choosing."

But Dante teaches us something different.

When he finally faced the giants at the edge of the pit—Nimrod, Ephialtes, and Antaeus—he saw that these towering beings had no power of their own anymore. They were chained, restricted, and bound by their own rebellion. They were not rulers of the journey—they were obstacles, collapsed and defeated by the very sins they once embodied.

And that's the same truth we must accept: The giants from our past only feel powerful when we approach them with old wounds.

Unrequited affection triggers doubt, insecurity, and questions of worth not because of the other person but because their silence echoes an older silence we never healed. That's why it hits so deeply. That's why it feels like rejection from the whole world.

But here is the truth you must anchor yourself in: Someone else's inability to see your value does not diminish it. Their limitations are not your identity. Their silence is not your reflection.

When Dante walked forward, he didn't ask the giants to approve of him or change their minds. He simply moved past them. And God calls us to do the same.

When you begin to see yourself the way God sees you—intentional, handcrafted, purposeful—you stop measuring your worth by how someone treats you. You stop trying to convince the wrong people to stay. You stop confusing attention with affection, and affection with identity.

Sometimes God allows distance, not to punish you, but to protect you. Sometimes He removes what you were reaching for so He can make room for what He ordained. Sometimes the affection that fails is the very thing that frees you.

My situation with Linda didn't crush me—it clarified me. It revealed where I was still vulnerable, still seeking validation, still tying my worth to someone else's response. It woke up something inside me. It pushed me toward compassion. It made me pay attention to the pain in others.

That brief moment of disappointment became a doorway to purpose. The healing I needed became the message I now carry. The brokenness became a lantern I use to guide people through their own shadows.

And that is exactly how Dante's journey worked—every wound became wisdom, every sorrow became direction, and every loss became part of his ascent.

Nothing that happens to you is random. Every shift, every silence, every closed door is allowed by God to shape the person you are becoming. Even unrequited love has purpose. It refines you. It strengthens you. It cuts the cords to lesser things so you can rise without carrying dead weight.

When someone leaves, let them go. When someone cannot match your effort, release them. The right people recognize your value immediately—not eventually.

Your worth is not up for negotiation. Not with people. Not with rejection. Not with your past. God already settled it.

He who rules his spirit is mightier than he who takes a city.

Proverbs 16:32 (ESV)

Chapter 25

Building the Kingdom: The Structure of Mastery

Steps to Transforming the Mindset

Transformation begins in the mind long before it manifests in behavior. The following steps are not a checklist—they are a process of renewal. You do not rush them; you embody them. Each one builds upon the last, moving you from awareness to authority and from awakening to action.

Awareness: Seeing the Old Patterns

You cannot change what you refuse to see. Awareness is the first light that breaks through the fog of habit. It is the courage to observe your thoughts, your reactions, and your repeated cycles without judgment. When you recognize how often you replay the same story—the same fears, the same excuses, the same emotional responses—you begin to reclaim power.

Awareness does not condemn; it clarifies. It shows you where energy leaks, where comfort hides, and where truth has been replaced by defense.

Truth illuminates what excuses conceal.

Acceptance: Facing Reality Without Resistance

Awareness without acceptance leads to denial.

Transformation cannot coexist with resistance. You must be willing to face your reality exactly as it is, not as you wish it were. Acceptance is not surrender; it is strength. It means saying, "This is where I am. Now I decide what to do with it."

When you accept your current state—the pain, the past, the patterns—you turn chaos into data. What was once an emotional storm becomes information for strategy.

Acceptance transforms chaos into clarity.

Ownership: Reclaiming Authority

Once you see and accept the truth, you must claim it. Ownership is where transformation takes root. You may not have caused every wound, but you are responsible for your healing. You may not have written every chapter of your past, but you are the author of what comes next.

Stop waiting for permission to change. Stop assigning blame for your stagnation. When you take full ownership of your choices, your emotions, and your direction, you stop living reactively and start leading your life like a kingdom under your command.

You cannot master what you refuse to own.

Intention: Redefining Who You're Becoming

Transformation fails when the goal is only to stop old behavior. True change begins when you define *who you are becoming.* Intention gives the mind direction and the soul focus. Decide what kind of person embodies your new mindset and how they think, speak, move, and respond.

Every decision then becomes a question of alignment: *Does this action match who I am becoming?*

Transformation sticks when identity shifts from who you were to who you are becoming.

Action: Repetition Creates Renewal

You cannot think your way into transformation; you must act your way into it. Every small, consistent action rewires the brain and rebuilds the spirit. Progress is not built through intensity but through repetition.

Discipline is not punishment; it is reinforcement. Every time you follow through on a new habit or resist an old temptation, you declare to your mind, "This is who I am now."

Transformation is not in the thinking; it's in the doing.

Reflection: Reinforcing the New Mind

Growth without reflection collapses into noise. Pause daily to measure the distance between who you were and who you are becoming. Reflection stabilizes transformation. Ask yourself each night:

- What did I learn about myself today?
- Where did I live in alignment with my new mindset?
- What needs reinforcement tomorrow?

Gratitude amplifies progress. Celebrate the smallest victories—they are proof that change is working.

Reflection turns progress into permanence.

Purpose: Anchoring Transformation in Meaning

Mastery is not abstract. It's built on structure, and it is steady, deliberate, and lived. Just as a kingdom rests on its pillars, so does a life of self-command. Without these supports, even the strongest willpower crumbles under distraction, temptation, or chaos. But with them, your life becomes immovable—a fortress of focus, wisdom, and peace.

These five pillars—Clarity, Discipline, Influence, Boundaries, and Contribution—are not ideals to admire; they are systems to live by. They determine whether your rule over yourself will be fleeting or eternal.

1. **Clarity: The North Star of the Mind**

No ruler can lead without vision. Clarity defines your direction, reveals your values, and protects you from confusion. It's not about knowing *everything*—it's about knowing what matters most.

Without clarity, effort becomes exhaustion. You chase a dozen goals and reach none. But with clarity, even small actions become powerful because they align with a single purpose.

Ask yourself

:

- What do I stand for?
- What am I unwilling to compromise?
- What vision governs my decisions?

Clarity is not discovered; it is chosen. You decide what your life stands for, and then you live in allegiance to that decision. Every day becomes a reaffirmation of purpose.

Clarity cuts through chaos like light through fog.

2. **Discipline: The Backbone of Freedom**

Freedom is not doing whatever you want—it's the power to do what's right, even when it's hard. Discipline is the daily act of loyalty to your highest self. It's the quiet consistency that builds unshakable strength.

The undisciplined ruler is a slave to emotion. The disciplined one commands results.

Discipline isn't intensity; it's integrity. It's waking up when you don't feel like it, following through on your word, and honoring commitments when no one is watching. Over time, it transforms effort into ease because what was once forced becomes natural.

Discipline is devotion disguised as repetition.

3. **Influence: The Ripple of Your Authority**

True power is not domination—it's direction. Influence is the art of shaping what's around you without coercion or ego. It's the invisible force that flows from character, consistency, and contribution.

You cannot command respect through fear and expect loyalty. Influence is built through credibility—the alignment between what you say and who you are.

Every conversation, every decision, and every moment of presence leaves an imprint. The question is: What kind of imprint are you leaving?

Influence is not about being followed—it's about being worth following.

4. **Boundaries: The Walls That Guard the Kingdom**

Without boundaries, even the richest kingdom falls to ruin. Boundaries are not walls of isolation—they are walls of integrity. They define what belongs within your peace and what must stay outside.

Saying "no" isn't rejection—it's protection. Saying "yes" without discernment drains your strength.

Boundaries protect your time, your energy, and your purpose from erosion. The wise ruler guards what is sacred. The weak one lets everyone and everything walk through the gates.

Ask yourself:

- What am I allowing that weakens me?
- What needs to be removed so peace can reign?

Boundaries don't limit your freedom—they preserve it.

5. **Contribution: Turning Power into Purpose**

The final pillar of mastery is contribution. A kingdom that exists only for its ruler soon collapses. Power without service is vanity; influence without generosity is emptiness.

True mastery over life culminates in what you give, not what you gain. Every gift, every lesson, every act of compassion extends your rule beyond yourself.

When your focus shifts from accumulation to contribution, your life becomes a legacy. And in that legacy, your influence outlives you.

The ruler who serves others multiplies his kingdom beyond time.

Each of these pillars is both a structure and a mirror. They reveal where your strength lies and where your foundation may still be cracked. Strengthen them daily. Walk your walls, check your gates, and feed your people—for your "kingdom" is every thought, action, and life you touch.

The Enemy of Mastery

Even after confronting giants and rising from ashes, there are threats that lurk in your kingdom.

- **Distraction:** The endless noise of modern life can erode focus. Every unchecked notification, every idle habit, every habit of comparison weakens your sovereignty.
- **Complacency:** Comfort is seductive. The moment you stop challenging yourself, the kingdom stagnates. Giants of fear and doubt can regain territory.
- **Toxic Influence:** Relationships, environments, or systems that drain energy or compromise your values are insidious invaders. They erode morale, distort perception, and sabotage progress.
- **Internal Saboteurs:** Old fears, shame, and resentment are never fully gone. They can manifest subtly, redirecting your decisions, undermining your authority, or freezing your action.

To command your kingdom, you must recognize these threats, name them, and actively defend against them.

The Warrior's Map

Mastery begins with assessment.

1. **Inventory Your Territory:** Map out every area of your life—health, relationships, finances, career, spiritual growth, and personal development. Identify where control is strong and where it is weak.

2. **Identify Allies and Adversaries:** Who supports your vision? Who drains it? Which relationships, habits, or environments empower you, and which ones hinder you?
3. **Strategize Resource Allocation:** Time, energy, and attention—these are your most finite resources. Deploy them with intention. Protect them fiercely.
4. **Set Tactical Boundaries:** Create rules for yourself and your interactions. Enforce them consistently. Boundaries are not optional—they are the framework of your kingdom.
5. **Expand Influence:** Every action you take should strengthen your domain and radiate outward. Mentor, teach, guide, inspire. Your personal mastery is meaningless if it does not elevate others.

Leadership Begins Within

Mastery is often misunderstood as domination. True mastery is not control over others—it is control over yourself, your environment, and the energy you emit. Leadership without integrity is tyranny. Leadership with integrity is transformative.

A ruler of a kingdom who hoards power, fears transparency, or manipulates subjects is a weak leader in disguise. But a ruler who leads with authenticity, courage, and generosity strengthens the entire realm. Influence grows, loyalty flourishes, and contribution becomes exponential.

Your kingdom thrives when you lead with love, clarity, and courage.

Practical Exercises for Mastery

1. **Daily Survey**

Spend ten minutes each morning mapping your kingdom. Ask:

- What needs my attention today?
- Which territories are under threat?
- Which areas are flourishing?

2. **Boundary Audit**

List all relationships, commitments, and environments. Identify where your energy is being drained or misused. Decide what to cut, limit, or adjust

.

3. **Power Deployment**

Write down three actions today that assert your influence positively—a conversation, a decision, or an act of service. Execute them.

4. **Reflection on Contribution**

Each night, journal:

- How did my actions strengthen my kingdom?
- Where did I uphold my values?
- Who benefited from my presence, wisdom, or support?

5. **Influence Expansion**

Seek one opportunity per week to mentor, teach, or guide. Even small actions ripple outward. Your mastery becomes a spark for others.

Reflection Questions

1. Which areas of my life are truly under my control, and which are neglected?
2. How do my habits, routines, and relationships support or sabotage my kingdom?
3. Who do I influence, and how can I do so more consciously?
4. Where have I been giving power away unnecessarily?
5. How can I create structures and boundaries to protect my energy and purpose?
6. What action today asserts my mastery and contribution simultaneously?

Closing

Commanding your kingdom is not about arrogance or ego. It is about responsibility. It is about rising fully into the role you were born to inhabit. Every giant defeated, every ash transformed, every shadow illuminated: They are the tools of authority.

A kingdom that is masterfully governed is a life fully lived. Your influence is felt far beyond your immediate surroundings. Your presence, your energy, and your contribution are transformative. You become a living example of victory, resilience, and power.

Step into your role. Survey your realm. Deploy your resources. Strengthen your borders. Expand your influence. Lead with integrity. Serve with courage.

Your life is your kingdom. Command it. Protect it. Elevate it.

The purpose of life is not to be happy. It is to be useful, to be honorable, to be compassionate—to have it make some difference that you have lived and lived well.

attributed to Ralph Waldo Emerson

Chapter 26

Living Unchained: Purpose, Presence, and Contribution

Living Unchained

Before Dante could rise into new understanding, he first had to face what lived within him. Your journey has been the same. The dark wood revealed your confusion. The circles exposed your patterns. The giants confronted your fear.

Now, just as Dante emerged ready to climb, this is where your ascent becomes structure. This is just the continuation of the same journey, moving from surviving your inner world to ruling it.

You've walked a long and merciless road through the fire that sought to consume you, through the storms that battered your faith, and through the silence that almost convinced you to quit—yet here you stand. The air is still, but it hums with something new. Power. Peace. Clarity.

You've fought giants that towered over your confidence. You've stared into darkness and refused to blink. You've watched the illusions burn away—the false identities, the borrowed beliefs, the noise that once drowned your purpose. And what remains is something unshakable: you.

The ground beneath you no longer feels like a battlefield. It feels sacred—the soil of transformation. The ashes of your pain have become the foundation of your power. The scars that once embarrassed you are now your armor. The same darkness that tried to bury you has become your teacher.

But this moment, right here—this stillness—is not the end. It's the beginning of everything. Freedom isn't what you thought it would be. It's not the absence of struggle or the disappearance of fear. It's waking up to the truth that you no longer have to be ruled by them. It's realizing that the chains were never around your wrists—they were in your mind, and now they're broken.

Living unchained means walking forward with purpose—not because life has become easier, but because you have become stronger. You move differently now. You speak differently. You think differently. You no longer react—you respond. You no longer beg for peace—you *create* it.

Every battle you've fought has brought you here to this clearing after the storm, where the air smells of new beginnings and the horizon stretches open like an unwritten story. The giants are gone, but their lessons remain. The fear is quieter, but it still whispers, testing your resolve. That's how you know you're alive.

Now comes the final act. This isn't about finishing another chapter or completing another reflection. This is about *embodying* everything you've learned; about living unchained, awake, and alive. It's about showing up as the version of yourself that can no longer be shaken by what once destroyed you.

You are no longer a survivor of your past. You are the architect of your future. You are no longer chasing worth—you *embody* it. You are no longer trying to find the light—you *carry* it.

Just as Dante, after confronting every layer of his inner darkness, finally emerged at the base of Mount Purgatory, blinking into the light of a world made new, this moment marks your own ascent. Dante did not rise because the journey grew easier; he rose because he grew different. His climb began the moment he realized Hell could not hold a man who refused to bow to it. In the same way, your rise begins here: not in perfection, but in awakening.

So as you turn the page, don't look for an ending. Look for a beginning. Because this moment right now is where your real story begins.

The Parable of the Caged Bird

There was once a bird born inside a cage. It had never known the feel of wind beneath its wings, only the rhythm of footsteps approaching with food and the faint shimmer of sunlight on metal bars. The cage became its world, its home, its safety, its prison.

Every morning, the bird watched the sky through the small square of light that reached its corner. It would see other birds soaring freely—wings open, voices echoing in the distance—and for a moment, something inside it stirred. But that stirring quickly gave way to fear.

One day, the keeper left the door open. No sound. No movement. Just an open space where the lock had always been.

The bird tilted its head, staring at the light beyond the door. Freedom, the very thing it had dreamed of, was right there. But its heart pounded, unsure. The outside was vast. Unpredictable. The cage was familiar. Safe.

So it stayed.

Hours passed. The sun shifted. Shadows stretched across the floor until the light disappeared. The open door creaked slightly in the wind, whispering a truth the bird was not yet ready to face: Captivity had become its comfort.

Days turned into weeks, and though the door was sometimes left ajar, the bird never left. It sang, it slept, it dreamed of the sky, but it never took flight.

In time, the bird grew old—still in its cage, still surrounded by freedom it never touched. And when the cage was finally empty, the wind that drifted through it carried no trace of sorrow—only the faint echo of a lesson: Freedom is not given; it is chosen. And sometimes, the door has been open all along.

The Invisible Chains

The greatest chains are not made of iron. They don't rattle or clank when you move. They live quietly in your routines, your fears, and the versions of yourself you've grown too used to carrying.

These are the invisible chains, the ones we mistake for comfort because we've worn them so long they start to feel like skin.

Fear is the first. It whispers that safety is better than growth, that comfort is wiser than courage. It keeps us loyal to small spaces and predictable days. Guilt is another. It binds us to the past, convincing us that we are undeserving of new beginnings. It punishes us for wounds that were meant to teach, not define.

Routine can be a quiet captor. It convinces us that repetition equals stability, when in truth it often hides stagnation. Life becomes a loop instead of a journey. And then there is identity, the most deceptive chain of all. We hold on to who we were because it feels certain, even if it's suffocating. We defend old versions of ourselves long after they've stopped serving the future we're called to build.

The tragedy is not that these chains exist; it's that we grow comfortable wearing them. They give us the illusion of control while quietly draining the pulse of life.

We all wear chains we can't see. They don't lock us in a room—they lock us inside ourselves. And when the door to freedom finally swings open, most of us don't rush out. We hesitate. Because freedom, at first, feels terrifying. It demands accountability, courage, and surrender.

Dante saw this same tragedy throughout the *Inferno*—souls who weren't chained by force but by attachment. They clung to illusions of identity, to patterns they refused to release, to cages they convinced themselves were kingdoms. Their suffering was not the fire around them but the lies within them. Freedom was always possible, but it was never chosen. And like those wandering souls, we must recognize when we are holding the lock to our own cages.

That's where the story of the caged bird begins—a story not of captivity but of choice.

The Unchained Life

To live unchained means to stop letting the past, the giants, the betrayals, or the frozen hearts dictate your actions. It means to stop letting fear, shame, guilt, or resentment rule your decisions.

You are free. Not because life suddenly became easy, or because giants no longer exist. You are free because you have learned to rise in spite of them. Freedom is born from mastery, courage, and choice. It is the fruit of all the work you have done.

Living unchained is not a state of comfort; it is a state of clarity, courage, and contribution. It is not passive. It is relentless, intentional, and alive.

Purpose As the Guiding Flame

Purpose is more than a goal. Purpose is the energy that drives your life, the fire that fuels your choices, and the compass that guides your actions. Every giant you faced, every mask you removed, every betrayal you processed, and every boundary you set was preparation for aligning your life with your true calling.

Without purpose, mastery becomes arrogance. Without contribution, freedom becomes selfish indulgence. Purpose without action is wasted energy.

Ask yourself:

- What am I here to do?
- How can my experiences—the pain, the victories, the lessons—serve others?
- What impact do I want to leave behind?

Purpose is not something you find outside yourself. It is discovered within through courage, self-reflection, and deliberate action.

Nelson Mandela: The Man Who Walked Out Free

Nelson Mandela's freedom did not begin when he left prison—it began while he was still inside it.

For twenty-seven years he lived in a small cell on Robben Island, forced into hard labor, cut off from family, and often humiliated by guards who tried to break his spirit. The days were filled with salt air and stone dust, and his nights were filled with silence. Yet through it all, Mandela refused to let bitterness take root. His body was confined, but his mind remained sovereign.

They took away his freedom, but they could not take away his choice—the choice to forgive, to learn, to rise. He studied law under a dim prison light, taught younger prisoners about justice, and treated his captors with dignity. He said, "No one is born hating another person."[5] Even surrounded by hate, he chose to believe in the power of reconciliation.

When he finally walked free in 1990, he did not walk out seeking revenge. He walked out with peace in his heart.

"As I walked out the door toward the gate that would lead to my freedom," Mandela later wrote, "I knew if I didn't leave my bitterness and hatred behind, I'd still be in prison."[6]

That is what it means to live unchained.

Mandela proved that freedom is not granted by the

---

5 Nelson Mandela, *Long Walk to Freedom* (Little, Brown, 1994).

6 Mandela, *Long Walk to Freedom.*

world—it is cultivated within. The chains that hold us are rarely made of steel. They are made of resentment, pride, and fear. He could have left prison a broken man, but he left a liberated one. He forgave those who harmed him and led a nation toward unity instead of vengeance.

He showed that true power is not domination but restraint. True victory is not survival but peace.

Freedom is not walking out of a cell; it's walking out without carrying the cell with you.

Mandela's life reminds us that living unchained means choosing forgiveness over fury, hope over hatred, and contribution over control. It means freeing not only yourself but also those who once opposed you because liberation that stops with you is incomplete.

The Practice of Purpose

Purpose isn't something you stumble upon one day—it's something you practice daily. It's shaped, refined, and strengthened by consistency. Living unchained doesn't mean you suddenly know all the answers; it means you've committed to showing up with intention every single day, even when clarity feels distant.

Purpose grows in motion. Every small act of service, every honest word, every courageous decision—they all build momentum. The most fulfilled people aren't those who found purpose overnight, instead they are those who practiced it through trial, failure, and faith. They turned ordinary choices into sacred ones.

To live with purpose means to wake up and ask, "What can I give today? Who can I lift? What can I create that outlives me?" It means aligning your actions with your values so that even your smallest moments echo eternity.

When you live this way, even mundane tasks take on meaning. The way you speak to others, the way you handle challenges, the way you carry yourself—all become part of your ministry. Your purpose stops being a destination and becomes a rhythm, a way of moving through the world with clarity and compassion.

Living with purpose doesn't require perfection—it requires presence. It's not about doing everything right; it's about doing the right thing for the right reason. It's knowing that progress, not performance, is what builds legacy.

And as you continue to practice purpose, something extraordinary happens: Your life starts to overflow. Peace stops being something you chase and becomes something you radiate. You stop striving to be significant and start focusing on being sincere. You stop measuring your worth in what you achieve and begin seeing it in what you give.

Purpose is not found in grand gestures; it's built in the small, faithful moments when no one is watching, when nothing glamorous is at stake, and when your only audience is God.

Presence As the Power of Now

To contribute fully, you must be present. Presence is not about perfection or control. It is about awareness, engagement, and authenticity.

A distracted, resentful, or fearful person cannot give fully. Only when your attention is grounded in the now can you recognize the needs of others, the opportunities for action, and the ways your energy can flow outward.

Presence is cultivated through:

- **Mindfulness**—noticing your thoughts, emotions, and reactions without judgment.
- **Emotional integrity**—acknowledging feelings but not being ruled by them.
- **Authentic action**—choosing steps that align with values and purpose.

Contribution As the Measure of Victory

All the work you have done—facing giants, mastering your kingdom, thawing betrayal, and transforming anger—was never just for you. True transformation is always relational and generative. It's measured by the lives you touch, the hope you instill, the guidance you give, and the example you set.

Your contribution is the outward expression of your inner work. The light you have reclaimed, the courage you have built, and the freedom you have earned become the spark that ignites transformation in others. In this way, what began as your own journey of healing and pain evolved into a mission of empathy and genuine care.

I wrote from a place of pain. Every chapter, every word came from the depths of what I once had to overcome. But over time, that pain transformed into purpose. Writing became an act of healing—not just for me, but for others who would one day walk the same road. What started as therapy became testimony. What began as survival became service.

The pages that once carried my brokenness now carry light for those still lost in their storms. That is the power of contribution—it turns your scars into lamps, your suffering into strategy, your story into strength for others to rise.

And that's when you realize: This journey was never just about you. Every time you speak truth, forgive, encourage, or lead, your healing multiplies. You become living proof that pain can be repurposed into power and that every wound can become a weapon for good.

The highest purpose of victory isn't self-celebration; it's self-giving. To serve, to guide, to lift—that is the true reward. The same fire that once burned you now fuels your compassion. And that, more than anything, is what it means to live unchained.

The Ripple Effect of Freedom

Freedom is never meant to end with one person. When you rise, the atmosphere around you shifts. Your peace begins to influence the rooms you walk into. Your discipline becomes a quiet sermon. Your compassion begins to heal people who may never know your full story—they just feel your presence and sense something different.

Every healed person becomes a lighthouse. Every moment of authenticity becomes an invitation for others to remove their masks. The more you live unchained, the more you unconsciously give permission for others to do the same.

The world doesn't need more noise—it needs more examples. People don't change because they've been lectured; they change because they've seen what freedom looks like. That's the beauty of the ripple effect—one act of forgiveness can inspire ten more, one story of healing can break a thousand silent chains, and one courageous life can open countless locked doors.

You never truly know who's watching you. Someone may be drawing strength from your story without ever telling you. They see your consistency, your resilience, and your calm in storms and they think, *If they can overcome, maybe I can too*. That's the unseen ministry of living unchained.

Your words, your choices, your presence—they become living seeds. Some will take root immediately, others years later. But every one carries the potential to change a life. You may never see the harvest, but the impact remains.

And so, freedom becomes contagious. Not because it's loud but because it's lived.

The Daily Practice of Living Unchained

Living unchained is not a one-time declaration. It is a daily commitment to act with integrity, clarity, and purpose.

1. **Daily Alignment:** Each morning, identify one act that aligns with your purpose. Let this guide your day.
2. **Face the Subtle Giants:** Even now, minor fears, doubts, or resentments will arise. Name them. Do not let them control you.
3. **Engage Fully:** Approach every interaction and responsibility with presence. Listen deeply, act intentionally, and contribute freely.
4. **Reflect and Adjust:** Each evening, review your day. Celebrate victories. Correct misalignments. Strengthen boundaries. Reclaim lost energy.
5. **Radiate Contribution:** Seek opportunities to uplift others. Share wisdom, encourage, mentor, or provide support. Your growth is magnified through the impact you create.

The Communion of the Unchained

Living unchained is not meant to be a solitary pursuit. Freedom expands when it's shared. The same way light spreads from candle to candle without losing its flame, your liberation carries the power to awaken others. You are not meant to walk this road alone—you are part of a communion, a fellowship of the unchained.

Every person who chooses truth over illusion, forgiveness over bitterness, and love over fear becomes part of a quiet revolution. Together, these souls form the living fabric of transformation—a collective heartbeat that reminds the world that light still wins.

When you live freely, your courage becomes contagious. People who once hid their pain begin to open up. Those who doubted their strength begin to believe again. You start to see that your healing was never just for you—it was for the countless lives connected to yours in ways you may never fully understand.

To live unchained in community means to uplift, not to compete. It means seeing others not as rivals but as reflections. It means celebrating their victories as your own because freedom multiplies when shared. The communion of the unchained is a movement of authenticity—people walking together, each carrying a piece of the light forward.

No one ascends alone. The climb is steep, but it becomes sacred when shared. In your words, your example, your compassion, you become both student and guide—learning as you lift and growing as you give.

And perhaps that's the truest form of legacy: not just breaking your own chains, but helping others see that theirs were never locked.

Legacy As Your True Measure

Ultimately, living unchained is about legacy. Not fame, wealth, or recognition but the enduring impact of your choices, actions, and presence.

Ask yourself:

- What patterns have I broken that will benefit the next generation?
- What lessons have I learned that can guide someone else through their storm?
- How can my life become a beacon for those still fighting giants in their own hearts?

Your legacy is not written in accolades. It is written in lives transformed, hearts healed, courage inspired, and love expressed. Every act of integrity, every victory over fear, and every contribution is a stone in the foundation of the world you leave behind.

Legacy is not about what people say when you're gone—it's about what still lives because you were here. It's written not in monuments or titles but in the quiet ripples your life creates. The smile you restored. The hope you sparked. The faith you reignited in someone who had nearly given up.

You've fought hard to reach this point through storms of anger, betrayal, and self-deception, and each battle has shaped the light you now carry. That light is not meant to stay with you. It is meant to spread. The greatest test of freedom is not what you do for yourself but what your freedom empowers in others.

Legacy isn't loud. It's often invisible: the student who remembers your encouragement ten years later, the friend who finally forgave because you showed them how, the child who learned courage from watching you rise after you fell. It's the echo of integrity that travels long after the applause fades.

When you live unchained, your very existence becomes a testimony. People watch how you handle loss, how you speak to strangers, how you honor your word. You are teaching—even when you don't mean to—what freedom looks like in motion.

And this is where the story turns from survival to stewardship. The life you've rebuilt is no longer about proving worth; it's about multiplying value. Your scars become maps for those still wandering. Your pain becomes permission for others to heal. Your victories become the blueprint for those who doubted they could rise.

Legacy isn't something you leave behind—it's something you live right now. Every conversation, every act of kindness, every decision aligned with your values writes another line of it.

Remember this truth: You are someone's answered prayer. You are walking proof that healing is possible. You are the evidence that transformation is real.

So live intentionally. Speak truthfully. Love relentlessly. Because one day, when the world remembers you, it won't be the battles you fought that define your name—it will be the lives you touched, the courage you shared, and the light you refused to hide.

Legacy isn't something that waits for the end of your life—it unfolds in the ordinary moments that make up your days. Every sunrise offers you the chance to write another line, to love more deeply, to forgive more freely, to lead more courageously. Your life is your message, written in actions, not words.

So before you move forward, take a breath. Look at the story you've already written—the battles you've fought, the peace you've reclaimed, the lives you've touched—and ask yourself what the next chapter will say. Because the greatest legacies are not left by those who merely lived but by those who *lived awake*.

Now it's your turn to reflect—not as a survivor, but as a builder. Not as someone who endured but as someone *who transformed.*

Reflection Questions: Living Unchained

1. Where in my life am I still chained by fear, guilt, shame, or resentment?
2. How does my purpose guide my daily actions?
3. How present am I in my interactions, choices, and contributions?
4. What steps can I take today to serve others more fully?
5. How can I use my story, experiences, and victories to guide or inspire others?
6. What legacy do I want to leave, and what action today brings me closer to it?

Reflection Exercises: Living Unchained

Identify the Chain: Write down one resentment, memory, or fear that still holds space in your heart. Be honest.

What emotion still tugs at you when you think of it—anger, guilt, shame, or pain?

Freedom begins with truth. You can't release what you refuse to name.

Redefine Power: Ask yourself what it would mean to reclaim your power from this chain. Mandela's power wasn't in vengeance; it was in choice. How can you turn your pain into power, not by controlling others, but by mastering yourself?

Choose Forgiveness, Not Permission: Forgiveness doesn't justify what happened—it releases you from it. Write a short letter (you don't have to send it) to the person, memory, or version of yourself you need to forgive. End it with: "You no longer define me."

Practice Internal Freedom: Each morning, tell yourself that "Today, I will not live from fear. I will live from freedom." When anxiety or resentment arises, pause and breathe. Ask yourself, "What would freedom choose in this moment?" Acting from that place retrains the mind toward peace.

Expand the Liberation: Living unchained isn't only personal—it's relational.

- Who around you still lives behind invisible bars of fear, doubt, or bitterness?
- How can your words, empathy, or example help them unlock their own gates?

Anchor in Purpose: Reflect on how your freedom can serve others. Mandela's release wasn't just for himself—it became a movement. Ask yourself, "Who is waiting for my courage to inspire theirs?"

Remember: Living unchained is not a single act of breaking free—it's a daily choice to live from love, not limitation.

Closing: Step into Fullness

This is the moment you have been preparing for—the life unchained, fully present, fully awake, and fully contributing. It is not without challenge. Giants still exist. Life will always demand courage. Pain will arrive. Betrayal may surface.

But now you are armed with clarity, mastery, courage, and resilience. You have walked through fire and ice, faced your shadows, mastered your kingdom, and confronted giants. You are free.

And now, your life is no longer about mere survival. It is about living fully, loving without hesitation, and giving without restraint.

Step into your freedom. Live unchained. Stand in purpose. Radiate presence. Contribute relentlessly. Your life is no longer just yours—it is a force of transformation for the world

The meaning of life is to find your gift, the purpose of life is to give it away.

attributed to Pablo Picasso

Chapter 27

The Armor of Integrity

The Forging of Armor

By now, you have walked through fire and storm, crossed rivers of blood, stood in the frozen silence of betrayal, and faced the giants that haunted your soul. You have stared into the shadows of greed, anger, deception, and fear and found within them the raw materials of transformation.

Now comes the forging.

This is where strength becomes substance and where lessons harden into protection. This is the moment you take everything you've learned and shape it into something that can carry you through the battles ahead.

Dante experienced the same truth on his descent through the *Inferno*. The circles he walked were not just punishments—they were revelations. Every circle exposed a different fracture of the human soul.

Dante wasn't merely observing the damned; he was confronting the very tendencies that once lived in him. By witnessing the cost of deception, rage, illusion, and misplaced desire, he began to form something within himself: a clarity that could only be forged in darkness. He entered Hell confused and divided, but with each circle, his understanding sharpened, his resolve strengthened, and his character became more whole. His descent became his shaping. His confrontation became his forging.

Integrity is the armor that guards your purpose. Without it, your victories are hollow. Without it, your calling collapses under the weight of ego and compromise. Integrity is what keeps your power clean. It protects the gift you were given so that when you share it with the world, it remains pure.

To walk unchained is to live with freedom. To walk armored is to live with responsibility. Together, they form the balance of a life that cannot be shaken.

Integrity is not perfection; it is alignment. It is living in such a way that your private life and your public voice echo the same truth. It means your actions whisper the same faith your words declare. It means you are trustworthy even when no one is watching, steadfast even when it costs you, and faithful even when it hurts.

This chapter is about protecting what you've become: the light you've fought to reclaim, the purpose you've rediscovered, and the truth you now carry. Because the battles don't end when you find freedom. The enemy simply changes form.

Your armor is what keeps you whole when the world tries to fracture you.

What Integrity Really Means

Integrity is more than honesty—it's alignment. It is the rare harmony between your beliefs, your words, and your actions. It is being one person—not a version for the public and another in private. When integrity governs your life, there are no hidden corners, no secret exceptions, no quiet negotiations with your conscience.

Integrity is the invisible witness of your soul. It speaks when you are silent. It tells the truth when no one is listening. It's what you rely on when applause fades and temptation whispers.

It's easy to appear noble when life is simple. The test comes in pressure—when truth costs comfort, when honesty risks rejection, and when doing what's right means losing what's convenient. In those moments, integrity doesn't just reveal who you are; it shapes who you become.

Dante understood this better than anyone. As he descended through the *Inferno*, he encountered souls who had not fallen in a single catastrophic moment—they had eroded slowly, one compromised choice at a time. A lie told here, a boundary ignored there, a desire justified "just this once."

Their punishments were not arbitrary; they were the natural outcome of lives lived out of alignment. The *Inferno* wasn't a portrait of monsters—it was a warning of what happens when a person stops listening to the truth inside them.

Dante saw how integrity, once fractured, becomes a chain that drags a soul deeper and deeper into confusion. His journey through darkness became the mirror that taught him the cost of compromise and the necessity of living whole.

Every time you bend the truth, your armor thins. Every unkept promise leaves a crack. Every compromise of principle—no matter how small—corrodes the structure from within. But each moment of courage, each decision to stay true when no one would blame you for folding, reforges that armor in fire.

Integrity is both a shield and a sword. As a shield, it guards your heart from corruption and from the slow erosion of excuses and self-deception. As a sword, it cuts through confusion, illusion, and hypocrisy. It brings clarity when the world offers chaos.

Integrity doesn't demand perfection—it demands presence. It's the daily discipline of staying awake to what you believe and letting those beliefs govern your behavior.

So ask yourself:

"Do my actions echo my values?"

"Do my private thoughts honor the same truth I speak aloud?"

"Am I whole or am I performing pieces of myself for approval, comfort, or gain?"

To live with integrity is to live without disguise. It is to move through the world unmasked, unashamed, and unafraid—knowing that your life, in all its seasons, stands for something that cannot be bought or broken.

Layers of Integrity

Integrity is not a single decision—it's a structure. Each layer you build strengthens the one beneath it, forming an armor that guards both your peace and your purpose. These layers aren't made of metal; they're forged from choices—small, daily decisions that decide who you become when no one is watching.

Dante saw the danger of neglecting these layers as he moved deeper through the Inferno. Each circle showed him the accumulated weight of unexamined habits (small lies, unchecked desires, ignored convictions), not a single catastrophic failure. No soul fell all at once; they slipped gradually, one layer at a time, until the absence of integrity solidified into identity.

Dante realized that every step downward was simply the natural result of choices never corrected. His journey revealed a truth we often avoid: Integrity doesn't collapse overnight—it erodes slowly and silently when we stop tending to the layers that protect us.

1. **Truthfulness: The Core Layer**

Truth is the foundation of integrity. Without it, nothing holds. Truth begins with yourself—acknowledging what's real, even when it's painful. It's easier to lie to others than to face our own reflections. But the moment you speak truth within, you begin to heal. Every deception—even one told to protect your ego—weakens your armor. Every truth spoken strengthens it. Truthfulness is not about brutality; it's about clarity. When you stand in truth, you no longer have to remember what you said—your life simply tells the story for you.

2. **Consistency: The Tempering Layer**

Integrity is tested in repetition. Doing the right thing once is easy. Doing it again tomorrow is character. Consistency transforms conviction into credibility. It means showing up the same way in the shadows as you do in the spotlight. Ask yourself: "Do my actions echo my words?" When they do, you become dependable to others and to yourself. And that dependability builds trust, the invisible currency of every relationship and every calling.

3. **Boundaries: The Shield Layer**

Boundaries protect your integrity from erosion. They are not walls that isolate; they are gates that guard what's sacred. Without boundaries, compassion becomes exhaustion, generosity becomes resentment, and conviction turns into compromise. Saying "no" to what threatens your peace is saying "yes" to what sustains your purpose. Every boundary you honor reinforces your armor; every one you ignore leaves a seam open for doubt, manipulation, and fatigue.

4. **Responsibility: The Refining Layer**

Responsibility is the weight that makes armor real. It's the refusal to hide behind excuses or blame. When you own your mistakes, you reclaim your power. When you correct them, you reinforce your character. Responsibility doesn't weaken you—it grounds you. True responsibility says, "I did this. I can learn. I can make it right." It turns failure into refinement, shame into wisdom, and chaos into order.

5. **Courageous Action: The Outer Layer**

All the previous layers mean nothing without courage. Courage is the heat that seals the armor. It's the strength to stand when it would be easier to yield, to speak when silence would keep you safe, to live by conviction even when it costs you comfort. Courage transforms integrity from a belief into a lifestyle. It's the quiet defiance that says, "I will not bend, even if I stand alone."

Why Armor Matters

Life does not stop testing you once you find peace. Even after clarity comes, the world still throws storms, and old giants still whisper from the shadows. That's why your armor matters—because peace without protection is fragile, and freedom without discipline is fleeting.

Dante understood this deeply as he moved through the *Inferno*. He saw souls who had once known truth but failed to guard it—men and women who began with conviction yet ended imprisoned by habits that slowly corroded them. Their torment was not the flames or the darkness but the realization that they had been undone by small compromises.

Each circle revealed the same warning: The danger is not the battle you survive but the weakness you ignore. Even the strongest soul can fall when its integrity cracks, not in grand betrayals, but in the quiet moments where truth is abandoned for comfort.

Dante learned that the greatest threat was never the demons around him—it was the erosion within. That is why armor is essential: Without it, even victory becomes vulnerable.

It allows you to:

- Face betrayal without becoming bitter.
- Tell the truth even when it costs you comfort.
- Protect your energy when others try to drain it.
- Love deeply without losing yourself.
- Serve faithfully without compromising your soul.

When your armor is strong, you stop reacting from fear and start responding from strength. You no longer live for approval or validation. You live from conviction.

Armor doesn't make you untouchable—it makes you unbreakable. It's what lets you walk through chaos with calm, speak truth in confusion, and remain grounded when others lose their way. It's not built for hiding from the world—it's what equips you to face it.

And perhaps most importantly, integrity keeps you close to God. When your inner world aligns with His truth, no external storm can shake you. You become both anchor and vessel—steady, guided, and purposeful.

So keep tending to your armor. Polish it daily with reflection. Repair the cracks with humility. Strengthen the joints with prayer. Every moment you live in integrity, your armor gleams a little brighter, reflecting not perfection but presence.

Because when the next battle comes—and it always does—it won't be your circumstances that determine your victory. It will be your integrity.

The Daily Practice of Armor

Armor isn't forged once and forgotten. It must be maintained, polished, and strengthened through deliberate practice.

Dante learned this as he journeyed deeper into the *Inferno*. At every level, he saw souls frozen in habits they never corrected; men and women whose downfall wasn't a single catastrophic failure but the daily neglect of their moral direction.

Some had drifted so subtly that they never noticed the slope beneath their feet until it became a cliff. Their fate wasn't sealed by one moment of rebellion but by thousands of small choices unexamined.

Dante realized that Hell was not filled with monsters—it was filled with consequences. Each soul was the final result of what they practiced daily.

That is why vigilance matters. Integrity is not built in dramatic moments; it is built in the quiet spaces where no one watches but God. Each day brings a choice: to guard your peace or give it away, to act in truth or drift into pretense, to live aligned or divided. Every choice either dulls your armor or sharpens it.

1. **Identify the Weak Points**

Integrity doesn't fail in explosions; it leaks through cracks. Take time each morning to reflect: *Where am I vulnerable? Is it fear, impatience, pride, or fatigue?* Awareness is the whetstone that keeps the blade sharp. You can't protect what you refuse to examine.

2. **Journal Your Observations**

Writing turns self-awareness into accountability. At the end of each day, record moments when you stood firm and moments when you didn't. Ask what emotions or pressures pulled you off-center. Journaling doesn't condemn; it clarifies. It turns the invisible into insight.

3. **Take Corrective Action**

When you notice a fracture, repair it quickly. Apologize where needed. Re-establish a boundary. Speak the truth that went unsaid. Integrity is rebuilt not through guilt but through course correction. Every repair restores strength and resets alignment.

4. **Celebrate the Small Victories**

Discipline can feel heavy; gratitude keeps it light. Acknowledge each act of integrity—every time you told the truth, kept a promise, or honored a boundary. These are not small things; they're spiritual weightlifting. They train your soul to carry conviction with ease.

5. **Teach Through Example**

Integrity multiplies through influence. When people witness honesty lived out with consistency and humility, it awakens something in them. You become a mirror that reflects what courage looks like in real life. Your actions preach louder than any sermon.

Daniel: The Unshakable Signature

Daniel was a senior architect overseeing a multimillion-dollar project. Everything was on track until his supervisor asked him to "adjust" a few numbers before an inspection deadline. "It's not lying," the supervisor said, "just smoothing the paperwork."

Daniel went home restless. He thought of his mortgage, his family, the years he'd invested in the company. Then he remembered something his mentor once told him: "If you bend once for convenience, you'll bend forever for approval."

The next morning, Daniel refused to sign. Calmly. Respectfully. Unapologetically. He didn't shout or moralize. He simply said, "My name means something. I want it to keep meaning something."

He lost the promotion, but he kept his peace. Months later, the adjusted data was exposed as part of a larger cover-up and Daniel's integrity became the benchmark for trust inside the company.

His quiet refusal became its own kind of leadership.

My Son Mikey: Tested by Truth

My son Mikey's first job was at a ticket booth by the beach.

Nothing complicated, just checking tickets and making sure people paid before entering. It wasn't glamorous, but it was his first real taste of responsibility.

When he told me he got the job, I joked, "Nice! That means I can get into the beach for free now." We both laughed, but soon after I pulled him aside and said, "Don't ever compromise your job for anyone, not even for me. Integrity isn't about convenience. It's about who you are when no one's watching."

A few days later, that lesson became real. The beach office received a report: Someone had been taking cash under the table, letting people in without recording the sale. Management began investigating, questioning each worker. Mikey was one of them.

He didn't panic. He didn't deflect. He told the truth—calmly, clearly, and unwaveringly. After reviewing the logs and cameras, the managers cleared him completely. He had done everything right.

The irony wasn't lost on me: Our very first conversation about doing the right thing had become his first real test.

That's the rhythm of life: The moment you speak truth, the world gives you a chance to prove it. Doing the right thing isn't just moral—it's foundational. It builds trust, and trust builds legacy.

A kingdom built on integrity stands long after the noise fades. But one built on deception? It crumbles under its own weight. Every time you choose honesty, you reinforce your foundation. Every time you compromise, you build on sand—and the tide always comes in.

Alex: The Slow Erosion

Alex was a respected financial advisor—sharp, successful, and admired. His career began with integrity at the center. He treated clients like family and built his name on transparency.

Then the pressure came. New leadership. Aggressive quotas. The promise of bigger bonuses. "Everyone's exaggerating numbers," they told him. "It's just how the game works."

At first, it was small—rounding up performance stats, overselling minor details. Then the lies became habit. And habits became identity.

Years later, it all unraveled. An audit revealed falsified records. His license was revoked. Clients he loved felt betrayed.

When I met Alex at a retreat, he said quietly, "I didn't lose everything at once. I lost it one small compromise at a time."

That's how integrity dies—not in explosions, but in slow erosion.

But Alex's story didn't end there. He began rebuilding. One apology at a time. One truth at a time. He started volunteering, mentoring others about ethics in business. His life became proof that restoration is possible, but only through humility.

He said something I'll never forget: "You can rebuild money and reputation. But rebuilding trust with yourself—that's the real work."

Integrity As Contribution

Integrity was never meant to make you invincible—it was meant to make you useful. Your armor doesn't exist just to guard your peace; it exists to empower your purpose. Once you've learned to stand firm in truth, the next step is to serve from it.

Integrity creates capacity. When your heart is clean and your motives are aligned, your energy flows outward toward others, toward impact, and toward purpose. You stop wasting energy maintaining appearances, and you start investing it in something eternal.

Every person you meet is affected by the strength of your integrity. It's in how you handle conflict, how you keep promises, how you follow through when no one's watching. These quiet acts build invisible bridges: connections of trust that outlast any title or platform.

Integrity Expands Influence

True influence isn't built on charisma; it's built on consistency. People trust what they see you do repeatedly, not what they hear you say once. When your word becomes dependable, your presence becomes magnetic. That's how leaders are born: not by noise, but by steadiness.

Integrity Strengthens Relationships

Integrity doesn't just protect you; it protects others. When people know you'll tell the truth—even when it's uncomfortable—they feel safe around you. Honesty becomes oxygen. Transparency becomes trust. Your presence becomes a refuge in a world addicted to performance.

Integrity Elevates Purpose

Integrity turns daily routines into sacred acts. When you work, you're not just earning—you're honoring your calling. When you lead, you're not just directing—you're serving. When you forgive, you're not just letting go—you're setting someone free. Each choice to walk in truth widens your reach because people follow authenticity more than authority.

When you live this way, integrity becomes contagious. Your life quietly challenges others to rise, to do better, to hold themselves to the same invisible standard. And when enough people live like that, integrity stops being a moral idea—it becomes a movement.

So wear your armor not as a wall but as a light. Let your strength protect without hardening. Let your honesty inspire without condemning. Because when integrity becomes contribution, your life shifts from self-preservation to soul expansion.

That is where legacy begins—not with applause, but with alignment.

Reflection Questions

1. Where in my life have I compromised my integrity, even subtly?

2. What masks do I wear that weaken my armor?
3. Which boundaries do I need to set or reinforce?
4. How consistently do my actions align with my values?
5. What courageous act can I take today to strengthen my armor?
6. How will reinforcing my integrity allow me to serve others more fully?

Reflection Exercises: The Cost and Renewal of Integrity

1. **Recognize the First Crack**

Think of one area of your life—work, relationships, or personal goals—where compromise slipped through.

Ask yourself: "What did I justify at the time, and what did it cost me beneath the surface?"

Awareness is the beginning of repair. The cracks you ignore today become fractures tomorrow.

2. **Revisit Your Original Standard**

Return to the person you were before the compromise—the one who valued honesty above approval.

Write down what principles once guided you that you've stopped protecting.

Integrity is restored when you realign with your original standard.

3. **Name the Pressure**

Integrity bends under pressure: fear, finances, loneliness, ambition. Identify the force that tempted you to compromise.

Ask: "What fear or need drove my decision?"

Naming it disarms its power.

4. **Repair the Damage**

Integrity rebuilds through humility. Make amends where truth was abandoned—even quietly.

Ask: "Who deserves my honesty, apology, or correction?"

You can't rewrite the past, but you can redeem it through action.

5. **Rebuild the Routine**

Create one daily habit that anchors you in truth—morning reflection, evening journaling, or simply a private vow not to exaggerate.

Ask: "What action today will keep my armor polished tomorrow?"

The practice becomes your protection.

6. **Teach Through Transparency**

   Integrity grows when shared. Tell your story—your failure, your lesson, your renewal—to someone who needs courage. Your vulnerability might become the spark that strengthens their armor too.

Closing: The Armor That Shines

Integrity is not about being flawless; it's about being faithful. It's not about appearing strong; it's about staying true. Every act of truth, no matter how small, forges another plate of armor over your heart.

When you live this way, your presence commands quiet respect. People trust your words because they see your life behind them. And as you move through the world—unhidden, unbending, unafraid—you become living proof that light and strength can coexist.

Your armor is not just protection—it's reflection. It doesn't hide who you are. It reveals who you've become.

And just as Dante, standing at the very mouth of Hell, wiped the soot from his face and stepped forward with renewed clarity, so do you. He did not rise because the darkness vanished—he rose because he had become someone who could not be swallowed by it anymore. His armor was not forged of iron but of insight, courage, and unshakable truth. In the same way, your integrity becomes your shining armor—the proof that you have walked through fire and emerged not burned but refined. It is this armor that now carries you into the life ahead: steady, rooted, aligned, and unbreakably whole.

He who is not courageous enough to take risks
will accomplish nothing in life.

Muhammad Ali

Chapter 28

The Sword of Courage

From Armor to Action

Your armor protects you. It shields your heart, clarifies your mind, and stabilizes your spirit. But armor alone does not win battles. Armor allows you to stand, to resist, to survive. To conquer, to act, and to move forward, you need a sword—a force that cuts through fear, hesitation, and uncertainty. That sword is courage.

Courage is not the absence of fear. It is the choice to move forward despite fear. It is the spark that turns reflection into action, insight into contribution, and potential into results. Courage is what allows your armor—your integrity—to become effective. Without courage, armor is only protection; with courage, it is power.

Armor without motion rusts. You can polish it, hide behind it, and convince yourself that you're safe, but rust still forms in stillness. The same is true of the human spirit. Without movement, your purpose decays beneath layers of hesitation and self-doubt.

Dante knew this moment well. When he stood at the gate of Hell, armor would have done nothing for him. The only thing that pushed him forward was courage—the willingness to step into the darkness even though every instinct told him to turn back. The journey didn't begin when he understood the path. It began the moment he took a trembling step into the unknown. That's what courage is: the decision to move when fear insists you shouldn't.

Understanding the Giants You Face

You've met your giants before. You've seen them in the chapters behind you—those voices that whispered "not now... wait... it's too risky."

They wear familiar disguises: self-doubt that slows your steps, procrastination that hides as patience, fear that masquerades as wisdom, and comfort that poses as peace.

They're persistent. They don't vanish when you recognize them—they return each time you step closer to purpose. But this time, you are not meeting them unarmed. You carry the sword of courage.

Courage doesn't negotiate with giants; it exposes them. It shines a light on their lies and reminds you that hesitation is not humility—it's bondage. The moment you act, their size diminishes. What once towered over you becomes something you can step past.

Every giant has one weakness: movement. They feed on inaction and fear, but they starve in momentum. When you swing your sword—when you choose honesty, integrity, and forward motion—their power breaks.

You've already named your giants. Now, it's time to face them.

Dante's giants weren't metaphors—he literally faced the towering Titans chained in the pit of Hell. But those giants symbolized something deeper: the forces that once ruled him. Fear. Pride. Confusion. Temptation. They stood frozen, immobilized by their own rebellion. Dante learned something essential—giants only have power when you stand still. The moment you move past them, their size shrinks and their roar becomes irrelevant.

The Four Faces of Courage

Courage manifests in different ways:

1. **Moral Courage**

   This is the willingness to stand up for what is right, even when it is unpopular or risky. Speaking truth in the face of deception, defending someone who is being wronged, or refusing to compromise your values are acts of moral courage.
2. **Emotional Courage**

   This is the ability to feel deeply, to embrace vulnerability, and to face internal pain without running. Emotional courage allows you to grieve, forgive, and love fully. It is the courage to open your heart without guarantees.
3. **Physical Courage**

   This is the courage to act despite bodily risk or discomfort. It is not about recklessness but about moving into situations that challenge your safety or stamina in pursuit of a greater purpose.
4. **Spiritual Courage**

   This is the capacity to trust in life, purpose, or faith, even when the outcome is uncertain. Spiritual courage allows you to act with faith in the unseen, hope in the impossible, and love without reservation.

Preparing to Swing Your Sword

A sword in an untrained hand can harm as much as it protects. Courage must be cultivated. Your armor—your integrity, boundaries, and discipline—is the foundation. But courage requires practice.

Waiting feels safe. It convinces you that patience is wisdom, that timing will eventually align, and that maybe next week—or next year—you'll feel ready. But waiting can become a trap. A quiet paralysis disguised as preparation.

Courage rarely arrives fully formed. It meets you halfway, in motion. The longer you wait for perfect conditions, the heavier hesitation becomes. Each day you delay, fear grows roots. Each excuse strengthens the chains around your purpose.

Readiness is not a feeling—it's a decision. Every great move in history began before someone felt ready. David stepped onto the battlefield. Esther walked into the king's court. Peter stepped onto the water. None of them had certainty; they had faith.

The weight of waiting lifts the moment you take the first step. Even a trembling step forward breaks the silence that fear depends on. You don't need full confidence, just commitment. Once you move, momentum becomes your ally, and courage begins to flow.

Sharpening the Blade

A sword loses its edge when it's never drawn. Courage works the same way—it dulls in comfort but sharpens in challenge. Every obstacle you face is a whetstone. Every time you move through fear instead of around it, you polish the edge a little more.

Discipline, repetition, and faith are the forge. Heat and friction aren't punishment; they're proof that you're being refined. The very resistance that frustrates you is the same force that is shaping you into something stronger.

You don't build courage by waiting for danger—you build it by practicing conviction in the ordinary. By speaking honestly when silence would be easier. By keeping promises when no one's watching. By choosing character over convenience.

A dull sword can't cut through fear. Keep yours sharp—through practice, prayer, and persistence—until bravery feels like instinct.

A sword is only as strong as the hand that wields it—and only as sharp as the effort that maintains it. Courage is the same. It dulls in comfort but sharpens in motion. Every challenge you face is a grindstone, shaping your edge and refining your discipline.

When life tests you, it's not to destroy you but to forge you. Heat, pressure, and resistance—those are the elements that transform metal into something unbreakable. Each fear you confront is a stroke against the stone. Each act of integrity, a polish to your edge. Each time you choose faith over fear, the blade gleams brighter.

You don't sharpen a sword by keeping it sheathed. And you don't build courage by waiting for the right moment. You build it by showing up and by doing the small, hard things every day until strength becomes second nature.

When you feel tested, remember: The forge doesn't destroy what's strong. It exposes what's ready.

Courage is sharpened the same way Dante grew stronger through each circle—not by escaping difficulty, but by walking through it. Every step he took, guided by truth, made him more discerning, more resilient, more prepared. By the time he reached the center of Hell, he wasn't the same man who had entered the dark wood. His courage had been forged in the very places that once terrified him, just like yours will be.

Courage in Action: The Story of Neerja Bhanot

Neerja Bhanot was a senior flight attendant for Pan Am in the 1980s. On September 5, 1986, Pan Am Flight 73 was hijacked while on the ground in Karachi by four armed terrorists.

The hijackers intended to use the plane and hostages for political leverage. Neerja, as senior cabin crew, found herself in the middle of chaos and danger.

But she didn't freeze or panic. At the age of only twenty-three, she took courageous, self-sacrificial action:

- She alerted the cockpit crew and helped prevent the terrorists from gaining full control of the aircraft.
- She hid American passports so the hijackers couldn't easily identify who to single out.
- During the crisis, she repeatedly helped passengers move toward exits, guided children, and prioritized others' safety even while under fire.
- In the final moments, when the terrorists began opening fire and setting off explosives, Neerja opened an emergency exit and helped as many passengers escape as possible—even though she knew it put her own life at risk.

Her actions cost her life. She was shot by the terrorists as she was assisting others.

Afterward, Neerja was honored as a hero. She became the youngest recipient (at the time) of India's Ashoka Chakra Award—the country's highest peacetime gallantry award.

Courage in Action: The Man in the Red Bandana

On September 11, 2001, when the South Tower of the World Trade Center was struck, Welles Crowther, a twenty-four-year-old equities trader, made a decision that would define his legacy.

Amid the chaos, smoke, and confusion, Welles could have escaped. He was young, athletic, and only minutes from safety. But instead of saving himself, he ran toward danger. Covering his face with his trademark red bandana, he began guiding survivors down the stairwells, carrying injured strangers, and returning again and again into the burning floors.

Witnesses remembered "the man in the red bandana"—calm, clear, giving orders when panic had taken over. Many lived because of his courage. Welles never made it out. His body was later found beside firefighters—proof that even in his final moments, he chose service over safety.

Welles's story isn't just one of heroism; it's a reflection of courage in its purest form. He didn't wait to feel ready or fearless. He acted in alignment with his integrity, guided by something higher than fear—purpose. That day, his courage became light in the darkest hour, and it continues to inspire generations long after his final breath.

Courage in Action: Dietrich Bonhoeffer—The Pastor Who Wouldn't Stay Silent

In the heart of Nazi Germany, when silence was survival, one man chose to speak. Dietrich Bonhoeffer, a young pastor and theologian, saw his country falling under the spell of fear and propaganda. Churches bowed to power, truth was twisted, and millions suffered under oppression.

Bonhoeffer could have escaped—he had the chance. He had friends, opportunity, and a ticket to freedom in America. But when he looked at the growing darkness, he couldn't leave. "I must share the trials of this time with my people," he wrote before returning to Germany—fully aware that his choice could cost him his life.

He joined the resistance, using his position to speak truth when it was dangerous to do so. He helped Jewish families escape, preached against hatred, and reminded the church that faith without action was hollow. His sermons weren't just words—they were fire in a time of fear.

Eventually, the Gestapo arrested him. Even in prison, Bonhoeffer wrote letters of hope, faith, and conviction that would inspire generations long after his execution in 1945. He died with peace in his heart, praying for his captors.

Bonhoeffer's courage wasn't about defiance alone—it was about obedience to truth. He understood something timeless: that courage is not always surviving the moment but instead standing firm in it. His life remains a reminder that when the world demands your silence, courage means speaking—even if your voice shakes.

Courage in Action: The Story of Desmond Doss

Desmond Doss was a US Army medic during World War II who refused to carry a weapon because of his religious convictions. He enlisted because he believed in saving lives, not taking them.

At the Battle of Okinawa, his unit came under fierce attack. Many soldiers were wounded and stranded on the battlefield under heavy fire. Despite being unarmed and under relentless enemy fire, Doss stayed behind. Bravo Company's position was precarious, and Doss repeatedly volunteered to go out into the open to rescue his fellow soldiers.

He carried the wounded one by one—lowering them down cliffs by ropes, navigating minefields, and running through gunfire. He stayed until the very end, making multiple trips, refusing to abandon those left behind.

It's recorded that he rescued seventy-five men (some sources say around fifty) without firing a single shot.

Eventually, he himself was wounded and unable to walk, but when he heard cries from injured men, he crawled to them and dragged them to safety—still under fire.

Desmond Doss's courage was not theatrical—it was consistent, sacrificial, and principled. He chose to act despite danger, because others' lives depended on it. Even in his wounded state, he refused to leave anyone behind.

He was awarded the Medal of Honor for his bravery—the first conscientious objector in American history to receive that honor.

The Courage of Everyday Life

These people certainly showed amazing acts of courage. However, you don't need to run into burning buildings, stand before gunfire, or risk your life on an airplane to show courage. The world doesn't always test us with explosions or hijackings—it tests us quietly. In the moments no one sees.

Courage is the decision to show up when it would be easier to hide. It's the strength to tell the truth when a lie would protect your reputation. It's the choice to keep believing when everything in you wants to give up. It's the heart to forgive, to love again, to start over.

Courage is in everyday choices—saying "no" when your old self whispers "yes." It's walking away from distractions that numb your purpose. It's facing your reflection and deciding, I will no longer be my biggest stranger.

The courage this book asks of you isn't about battlefields or heroics. It's about becoming who you were always meant to be. It's the courage to dig deep, to face yourself honestly, and to stop playing small. It's the courage to build the life that matches the greatness already inside you.

It takes courage to change your habits, courage to silence the noise, and courage to follow this path—not because it's easy, but because you know you're called to more.

Courage isn't free. Every bold step asks for something in return. Sometimes it costs you comfort. Other times, connection. There are moments when courage will isolate you—not because you've done something wrong, but because you've finally done something real.

When you speak the truth, some people will pull back.

When you choose growth, the familiar will resist. When you follow conviction, convenience disappears.

But what courage takes away, it replaces with clarity. You might lose the approval of others, but you'll gain alignment with yourself. You might lose the crowd, but you'll find your purpose.

Courage strips you bare so that only what's genuine remains. It exposes who's meant to walk beside you and who was only drawn to your silence. It tests your faith until it becomes unshakable.

So when the cost feels heavy, when loneliness or loss begins to whisper that you've made a mistake, remember: Courage never leaves you empty. It refines you. It removes what can't endure truth. And what remains afterward is real—stronger, cleaner, lighter, and whole.

When you act with courage born from truth, your life becomes your greatest contribution. Not through fame, applause, or recognition but through the quiet influence of integrity, presence, and purpose.

The world doesn't need more perfect people. It needs courageous people: people who are willing to live honestly, love deeply, and lead from the heart. That's the courage that transforms not just your world but the world around you.

Daily Practices to Build Courage

1. **Small Acts of Bravery:** Start with manageable challenges—speaking up, setting boundaries, or acknowledging a fear.
2. **Reflection on Past Victories:** Recall moments where you acted despite fear. Internalize these as proof of your capability.

3. **Visualization:** Mentally rehearse confronting your giants. See the action, the challenge, and the triumph.
4. **Incremental Exposure:** Gradually face more intimidating situations, building your confidence and resilience.
5. **Accountability:** Share your intentions with a mentor, friend, or coach who can hold you to your commitments.

Courage in Action

True courage is active. It moves. It chooses, it risks, and it persists. It's the invisible decision that separates dreamers from doers and those who talk about change from those who create it.

Courage isn't loud or always heroic. Sometimes, it's quiet, trembling, and unseen. It's the push that gets you out of bed when your heart feels heavy. It's the whisper that says, "Try again" after another closed door. It's the steady voice that says, "Start anyway" when logic screams, "Wait."

You want to start a project that could help thousands, but fear tells you it will fail. Courage says, "Begin anyway." You may stumble, fall short, or face criticism—but movement born from conviction is never wasted. Every step forward is progress, even when it doesn't look like success.

Courage doesn't guarantee victory; it guarantees growth. Each attempt builds strength. Each setback sharpens discernment. Each act of persistence builds the muscle that fear cannot weaken.

To act courageously means not only accepting risk—the risk of rejection, misunderstanding, loss, or failure—but also recognizing that doing nothing is the greatest loss of all.

When you act in alignment with your purpose, you trade comfort for clarity. You trade fear for forward motion.

Courage doesn't wait for permission. It doesn't seek applause. It doesn't need certainty.

It simply moves.

Courage says, "I don't know how this will end, but I know I'm meant to begin." It's not about removing fear; it's about refusing to let fear make the final decision. And when you act from that place—with heart, integrity, and conviction—the result is always impact. Sometimes that impact changes the world. Other times, it simply changes you. Both are sacred.

Because every courageous act, no matter how small, shifts something. It creates momentum, ignites faith, and proves that growth is possible. Courage is how ordinary people do extraordinary things—not because they feel ready, but because they act before they do.

Overcoming Paralysis

Fear is persuasive. It whispers that stillness is safety, that waiting will bring clarity, and that if you hold your breath long enough, the storm will pass. But hesitation is the giant's favorite weapon. It convinces you that you're thinking things through when really you're standing still.

Courage isn't reckless—it's responsive. It sees the risk, feels the fear, and moves anyway. The only cure for paralysis is motion, even if that motion is imperfect.

When you feel stuck, remember: Fear feeds on delay. Every small action you take weakens its grip. Every decision, every step, every "yes" to purpose chips away at the weight of hesitation.

To overcome paralysis:

1. **Name the fear.** Say it out loud. When fear is spoken, it loses its disguise.
2. **Clarify the risk.** Write down what could go wrong—but also what could go right. Let truth, not imagination, set the boundaries.
3. **Act immediately.** Even the smallest move forward is a declaration of freedom.
4. **Reflect and refine**. Progress isn't perfection; it's persistence. Adjust as you go, but never stop going.

Movement is the language of courage. The moment you act, you break the spell of fear. Courage doesn't promise comfort—it promises momentum. And once momentum begins, fear loses its throne.

The Ripple Effect

Courage doesn't end with you. Every time you act boldly, you create a ripple that reaches farther than you realize. A single choice to stand firm, to speak truth, or to follow conviction becomes a signal of permission for someone else to do the same.

Fear spreads quietly, but so does faith. When you move despite fear, you remind others that it's possible. Your strength becomes their spark, your perseverance their proof.

You might never see the impact—a stranger who read your words, a child who watched your consistency, a friend who found hope because you refused to give up—but it happens. Courage multiplies itself.

The same sword that carves your path forward cuts a trail through the darkness for others to follow. That's the hidden beauty of courage: its legacy. You don't just change your story—you change the atmosphere around you.

Courage and Contribution

Courage is not selfish. Its highest purpose is contribution. Every act of courage—speaking truth, defending boundaries, creating opportunities—empowers others. It becomes contagious. When one person acts boldly, they show what is possible for everyone around them.

Your sword of courage allows the life, love, and grace you have cultivated to flow outward. It is the tool through which your victories become the victories of others.

Reflection Questions

1. Where in my life am I hesitating because of fear?
2. Which giants are I avoiding that require courageous action?
3. How can I practice courage today in a small, manageable way?
4. What would happen if I acted boldly in alignment with my purpose?
5. Who can benefit from my courage? How does it ripple into the lives of others?

Reflection Exercises: The Sword of Courage

Name Your Fear: Write down the one fear that most often stops you from acting—fear of failure, rejection, loss, or judgment.

What story do I tell myself that keeps this fear alive? Seeing fear on paper exposes its limits; unspoken fear grows stronger.

Trace Its Origin: Every giant has roots. Think back to where this fear first appeared—a failure, criticism, or moment you felt unprepared.

What memory still holds power over my confidence? Awareness begins the unchaining process.

Record Past Courage: List three times you acted bravely, even while afraid. They don't have to be dramatic—just moments when you moved forward anyway.

What did I feel before, during, and after each act? Patterns of courage remind you that bravery already lives within you.

Plan Your Next Strike: Choose one small action you've delayed because of fear. Commit to a single, visible step toward it today.

What would courage look like in motion? Action, not thought, weakens giants.

Reframe Failure: Write a short paragraph beginning with the following phrase.

If I fail, I will still have learned... Failure is never final when it's reframed as training. Each attempt strengthens your swing.

Anchor in Purpose: Ask yourself the following each morning.

Who could benefit if I act with courage today? When courage becomes service, fear loses its grip.

Evening Reflection: At the end of each day, record one courageous act—no matter how small.

Where did I move despite fear today? Over time, these moments become your personal proof of progress.

Remember: Courage is not something you wait to

feel—it is something you choose to wield. Each deliberate act of bravery sharpens your sword and expands your reach.

The Courage to Face Yourself

The greatest act of courage isn't running into battle or standing before giants. It's standing before your own reflection—unguarded, honest, and unwilling to turn away.

Every external victory is only a mirror of an internal one. You can conquer enemies, win accolades, and earn recognition, and yet still live as a stranger to your truest self. Real courage begins when you decide to meet that stranger—not with judgment, but with compassion and truth.

Facing yourself requires more bravery than facing the world. Because the world will forgive your failures long before you forgive yourself. But the mirror doesn't lie; it invites you to grow.

That's the essence of the sword—not to destroy who you were, but to cut away what no longer serves you. To sever the cords of fear, shame, and self-doubt that once dictated your steps.

When you wield that sword inwardly, something powerful happens: Peace replaces guilt. Conviction replaces confusion. Identity replaces insecurity.

The same courage that pushes you toward your dreams must also pull you into your healing. You cannot become who you were created to be while avoiding who you've been.

So lift your sword. Not to strike the world but to confront the self that settled, doubted, and delayed. Forgive that version. Thank it for surviving. Then, let it rest. You are not here to hide behind armor anymore. You are here to live as a warrior of light—refined, honest, courageous, and whole.

When Dante finally emerged from the pit and saw the stars again, he wasn't celebrating escape—he was celebrating transformation. Courage didn't remove his fear; it gave him authority over it. The same is true for you. The goal isn't to eliminate darkness, but to walk through it with a light that refuses to die. That is the sword you carry now.

Closing

Your armor protects. Your sword cuts. Courage is the bridge between preparation and contribution. Without it, potential remains unrealized. With it, your life becomes a force for change, a beacon of possibility, and a source of light in a world that desperately needs it.

The giants will test you. They will whisper, threaten, and try to stop you. But armed with integrity and wielding courage, you are unstoppable. Your purpose, your potential, and your ability to serve are now ready to manifest.

Stand tall. Hold your sword. Move forward. Face your giants. Live boldly. Love courageously. Contribute relentlessly.

When what you think, what you say, and what you do are in harmony, you are at peace.

attributed to Mahatma Gandhi

Chapter 29

The Power of Alignment: Living in Harmony with Purpose

Mastering your mind and confronting your giants is vital, but it is not enough. Courage without direction is wasted. Strength without alignment can scatter. Clarity without action is meaningless. The next step, the step that transforms personal victories into a life that matters, is alignment.

Alignment is the harmony between your inner world—your values, beliefs, and vision, and your outer life—your actions, choices, and relationships. It is the bridge that connects who you are to what you do, creating power, peace, and purpose.

Understanding Alignment

Alignment is not about perfection—it's about *direction.* It's the moment when your beliefs, actions, and emotions all point toward the same truth. It's when your inner world and outer world stop arguing.

Think of alignment as spiritual physics—when every force within you moves in the same direction, momentum happens. You stop leaking energy into worry, confusion, or contradiction. Life stops being a tug-of-war between who you are and what you do.

You've met people who seem peaceful even when life is chaotic. That's alignment. Their circumstances aren't easier—they're just not at war with themselves. They've stopped trying to live two lives: the one they show the world and the one that actually exists inside.

When you are aligned, your words match your values, your work reflects your calling, and your choices echo your beliefs. You stop chasing validation because peace replaces performance. You stop trying to prove something because you already know who you are.

But when you're *out of alignment*, even success feels hollow. You can have a great job, followers, and money and still feel like you're pretending. That's because misalignment is the silent thief of peace. It's when you do things that contradict your inner truth—when you say "yes" when your soul is screaming "no," stay where you no longer belong, or compromise who you are to be accepted.

Alignment is the bridge between clarity and movement. Without it, courage and discipline scatter like arrows shot in different directions. With it, everything you've built—integrity, purpose, and courage—moves in harmony.

You can feel alignment. It shows up as ease in your chest, peace in your decisions, and consistency in your choices. You can also feel misalignment—the anxiety before you answer "yes" to something you don't want, the guilt that lingers after ignoring your intuition, and the burnout that comes from chasing something that doesn't fulfill you.

Living in alignment is not about being flawless; it's about being honest. It's not about doing everything right; it's about doing the right things for the right reasons.

When your spirit, mind, and actions move in the same direction, you don't need to chase peace—you become it.

Why Alignment Matters

Imagine a bow without an arrow. The tension exists, the energy is real, but it cannot release into motion. That is a life out of alignment.

When your thoughts, emotions, actions, and goals are aligned:

- You move with clarity and purpose.
- Decisions are easier because they are guided by your true north.
- Energy flows naturally instead of leaking through indecision, conflict, or distraction.
- Your life becomes a source of influence and contribution rather than chaos and compromise.

When you are out of alignment:

- Fear, doubt, and frustration dominate.
- You feel heavy, stuck, or depleted.
- Relationships suffer because your actions do not reflect your truth.
- Opportunities pass by because indecision and contradiction blur your path.

Alignment is not about perfection; it is about coherence—your inner world reflected in your outer life.

Dante understood misalignment long before he understood salvation. When he woke in the dark wood, he wasn't there because he was evil; he was there because he had lost alignment. He had strayed from "the straight way," drifting little by little until he no longer recognized himself.

That's what misalignment does: It doesn't destroy you all at once; it slowly pulls you into a place where your soul can't breathe. Dante's entire journey begins with that realization—that before he could rise, he had to realign.

When Dante looked around Hell, he saw souls twisted by misalignment; people whose outer actions contradicted their inner truth. Each punishment wasn't arbitrary; it was an outward expression of an inward contradiction. They did one thing but believed another. They spoke one truth but lived another. Dante's lesson was clear: Misalignment is its own prison.

The Pillars of Alignment

Dante didn't climb out of the dark wood by accident; he walked with Virgil step by step, circle by circle. Their journey mirrors the four pillars: values, vision, consistent action, and integration. Each circle confronted a different fracture in the human spirit, and with every descent, Dante became more aligned within himself. The deeper he went, the clearer he became.

To live in harmony with your purpose, you must anchor yourself to four pillars:

1. **Clarity of Values**
   - Know what matters most. Define your nonnegotiables.

- When your values guide decisions, even difficult choices become clear.

2. **Clarity of Vision**
   - Define what a meaningful life looks like for you.
   - Vision without alignment leads to burnout; alignment without vision leads to stagnation.
3. **Consistency of Action**
   - Actions must reflect values and vision.
   - Small, deliberate choices compound into habits that shape destiny.
4. **Integration of Self**
   - Every aspect of you—your past, strengths, weaknesses, emotions, and mind—must be acknowledged and integrated.
   - You cannot truly act in alignment while denying parts of yourself.

Integration is exactly what transformed Dante. He entered Hell fragmented—afraid, ashamed, and confused. But as he witnessed the consequences of divided living, he began to integrate his past, his fears, and his purpose. By the time he reached the very center of Hell, he no longer ran from himself. Integration made him whole enough to climb.

Why Alignment Matters

Imagine driving a powerful car with one tire turned inward. The engine roars, the wheels spin, but you're fighting the steering wheel the entire way. That's what life feels like when you're out of alignment. You can have strength, speed, and even success, but progress feels forced.

Alignment is what turns motion into momentum. It's what allows your energy, focus, and intention to flow in the same direction instead of being divided between "who I am" and "who I pretend to be." When your inner truth and outer action collide, peace disappears. You don't need more effort—you need alignment.

Story: Howard Schultz and the Soul of Starbucks

In the early 1980s, Howard Schultz left a secure corporate position to join a small coffee company called Starbucks. He believed coffee could be more than a product—it could be an experience, a way of connecting people. For years he built Starbucks on that belief: a sense of community, warmth, and authenticity.

But as the company grew, its mission blurred. It became obsessed with expansion and profit, not connection. Schultz stepped away for a time, and when he returned years later, he found that Starbucks had lost its heart. Stores felt transactional. Baristas were discouraged. The culture was efficient but hollow.

He realized that Starbucks's success had come at the cost of its alignment. The brand no longer reflected its original values. Schultz made the hard choice to slow growth, refocus on quality, and rebuild the culture around human connection. It was risky, but alignment restored life to the business.

The result? A resurgence that made Starbucks not only profitable again but purposeful. When a company realigns with its values, it regains its soul. The same is true for people.

The Energy of Alignment

When you are aligned, energy flows instead of leaks. Decision-making becomes clear because you no longer weigh every choice against fear, guilt, or other people's opinions—you weigh it against your truth.

Alignment is freedom disguised as discipline. It feels like peace because your inner and outer worlds finally agree. You stop needing constant validation because you are living from conviction. You stop hustling for worthiness because you know who you are.

When you are misaligned, life feels like resistance training—every step takes twice as much energy. You say "yes" when your spirit says "no," chase opportunities that don't fit your calling, or stay in environments that drain you. You can be successful and still be starving internally. That's the cost of misalignment: burnout, confusion, and quiet resentment.

Alignment and the Human Spirit

The soul was designed for coherence. Even nature itself operates in alignment—the tides, the seasons, the rotation of the planets. When anything in creation goes out of rhythm, imbalance appears. Humanity is no different. We were meant to live with spiritual, mental, and emotional unity.

That's why scripture warns, "A double minded man is unstable in all his ways" (James 1:8, KJV).

Double-mindedness isn't just indecision; it's internal division. Alignment restores stability because your choices no longer argue with your convictions.

A Personal Reflection

Think back to a time when you were fully aligned—when your actions, beliefs, and energy all pointed in the same direction. Maybe it was a season of faith, creativity, or deep connection. You likely felt alive, clear, and unstoppable. That's not coincidence. That's coherence.

Now recall a season of misalignment—saying "yes" to something that didn't feel right or staying silent when you should've spoken truth. The tension, the fatigue, the emotional drain—all of those all symptoms of an inner misfire.

Alignment matters because it determines whether you live by intention or by inertia.

The Four Pillars of Alignment

Alignment is not achieved overnight; it's cultivated through conscious choices that bring your inner truth and outer actions into harmony. These four pillars act as the foundation of a life in alignment—each one strengthening the bridge between purpose and peace.

1. **Clarity of Values: The Compass of Integrity**

Values are your internal compass. They are not wishes or ideals; they are principles that determine your direction when life feels foggy. Without them, you drift.

When you know your values, decisions become simpler—not easier, but clearer. The moment of choice becomes less about what feels convenient and more about what feels true.

Story: The Uncompromising Line

Years ago, a small-town accountant discovered that his boss was manipulating numbers to cover losses. Everyone in the office knew, but no one said anything. The accountant wrestled internally—loyalty versus honesty. Finally, he reported it, knowing it would cost him his job.

He was fired, but the story didn't end there. Months later, the company collapsed and his integrity became his reputation. A local business hired him because they wanted someone "they could trust."

Values aren't what you post online; they're what you live when it costs you something.

Reflection:

When you live by your values, you move through life without fear of exposure because there's nothing to hide. Alignment begins where compromise ends.

2. **Clarity of Vision: The Destination of Purpose**

Vision is the map that gives your values movement. It's not just what you want to achieve—it's who you want to become.

Without vision, life becomes reactionary. You wake up responding to demands instead of designing direction. With vision, even setbacks have meaning because you know where you're going.

Story: Nelson Mandela's Vision of Reconciliation

During his twenty-seven years in prison, Mandela's captors tried to break his spirit. They isolated him, stripped him of comfort, and hoped bitterness would replace belief. But Mandela had a vision larger than revenge: a South Africa united, not divided.

That vision became his anchor. When freedom finally came, he didn't seek vengeance; he sought restoration. His vision outlasted his suffering. A clear vision doesn't remove pain; it redeems it. When your goals are tied to purpose, obstacles become teachers, not enemies.

3. **Consistency of Action: The Proof of Discipline**

If values are your compass and vision your map, consistency is the movement that gets you there. Alignment doesn't happen through grand gestures—it's built through daily faithfulness.

Every time you choose discipline over distraction, truth over convenience, and purpose over comfort, you are aligning your future self with your highest potential.

Story: Captain "Sully" Sullenberger and the Miracle on the Hudson

When both engines failed after takeoff, Captain Sullenberger had seconds to act. Years of repetitive training, quiet discipline, and consistent preparation guided his calm under pressure. He landed Flight 1549 safely on the Hudson River, saving every life onboard.

He later said, "We didn't have time to make new decisions — we relied on thousands of small ones we had made before."

Reflection:

Alignment isn't proven in crisis—it's practiced long before the crisis arrives. The habits you repeat in peace become the instincts you rely on in chaos.

4. **Integration of Self: The Wholeness of Authenticity**

Alignment cannot exist where you are fragmented. Many people live split between personas—the public self, the private self, and the wounded self. But to live aligned, you must integrate them.

Integration means accepting your past, embracing your weaknesses, and uniting your heart and mind. When you stop rejecting parts of yourself, peace follows.

Story: Courage in Alignment—The Story of Michael Phelps

Michael Phelps, the most decorated Olympian in history, once stood as the embodiment of success—gold medals, global fame, and financial security. But behind the medals was a man drowning in his own mind.

After the 2012 Olympics, he spiraled into depression. He described it as "carrying weight that no amount of gold could lift." For years, his identity had been built entirely around winning. Every race, every record, was an attempt to prove he was enough; it was a wound born from years of pressure and perfectionism. When the competition stopped, the silence became unbearable.

Phelps later revealed that he considered ending his life in 2014. That moment of darkness became a turning point. Instead of running from his pain, he faced it. He entered therapy, embraced vulnerability, and began to rebuild not as "Michael Phelps the swimmer," but as Michael Phelps the human being.

Through counseling, meditation, and open conversations about mental health, Phelps found freedom in honesty. He said, "I was so afraid to ask for help, and when I finally did, that's when I realized how powerful it is."

Now, his mission is no longer to win races—it's to help others heal. Through his foundation and advocacy, he champions mental wellness, encouraging others to seek balance, purpose, and alignment between success and peace.

Phelps's story reminds us: You can master the body, the world, even the podium, but if the mind is out of alignment, victory feels empty. True freedom comes not from performance but from peace within.

Signs You Are Out of Alignment

- You feel exhausted despite effort.
- You frequently compromise your integrity for convenience or approval.
- Your work, relationships, or personal life feels fragmented.
- You chase external validation rather than internal truth.
- Fear, doubt, or resentment quietly directs your decisions.

How to Reclaim Alignment

Realignment doesn't happen in a single moment of clarity—it happens through consistent awareness, correction, and courage.

The process is less about fixing yourself and more about *returning to yourself.* Every act of alignment brings you closer to peace, purpose, and power.

1. **Audit Your Life**
   - Examine your habits, relationships, work, and goals.
   - Identify where choices contradict your values or vision.
2. **Set Boundaries**
   - Alignment requires protection. Say "no" to what distracts or misaligns you.
3. **Daily Reflection**
   - Morning or evening, ask: Did my actions today reflect my values? Did I honor my purpose?
4. **Adjust Continuously**
   - Alignment is not static. Life changes, as do you. Periodically recalibrate.
5. **Celebrate Integrity**
   - Every small act of alignment strengthens your ability to act with clarity and courage in bigger decisions.

Misalignment is often revealed not through failure but through fatigue. When something constantly drains you, it's usually out of sync with your values or calling. Awareness is the first act of alignment.

Alignment Amplifies Contribution

Purpose is not merely a personal achievement; it is a gift to the world. When your life is aligned:

- Your energy is available for meaningful work.
- Your influence is felt without force because integrity attracts trust.
- Your actions serve as a model, inspiring others to face their own giants and align their lives.

In alignment, your victories are not just personal triumphs; they are opportunities for others to rise. The life, love, and grace you have cultivated flow outward naturally.

Reflection Questions

1. What are my core values, and how clearly do I live by them?
2. Where in my life am I out of alignment, and why?
3. Which daily actions could better reflect my purpose?
4. How do my relationships either support or hinder my alignment?
5. What steps can I take this week to create greater coherence between my inner world and outer life?

Reflection Exercises: Realigning Your Life with Purpose

1. **The Alignment Audit:** Take ten quiet minutes to assess your current season of life.
   - Which areas (career, relationships, habits, faith, or health) feel peaceful and aligned?
   - Which feel heavy or forced? Write each one under *Aligned or Misaligned.*

   Reflection Prompt: *What small shift could bring each misaligned area closer to my values?*
2. **The Values Check-In:** List your top five nonnegotiable values—the principles that define who you are. Next to each, write one daily action that either honors or contradicts it.
   - Value: Integrity → Action: "Speak honestly, even in discomfort."

- Value: Family → Action: "Be fully present at dinner with my phone off."

3. **Alignment Through Stillness:** Set a timer for five minutes each morning. Sit in silence and ask: "What would peace choose today?" Record the first thought that arises. Stillness allows your intuition—your spirit's compass—to speak before the world's noise drowns it out.
4. **Re-Center with Boundaries:** Choose one area of life where you've said "yes" when you meant "no." This week, practice saying "no" respectfully but firmly. Alignment requires courage to protect what matters most.
5. **Alignment Gratitude Journal:** Each evening, list three moments where you lived in alignment—even small ones. Gratitude for these moments reinforces new neural pathways of peace and authenticity.
6. **Weekly Realignment Ritual:** Every Sunday evening, review your week.

- Where did I feel peace?
- Where did I feel tension?
- What decision or boundary can restore harmony next week? This rhythm keeps you recalibrated before misalignment grows into burnout.

7. **The Mirror Exercise:** Stand before a mirror and say aloud: "I am proud of the person I am becoming. I choose truth over approval, purpose over comfort, and alignment over illusion." Speaking truth into reflection anchors identity in conviction, not perception.

Dante's ascent toward the stars didn't begin when Hell ended—it began when his inner world aligned. Only when his heart, will, and clarity moved together could he start climbing the mountain ahead. The moment he reached equilibrium, the universe opened. That's the power of alignment: It turns darkness into a path and struggle into ascent.

Closing

Alignment transforms courage into action, mastery into influence, and clarity into contribution. When your inner world and outer life resonate in harmony, you live not by accident but by design.

Giants can still rise. Doubt can still whisper. Fear can still test. But alignment creates a foundation that cannot be shaken—a compass that points toward your true north.

By living in alignment, you turn personal victories into a life that matters. You take the courage, the insight, and the clarity gained from confronting your giants and direct it outward—helping others, inspiring transformation, and fulfilling your purpose with authenticity and power.

The path is clear: align, act, contribute. Live a life that is unshakable, undeniable, and unapologetically yours.

Alignment brings you peace, but it also awakens something deeper—flow. Once you are aligned, life no longer feels like striving; it feels like participation in something larger than yourself.

Next comes the Flow of Purpose—where alignment becomes effortless movement and your life begins to impact others with grace, rhythm, and momentum.

Carve your name on hearts, not tombstones. A legacy is etched into the minds of others and the stories they share about you.

Shannon L. Alder

Chapter 30

Living the Legacy: The Journey Continues

Living Beyond Survival

You have walked through the fire and refused to be consumed. You have crossed rivers that once threatened to drown you, faced the shadows that sought to silence you, and unearthed the strength that was buried beneath your pain. You have looked your giants in the eye and discovered that victory was never about destroying them—it was about transforming yourself in their presence.

Now, standing on the other side of the storm, the question is no longer "How do I survive?" but "How do I live?" Because survival is not the end—it is the beginning of legacy.

The path behind you was about healing, courage, and alignment. The path ahead is about *impact*. Your story is no longer just your own; it becomes the light that helps others find their way through their own dark wood. Legacy isn't built from what you own—it's built from what you give, from the lives you touch, from the truth you live out loud.

You are no longer walking to escape the past. You are walking to define the future.

Dante understood this transition better than almost anyone. When he awoke lost in the dark wood, his only goal was survival—to escape the confusion and fear wrapped around him. But survival didn't save him. It simply held him still long enough for clarity to arrive.

When he finally stepped forward and followed Virgil, the shift happened: He stopped moving just to escape and began moving because purpose had found him.

Every descent into Hell was a descent into himself—confronting illusions, fears, and wounds he had carried for years. Dante survived the dark wood, but he was transformed by the journey through it.

You are in that same transition now. Survival was necessary, but significance is calling.

The Turning Point: From Survival to Significance

There comes a moment in every journey when survival is no longer enough. It's the moment you realize you've spent years fighting to stay afloat but now you're called to learn how to fly.

For so long, your focus was on enduring: enduring pain, betrayal, loss, or silence. You learned to breathe underwater, and to withstand the storms that tried to erase you. That season had purpose; it taught resilience. But resilience is not the destination. It is the bridge.

The shift from *survival* to *significance* happens quietly at first. You begin to sense that the very strength that once protected you now feels too small for who you're becoming. You're not just meant to overcome anymore—you're meant to overflow.

Survival is reactive; significance is intentional. Survival says, "I made it." Significance says, "Now I'll make it matter."

To live a life of significance, you must take the lessons forged in pain and shape them into purpose. The scars you carry are not reminders of weakness—they are proof of endurance. They are the credentials of someone who has walked through Hell and still believes in Heaven.

Every battle you've faced was preparation, not punishment. You were being trained, tested, and tempered. The darkness taught you how to recognize light. The silence taught you how to listen. The pain taught you how to see others who are still trapped in it.

Now, the question is no longer "How do I get through this?" but "What will I build from this?"

The turning point is realizing that your life was never meant to end in recovery—it was meant to become revelation. The world doesn't just need survivors. It needs teachers, healers, and leaders who have survived and chosen to rise higher.

The battle that once tried to destroy you now becomes your platform. The voice you once silenced now becomes your message. The life that once felt broken now becomes your legacy.

You have been refined by fire, not ruined by it. Now it's time to use the light within you to illuminate the way for others.

There is a moment at the bottom of Hell where everything changes. After climbing down Lucifer's massive form, Dante and Virgil suddenly feel gravity flip—what was once downward becomes upward.

In that instant, Dante realizes that he is no longer descending. He is rising. He is moving toward air, toward clarity, toward the stars.

That shift from downward despair to upward purpose is the moment survival becomes significance.

Your gravity has flipped too. Your story is no longer pulling you down; it is lifting you up. Your past is no longer a prison; it is a platform. Your scars are no longer shame; they are strength.

You are rising now.

Your Life As a Legacy

Every thought, every choice, every action carries weight. Life is not measured by time alone but by the impact of your presence. The legacy you leave is the sum of the lives you touch, the hearts you heal, and the courage you model.

Legacy is living intentionally. It is acting with awareness that your words and actions ripple beyond your immediate life. It is understanding that the inner work—confronting fear, betrayal, anger, and self-doubt—is not just for you. It is for the people around you, for the generations who will follow, and for the world that is watching, often in silence.

The Story of Charlie Kirk

When Charlie Kirk was just eighteen years old, he stood in a small garage in Illinois, convinced that his generation needed a new kind of voice. He had already felt the friction—rejection from military pathways, pressure from peers, frustration with institutional politics. But he was done waiting. He co-founded Turning Point USA to channel his convictions into action.

From those humble beginnings, Kirk poured energy into campus halls, student meetings, and social media circuits. He debated professors, organized chapters, and spoke loudly about free markets, limited government, and challenging liberal dominance on campuses.

As Turning Point grew, so did his influence. What he built was more than a political movement—it was a cultural force. Thousands of students, disillusioned with conventional politics, heard his voice, echoed his message, and carried his banner. He became a lightning rod who was hailed by supporters as a brave change-agent and denounced by critics for polarizing stances.

But success carried hidden costs. As his influence expanded, every inconsistency, every compromise, and every criticism was amplified. The spotlight magnified not just his victories but his blind spots. Legacy is never just carved in the successes—it is also written in how one responds to challenge.

In 2025, during a university event, Charlie Kirk was tragically shot and killed while addressing students. His death rattled the political world, sending shockwaves through campuses across the nation. In death, his legacy grew more complicated, more scrutinized, and more debated.

Now, as his widow, Erika Kirk, steps into leadership at Turning Point, his life's work is under new stewardship—continuing, evolving, but forever shaped by the man who founded it.

In the end, Charlie Kirk's legacy wasn't simply the organization he built or the audiences he gathered—it was the lives that were touched by the message of hope he carried. That is the truest measure of contribution.

The Story of Roberto Clemente

Roberto Clemente was more than one of baseball's greatest players—he was a man who believed success meant nothing if it didn't serve others.

Born in Puerto Rico, Clemente rose from humble beginnings to become a twelve-time All-Star and World Series champion. Yet, the more fame he gained, the less he cared about trophies or applause. To him, baseball was simply a platform—a way to lift others higher.

During off-seasons, he returned home to build schools, deliver food, and mentor young athletes who had grown up with the same poverty he once knew. He used every headline, every paycheck, and every ounce of influence to draw attention to those without a voice.

Then, on December 31, 1972, a massive earthquake struck Nicaragua. Aid was slow, and corruption threatened to keep supplies from reaching survivors. Clemente refused to stand by. He loaded a relief plane with food and medicine and joined the flight himself to make sure the goods reached the people who needed them. Moments after takeoff, the plane crashed into the ocean. Roberto Clemente was thirty-eight.

His death stunned the world, but his life preached louder than any sermon. He had spent his final breath serving others.

Clemente's legacy isn't just written in baseball history; it's written in the spirit of giving. Stadiums still bear his name, but the greater monument is the way people remember him—not as a man who hit home runs, but as a man who gave until the very end.

His story teaches a simple truth: A legacy isn't about what you build for yourself—it's about what you're willing to give away for others.

The Story of Fred Rogers

Fred Rogers, known to the world as Mister Rogers, didn't chase fame or fortune. His mission was simple—to help people, especially children, understand that they are seen, valued, and loved just as they are.

In an era of fast entertainment and noise, he chose stillness and sincerity. His television show, Mister Rogers' Neighborhood, became a sanctuary for millions. He spoke gently about feelings—anger, sadness, fear—and taught generations how to process them with kindness and honesty.

But what most people didn't see were his quiet acts off-screen. He wrote letters to fans who shared their pain, visited families of children who were sick, and prayed for hundreds by name every day. He never viewed his platform as a stage; he saw it as a ministry.

One of the things that Fred taught was that the greatest thing we can do is to help somebody know that they're loved and capable of loving. That was his theology of contribution. He believed kindness could heal what systems could not.

When he died in 2003, stories poured in of handwritten notes, surprise visits, and moments of compassion that had changed lives forever. His funeral wasn't filled with celebrities or applause but with people whose hearts he had touched.

Fred Rogers's legacy wasn't loud, but it was lasting. He proved that gentleness is not weakness—it is power under control. His life reminds us that contribution doesn't always come from grand gestures. Sometimes it comes from the quiet decision to keep showing up, to keep caring, and to keep loving in a world that forgets how.

The Story of Chadwick Boseman

Chadwick Boseman lived like a man racing time—but few realized how literal that was. While the world saw the hero of Black Panther, Boseman quietly fought his own invisible war. In 2016, he was diagnosed with stage III colon cancer. Yet he chose silence—not out of denial, but devotion. He didn't want sympathy to eclipse his service.

Through surgeries, chemo, and exhaustion, he kept working. Marshall, 21 Bridges, Da 5 Bloods—each performance carried the weight of purpose. Between film sets, he visited children battling cancer, speaking hope into hospital rooms even while carrying the same pain in his own body.

He understood something sacred: Legacy isn't what you do when life is easy—it's what you give when life is breaking you. He once said, "Purpose is the essential element of you. It is the reason you are on the planet at this particular time in history."[7] He lived those words until his final breath.

When news of his passing came in 2020, the world wept—not only for a gifted actor, but for a man who showed what it means to live with integrity, humility, and conviction. He never sought attention; he sought alignment. His strength was quiet, and his impact was eternal.

---

7 Chadwick Boseman, commencement address, Howard University, May 12, 2018, Washington, DC.

Boseman's legacy reminds us that we don't choose the length of our lives, but we do choose the depth of our contribution. He didn't die unfinished—he finished what mattered most.

The Ripple Effect: How Legacy Outlives You

To paraphrase Mother Teresa, "I alone cannot change the world, but I can cast a stone across the waters to create many ripples."[8]

Legacy is not measured in moments; it's measured in momentum. In ripples. Every act of courage, kindness, or integrity you make sends out ripples—waves that move through time, touching people you may never meet.

You may think your influence ends with your words, your job, or your lifetime. But the truth is, impact doesn't end when the story seems over. It multiplies quietly through the lives you've touched.

The student you encouraged becomes a teacher who inspires hundreds. The act of forgiveness you modeled becomes a cycle of healing that breaks generational pain. The business you built with integrity becomes the foundation for others to thrive.

Legacy doesn't need applause to echo. It spreads in unseen ways—like roots underground, sustaining a forest you'll never walk through.

When Dante finally emerged from Hell, the first thing he saw was the sky—wide, open, and filled with stars. Not

---

8 Paraphrased from Mother Theresa, *No Greater Love* (New World Library, 1997).

because his journey was finished but because clarity, alignment, and courage had positioned him to rise.

Closing: The Legacy You Live Forward

Legacy is not something you leave behind when you die—it is something you live every single day. It is built in the quiet decisions, the unseen sacrifices, the love you offer, the truth you stand on, and the courage you model.

Dante ended his descent not by escaping darkness but by turning toward the light and letting the journey transform him into someone capable of ascent.

So it is with you. Your legacy is not measured by applause or achievements but by the people who rise because you refused to fall. By the lives that find hope because you chose healing. By the souls that see possibility because you walked out of your own dark wood and shared the map.

You have survived, overcome, and aligned. Now you are called to live forward and to let your life speak long after your footsteps fade. Legacy is not the end of the journey; it is the beginning of impact. Your story continues, and the world is different because you walked through it.

The journey is the destination.

attributed to Dan Eldon

Chapter 31

The Continuous Journey

The Power of One Life

History remembers kings and warriors, but the world is changed most by those who live with quiet consistency. A single word of encouragement, a single act of compassion, a single decision to forgive can shift destinies.

When Rosa Parks refused to give up her seat, she wasn't planning to spark a movement. She was simply aligned with her truth. When Mother Teresa picked up one dying man from the streets of Calcutta, she wasn't calculating influence; she was living her calling.

They weren't chasing legacy—they were living it. Because legacy is never built for recognition; it's built from conviction.

Invisible Ripples

You may never know who your courage healed, who your honesty freed, or whose faith was restored because you chose not to give up. But those ripples move. They expand through time and space, carried by the people you've inspired, the children you've raised, and the strangers who watched you stand firm when it mattered most.

Even the smallest alignment of action and purpose carries power. When your life reflects your values, others are drawn to the light in you—not because you preach perfection, but because you live authenticity.

The Eternal Principle of Multiplication

In scripture, Jesus said, "A good tree cannot bear bad fruit" (Matthew 7:18). That is the essence of legacy—the fruit of your character outlasting your breath. The quality of what you cultivate within yourself becomes the nourishment others receive long after you're gone.

When you pour truth into your heart and when you plant seeds of faith, kindness, and integrity, those seeds take root in the lives around you. People may forget your words, but they will never forget how your presence made them feel and how your example made them believe again.

Legacy is not built in moments of applause—it's grown in seasons of obedience. Every act of humility, every sacrifice made in silence, every time you choose love over bitterness becomes a seed in someone else's garden. You may never see the harvest, but Heaven does.

The giants you've slain are not just victories for your story; they are victories for everyone who comes after you. Every battle you've overcome becomes a bridge for another soul still fighting. Your healed heart becomes a refuge for those searching for safety.

Your forgiveness becomes a map for those still lost in resentment. Your courage becomes permission for others to be brave. Your peace becomes an atmosphere others can breathe in.

That is the divine design of legacy: It multiplies through the lives you touch. God never intended your transformation to stop with you. He intended it to echo through your children, your work, your relationships, and your influence. The light you cultivate becomes transferable, an inheritance of spirit that spreads farther than your reach.

The principle of multiplication means this: When you choose alignment over ego, truth over comfort, and purpose over fear, your life becomes a conduit of grace. The fruit of your character feeds generations you may never meet. The compassion you show today could spark healing in someone you'll never know. The wisdom you share could save a life you'll never see.

That's why living intentionally matters. You are not living in isolation—you are part of a divine chain of influence, a spiritual lineage of courage and grace. What you build in truth today becomes the foundation for others tomorrow. What you heal within yourself becomes freedom in someone else's future.

Legacy isn't an ending—it's a continuation. It's God's way of turning your obedience into someone else's awakening.

The Continuous Journey

You may feel like you are at the end of a journey, but the truth is that this is only the beginning of a new chapter—one that is lived, not written. The pages ahead are blank, waiting for the ink of your choices. What comes next will not be defined by what happens to you but by how you respond.

The giants you have faced will return in new forms: new fears, new doubts, new trials. Life doesn't stop testing you once you've learned the lesson—it simply shifts the questions. Each new challenge will ask, "Have you truly learned who you are?" and "Will you remember what you've become?"

But this time, you are different. You are no longer fighting to survive—you are living with awareness. You no longer swing blindly in panic—you move with precision, with wisdom, and with grace. You have the strength to pause before reacting, to breathe before speaking, and to trust before retreating.

You now understand that growth isn't linear; it's cyclical. There will be seasons of peace and seasons of stretching. There will be moments when you feel the old fear trying to return, and that's okay. The goal was never to eliminate struggle, but to meet it with new eyes.

Every fall still carries purpose. Every setback still holds instruction. Every storm that shakes your world still refines your foundation. Victory, you've learned, isn't a single moment of triumph—it's a lifestyle of alignment. It's showing up each day with courage even when motivation fades. It's honoring your values when no one is watching. It's living in truth even when it costs you comfort.

You have the tools now—courage, insight, and alignment. You've tasted the strength that comes from reflection, the power that comes from facing yourself, and the peace that follows integrity. You've seen that confrontation brings clarity and that intention births transformation.

Every time a giant rises, you are no longer unarmed. You carry the armor of experience and the sword of truth. You know that fear can roar, but it cannot rule. You know that pain can sting, but it cannot stop you. And you know that even when you fall, grace still reaches down and says, "Get up—your story isn't finished."

Because it's not. It never will be. The journey doesn't end with healing—it continues through purpose. It evolves with every breath, every act of love, every choice to keep going. The continuous journey is not about reaching perfection; it's about remembering progress. It's about living in rhythm with your purpose, knowing that every day you wake up, you are being invited to begin again—stronger, wiser, freer.

So walk forward. The road may twist, but it will never abandon you. You have walked through your fire and found your light. Now carry it boldly into the world.

Dante understood this truth intimately. After he faced every shadow in the depths, he didn't escape Hell by force—he rose out of it by clarity. When he and Virgil climbed down Lucifer's frozen form, they suddenly felt gravity flip. What had been descent became ascent. Dante realized he was no longer falling into darkness—he was rising toward light.

His first sight outside the pit wasn't victory or applause; it was the open sky filled with stars. This is a reminder that the journey doesn't end in the dark wood or the valley; it continues upward, guided by purpose.

Contribution As the Ultimate Measure

Your purpose is not fulfilled in isolation. It is realized in connection. Every giant you confront, every act of honesty, every moment of alignment, expands your capacity to contribute.

- **Teach:** Share your lessons without shame, without ego, without pretense. Your struggles, when shared with integrity, become a roadmap for others.

- **Serve:** Let your gifts and energy flow outward. Help others stand tall in their own battles.
- **Inspire:** Model courage, integrity, and alignment. Live in such a way that others are drawn toward the light you carry.

The true measure of your journey is not how much pain you endured or how many giants you defeated. It is how your transformation empowers others and how your life becomes a beacon of possibility.

The Power of Reflection

Even after this book, the journey continues because growth doesn't end with understanding; it continues through awareness. Reflection is how you stay aligned with truth when the noise of life tries to pull you away. It is not about dwelling on what went wrong; it is about staying awake to what is right.

Reflection is your compass. It reminds you where you've been, why you started, and where you are being called next. It brings stillness to the storm and clarity to confusion. It invites you to slow down long enough to hear what your soul is saying beneath the surface of routine.

Ask yourself often:

- "Are my actions still aligned with my values and purpose?"
- "Am I confronting new giants, or am I hiding behind old victories?"
- "Who in my life can I uplift today by sharing courage, insight, or love?"

- “How can I expand my contribution while remaining true to myself?”

Reflection is not a pause from life—it is participation in it. It is the moment you step outside the noise to recalibrate, to realign, to ask whether your direction still honors your destination. Without reflection, even success can become meaningless. With it, every step regains purpose.

True reflection demands honesty, not perfection. It asks you to look at yourself without judgment, to see not only what needs changing but also what deserves celebrating. It’s recognizing the progress hidden in small choices—the quiet victories that no one else sees.

Reflection also connects you to gratitude. When you look back through the lens of grace, you realize that every trial carried a lesson, every delay shaped your patience, and every heartbreak widened your capacity to love. You begin to see that nothing was wasted—everything was preparation.

But reflection is not meant to end in thought. Its purpose is transformation. It is not a mirror meant for observation; it is a window meant for movement. When you reflect deeply, you remember who you are and why you were called to begin. You gather wisdom from the past, courage from the present, and direction for the future.

So keep reflecting. Keep listening to the quiet voice that guides you. Let reflection become your rhythm—the sacred pause between doing and becoming. When you live reflectively, you live intentionally. And when you live intentionally, you live in alignment with purpose.

That is the power of reflection—not to look backward with regret, but to move forward with clarity.

The Gift of Forgiveness

Legacy cannot be built on resentment or frozen hearts. Bitterness may feel like protection, but it slowly corrodes the vessel that holds it. Forgiveness is not weakness; it is wisdom. It is the lifeblood of contribution and the decision to no longer let pain dictate the rhythm of your life.

Forgiveness is not about excusing the harm of others or pretending it didn't hurt. It is about releasing yourself from the grip of the past so that you can move freely into the future. When you forgive, you stop letting old wounds narrate new chapters. You acknowledge the pain, but you refuse to let it poison your purpose.

Forgiveness is a courageous act of surrender—a quiet declaration that says, "You no longer control me." It doesn't erase the memory; it redeems it. It takes what was meant for harm and transforms it into wisdom, compassion, and grace.

By forgiving, you create space for generosity, creativity, and love. You clear the clutter of bitterness so peace can move in. You reclaim the energy once trapped in anger and redirect it toward growth. And in doing so, you model strength—the kind that doesn't roar but radiates. Others see your freedom and begin to believe they can have their own.

Forgiveness is also an act of faith. It's trusting that justice, healing, and truth belong to something bigger than you. It's recognizing that grace multiplies when given, not when withheld. When you forgive, you align yourself with that divine current of mercy that keeps the world from drowning in revenge.

Your life then becomes a living testimony—a proof that freedom is not earned through payback but through release.

Forgiveness and courage, when combined, become the foundation of a lasting legacy. Because people may forget what was said or done, but they will never forget the peace they felt in your presence.

Living Boldly

The final lesson is this: Live boldly. Stand in the fullness of your truth. Speak it. Act it. Love it.

Bold living does not mean being reckless or cultivating your ego; it's about awareness. It's about living with conviction even when the path is uncertain. To live boldly is to rise each morning and choose to show up for life—fully awake, fully alive, fully present.

Boldness is saying "yes" to the call God placed within you, even when fear whispers "not yet." It's turning away from distractions that dilute your purpose and walking straight into the unknown with faith as your compass. Boldness means forgiving when your pride says "never again."

It means creating when doubt says "you're not ready." It means loving deeply even after loss, because you've learned that the risk of pain is far smaller than the regret of restraint.

Living boldly doesn't mean you'll always feel strong—it means you'll act even when you feel weak. It's a daily choice to keep moving, to keep building, to keep believing that there are more chapters to be written in your life. It's trusting that the same God who brought you through the storm is now calling you to walk on the water.

Every giant you have faced has prepared you for this moment. Every insight, every act of integrity, every step toward alignment has equipped you to live a life of impact. You've endured the dark night, and now you carry the dawn within you. You no longer live in reaction—you live in revelation. You no longer ask, "What if I fail?" but "What if I fly?"

The bold life is not about arriving at perfection; it's about refusing to stop at fear. It's knowing that your voice matters, your presence matters, and your courage can shift the atmosphere around you. To live boldly is to declare, "I was not created to merely exist—I was created to expand, to love, to serve, to shine."

So take the risk. Say the thing that needs to be said. Build the thing that only you can build. Forgive where it hurts. Try again where you've failed. Believe again where hope once broke.

The world changes when ordinary people decide to live extraordinary truth. And now—it's your turn.

Reflection Questions: The Legacy Path

1. What legacy do I want to leave in relationships, in work, and in the world?
2. How does my current life reflect the values and purpose I claim?
3. Which giants, though conquered once, could return to challenge me?
4. How can I use my lessons and victories to help others rise?
5. Where can I practice forgiveness to create space for love and contribution?
6. What daily choices will align me with the life I am meant to live?

Reflection Exercises: The Ripple Effect

1. **What ripples have I already created?** Think of one decision, one act of courage, or one moment of compassion that may have impacted someone else, even if they never told you.
2. **Who in my life has created ripples that reached me?** Reflect on a mentor, teacher, parent, or friend whose influence still echoes in your choices. What did they do that made such a lasting mark?
3. **Am I living in a way that multiplies good or or in a way that recycles pain?** Consider whether your words, habits, and energy inspire others to rise or cause them to shrink. What shift would align your influence with healing rather than harm?
4. **What is one small stone I can cast today?** Mother Teresa said, "I alone cannot change the world, but I can cast a stone across the waters to create many ripples." What small, intentional act—kindness, forgiveness, encouragement—could you offer today that might outlive you?
5. **Where have I underestimated my impact?** Legacy often hides in ordinary moments. Reflect on where your example, honesty, or perseverance might have inspired someone without you realizing it.
6. **What message do I want my life to send long after I'm gone?** Write a single sentence that summarizes the essence of your ripple—the truth you want your life to whisper into the world when your voice is gone.

Closing: Your Life, Your Contribution

The journey through fire, ice, and giants has not been easy, and it was never meant to be. The struggle was sacred. Every moment of pain shaped your strength. Every storm that shook you stripped away what was false, leaving only what was real. You walked through darkness not to prove your toughness, but to discover your light.

And now, you stand at the threshold of something greater—a life lived with authenticity, courage, and purpose. You no longer carry the weight of survival; you carry the wisdom of transformation. You have faced your fears, challenged your limits, and peeled back the layers that once hid your true self.

But this is not the end. It never was. The end of one journey is only the beginning of another—a higher calling, a deeper walk, a more intentional way of living. The process of becoming never stops; it expands. Life will keep inviting you to grow, to contribute, to give more of yourself to the world. Each day becomes another opportunity to live aligned with truth, to choose courage over comfort, and to transform experience into impact.

This is the rhythm of purpose: reflection, confrontation, alignment, and contribution. Again and again. With each cycle, your awareness deepens, your influence widens, and your legacy strengthens. You no longer see obstacles as punishments—you recognize them as portals to evolution.

Your life is your legacy. Every thought you think, every boundary you honor, every act of compassion you extend—it all matters. Every act of courage you demonstrate becomes a ripple of permission for others to rise. Every expression of love, forgiveness, and truth strengthens the foundation for a world that desperately needs people who dare to live fully.

So live boldly. Love deeply. Give relentlessly. Stand tall even when the winds of fear return. Confront your giants with grace, not aggression. Align your steps with purpose, not pressure. Let your story, your scars, and your strength serve as the spark that lights the way for others who are still finding their path through the dark.

Because you are no longer merely surviving. You are living. You are *contributing*. You are building something that cannot be frozen by fear, stolen by circumstance, or diminished by time.

You are becoming the very thing this world needs more of: a living example of courage refined by truth and of purpose ignited by love. So go forward. Keep walking. Keep giving. Keep becoming. Your journey continues, and through you, so does the light.

When you stop running from yourself, you don't just find peace—you find purpose. Because the stranger you feared was never your enemy; it was the part of you waiting to be known.

Unknown

Chapter 32

The Journey Beyond: Living With Purpose Every Day

Full Circle: From Darkness to Daybreak

The work doesn't stop because you've finished this book. In many ways, this is where the real work begins. The final page isn't a finish line; it's a doorway. Life doesn't hand you trophies for transformation; it hands you new battles, new responsibilities, new tests of faith. This isn't the end of the journey—it's the start of a higher one.

Life is not a checklist; it's a battlefield, a playground, and a sacred space all at once; it's a place where you practice courage when you feel afraid, integrity when no one is watching, and love when the world gives you reasons not to.

The giants, the fires, the ice; they never disappear. They simply change shape. New fears will come dressed as logic. New doubts will whisper, "You've done enough." But listen to me—you are not who you were when you started. You've been forged in the heat, tested in the silence, and refined by every tear you've cried and every truth you've faced. You are no longer unarmed. You are equipped. You are ready.

Your journey began, like Dante's, in the dark wood—in that moment of confusion when the old life no longer fit but the new one was still hidden in shadow. You stood there, unsure of where to go, but you took the step anyway. That first step was everything. Because it said, "I'm done hiding. I'm done running. I'm ready to rise."

Just as Dante wrote, "I found myself alone in a dark wood, for the straight way was lost." That moment wasn't a failure; it was an awakening. The dark wood didn't arrive to destroy him; it arrived to redirect him. And like Dante, the moment you stepped forward, you discovered that clarity doesn't come before movement; it comes because of it.

You faced your monsters—not the ones outside of you, but the ones that whispered within about your doubt, your guilt, your shame, and your fear. You walked through loneliness and through loss, through anger and temptation. You stumbled, yes, but you never stayed down. Every fall only strengthened your resolve. Every scar became a story.

Every descent was preparing you for ascent. Every failure was shaping your foundation. The pain that once felt like punishment was never meant to break you; it was meant to prepare you. It was fire with purpose. The very flames that once burned you now make you shine.

The giants that once towered over you—the fear, the betrayal, the heartbreak—they became your teachers. They taught you how to fight, how to forgive, and how to focus. They taught you how to keep moving when every part of you wanted to stop. They sharpened your faith, deepened your patience, and awakened your calling.

This is the rhythm of transformation—descent, confrontation, awakening, renewal. You've lived it. You've earned it. Just as Dante climbed from the depths to see the stars again, you too have emerged. And now you can see clearly what you could not before—that the darkness was never your enemy. It was your invitation to grow.

You have walked through Hell and discovered that Heaven was never a destination—it was awakening within you the whole time. Heaven is the peace that follows forgiveness. It's the strength that follows surrender. It's the love that remains after loss. That is self-mastery—not perfection, but peace in motion.

This is your daybreak. You've made it through the night, and you carry the light with you now.

But don't stop here. Don't you dare settle. You've come too far to turn back now. The world needs your story, your strength, and your light. You are a conqueror—not by title, but by endurance. You stood in the storm and refused to be moved. You were broken and rebuilt. You were lost and now you lead.

So hold your head high—not in pride, but in gratitude. You've proven what's possible when someone refuses to quit. You've risen from the ashes, walked through the fire, and discovered that the same God who led you through the darkness has now called you to shine in the light.

And this, right here, is only the beginning.

The Giants Revisited

The giants are never truly gone. They simply change faces. The same fear that once stopped you from taking your first step may now disguise itself as comfort, convenience, or control. The same pride that once shouted may now whisper, "You've done enough. Rest here." The battlefield looks different, but the strategy of your enemies remains the same—to keep you small, silent, and stagnant.

Dante faced giants too: literal ones. In the Ninth Circle, monstrous figures like Nimrod and Antaeus stood frozen in ice, symbols of pride, rebellion, and the consequences of refusing to grow. They weren't just obstacles; they were warnings. Dante showed us that giants don't just block the path—they reveal the parts of ourselves that must be confronted so the journey can continue.

In the early stages of your journey, your giants were loud and obvious. They taunted you with failure, shame, addiction, betrayal, or fear of rejection. You fought them with everything you had—raw courage, prayer, discipline, and persistence. But as you've grown stronger, the giants have grown quieter. They no longer attack from the front; they wait in the shadows, disguised as reason, comfort, and "good enough."

The danger now is not defeat—it's drift. When you've conquered visible battles, the temptation becomes complacency. The mind whispers, "I've healed enough... I've grown enough... I've done enough." But giants don't retire; they reinvent.

The giant of fear becomes the fear of success—the anxiety of what responsibility will require. The giant of anger becomes quiet cynicism—the dull belief that nothing can really change. The giant of self-doubt becomes perfectionism—an endless delay of purpose in the name of preparation.

That's why awareness must continue even after victory. The battlefield is not just external—it's mental, emotional, and spiritual. The moment you stop watching, the giants return to claim ground you once reclaimed.

But now you are different. You no longer swing your sword blindly or react in panic. You've learned discernment—when to fight, when to rest, and when to stand still. You've learned that victory isn't about destroying every enemy; it's about recognizing them and refusing to let them rule your life.

Every new season of growth brings new giants to face because every level of purpose demands a deeper level of courage. The battles may change, but the mission remains the same: To stand firm in truth. To walk in alignment. To love without fear.

This is not the return of war—it's the evolution of mastery.

The Armor of Integrity and the Sword of Courage

You have fought long enough to know this truth: Your armor and your sword are not relics from old battles—they are companions for life. Integrity and courage are not things you wear only in crisis; they are what sustain you in calm.

When you first put on your armor, it was heavy. You were uncertain, still learning what truth, discipline, and faith felt like in motion. You stumbled under the weight of accountability and conviction. But now, your armor has shaped itself to you—it fits your spirit. You don't just wear integrity; you *walk in it.*

Integrity is the stillness beneath the storm. It's what keeps you honest when no one is watching, faithful when no one applauds, and steady when temptation calls your name. It is not built in a day; it's forged in every small decision you make—the moment you choose patience over pride, forgiveness over fury, or humility over validation.

Your sword—courage—has changed too. It's no longer the wild swing of survival; it's the deliberate strike of wisdom. There was a time when courage meant rushing into battle—confronting everyone and everything that threatened your peace. But now you know true courage often means restraint. It's the quiet power to listen before you react, to stay kind when wronged, and to walk away from what no longer serves your calling.

Your armor protects your heart; your sword advances your purpose. Together, they remind you that you are both warrior and healer, both defender and builder.

Every battle you have faced trained you for the ones that come quietly—the battles in thought, emotion, and spirit. When fear whispers, your armor answers: "I am grounded in truth." When doubt presses close, your sword reminds you: "I move forward anyway."

Integrity without courage becomes safety. Courage without integrity becomes recklessness. But when both move in unity, you are unstoppable—not because life is easy, but because your foundation is unshakable.

So polish your armor daily. Keep your sword sharp. Because the giants will return, and when they do, they will find you not afraid, not uncertain, but ready.

The Battle Within: A War That Never Ends

The fiercest war you will ever fight is the one inside you. The world around you may grow calm, but within, battles still rise between faith and fear, humility and pride, peace and pressure. The noise of the world fades, yet the mind continues its restless chatter, asking, "Am I doing enough? Am I enough?"

You've learned by now that the journey to mastery doesn't end when the giants fall; it only changes terrain. The outer giants are easier to see—they roar, they challenge, they force a reaction. But the inner ones? They whisper. They wait. They take familiar shapes: resentment dressed as righteousness, comfort disguised as peace, anxiety masquerading as responsibility.

These are the wars of the second half of your journey—the subtle ones that test your discipline more than your strength.

Even Dante, after passing every external trial, faced his greatest battle in the quiet—the battle of clarity. As he climbed toward the mountain of Purgatory, he discovered that the hardest work wasn't defeating demons; it was purifying the heart, confronting the thoughts, motives, and attachments that lived within. His ascent teaches us that the truest war is internal and the truest freedom is too.

Every day, you stand at a crossroad within your own mind. Do you choose gratitude or grievance? Faith or fear? Forgiveness or judgment? Purpose or procrastination?

The mind is relentless, but it can also be renewed. You've already begun this renewal: through reflection, journaling, prayer, stillness, and truth. The key now is maintenance—to guard the gates of thought as diligently as a soldier guards a fortress. Because every great fall begins with a small compromise in thought.

When you notice anxiety rising, that's a call to center. When resentment knocks, that's an invitation to forgive. When old shame resurfaces, that's not regression—it's refinement. The battle within isn't a sign that you're failing; it's proof that you're still growing.

The mind, left untended, reverts to chaos. But when disciplined, it becomes your greatest ally. That's why scripture says, "Take every thought captive" (2 Corinthians 10:5). Because not every thought deserves to stay. Some are visitors meant to be shown the door.

Winning this inner war isn't about perfection—it's about awareness. It's about noticing when your peace starts slipping and then pausing long enough to ask, "What giant is trying to reclaim this ground?"

You've mastered many external battles, but the truest mastery is of self:

- The ability to stay calm in conflict.
- The ability to forgive before bitterness grows roots.
- The ability to keep faith when the outcome is uncertain.
- The ability to choose joy even when circumstances don't justify it.

That is the lifelong war. It is also the lifelong victory.

When your inner world is anchored, no storm can uproot you. Your courage endures, your purpose remains clear, and your contribution flows freely. The battle within will always exist, but now, so will your peace.

The Ripple Effect: Your Life As a Light

No act of courage ever ends with you. Every moment of truth you live becomes a current that moves outward—touching people you may never meet, shaping futures you may never see. This is the ripple effect: the quiet miracle that happens when one healed soul becomes a source of healing for others.

Mother Teresa once said, "I alone cannot change the world, but I can cast a stone across the waters to create many ripples." That's what your life does now. Each decision rooted in integrity, each word spoken in love, each act born of purpose sends ripples across time and space. You may never know their full reach, but Heaven keeps count.

When you forgave instead of retaliating, someone watching learned mercy. When you persisted after failure, someone found strength. When you told the truth even when it cost you, someone remembered what character looks like.

That's the paradox of impact: It's rarely seen by the one creating it. Ripples travel quietly through conversations, kindnesses, and choices that seem small but echo deep. You can't control how far they go, but you can control the heart that sends them.

Dante ended every stage of his journey by looking upward, guided by the light of the stars. Even in the darkest places, he reminded us that the smallest light can guide us home and that your life now carries that same guidance for others.

Your legacy is not built in applause but in influence—the unseen kind that multiplies through lives touched by your example. This is why your inner battle matters so much, because healed people heal people. The courage you cultivated becomes courage transferred. The peace you found becomes peace shared.

Think of the teachers who shaped generations not by fame but by faithfulness. The single parent who raised children in love despite exhaustion. The friend who listened without judgment when the world turned away. None of them made headlines, but their ripples became rivers of grace.

The world doesn't need louder people. It needs aligned ones. It doesn't need more noise; it needs light.

So keep shining. Even when no one praises it. Even when no one notices. Because in the divine design of life, light never dies—it only travels farther than the eye can see.

Your Life As a Beacon

Every step forward and every victory over fear or betrayal makes your life a lighthouse for others. People may not always say it, but your courage, integrity, and alignment influence those around you. You are proof that resilience can look like peace and that strength can sound like gentleness. Your life becomes a quiet revolution, an example of what is possible when someone refuses to be limited by giants, chains, or frozen hearts.

You may never see the full reach of your light, but it's there—guiding someone who's standing where you once stood. The way you choose to rise after disappointment shows others that healing is real. The way you respond with kindness instead of anger shows others that love is still stronger than ego. Even your silence, when rooted in wisdom, becomes a signal of strength in a world addicted to noise.

Legacy is not only measured in grand acts. It is measured in daily choices: the honesty in conversation, the courage to confront fear, the compassion you extend to others, and the forgiveness you practice quietly but consistently. These are the unrecorded miracles, the ripples that grow into waves over time.

Your presence can shift a room without a single word. The peace you carry becomes contagious. The consistency of your character reminds people that it's still possible to walk in truth even when it costs comfort. Every moment you live with intention, you are lighting the path for someone else who has lost their way.

Being a beacon doesn't mean being perfect; it means being visible, not in spotlight, but in authenticity. Light doesn't compete with darkness; it simply shines. It doesn't argue, it doesn't rush, it doesn't boast—it just is. When you live in alignment, your light speaks for you.

You are now a living testimony that transformation is real. You've faced the storm, stood your ground, and chosen peace over pride, purpose over distraction, and truth over illusion. The glow that follows you is not decoration—it is direction. It's how others find their courage to begin again.

So keep shining—not to be seen, but so others can see the way. Because your life, lived with purpose and love, becomes a map for those still walking through their own night.

Rest As Resistance: The Sacred Rhythm of Renewal

In a world obsessed with constant motion, rest becomes an act of rebellion. It is a declaration that your worth is not measured by your productivity but by your presence. The same strength that drives you to conquer your giants must also teach you when to lay down your sword and breathe.

Rest is not retreat—it is renewal. It is the pause between battles where you gather clarity, where your spirit exhales, and where your heart remembers why it fights. Even soldiers in holy wars must stop to sharpen their blades and mend their armor. You are no different.

The body and soul are sacred instruments. You cannot serve your purpose if you're constantly running on empty. Stillness is not weakness; it's wisdom. It's where alignment deepens, creativity returns, and peace reminds you that you are already whole.

When you rest, you honor the God who modeled it on the seventh day. You realign your pace with divine rhythm—work and worship, movement and stillness, giving and receiving. Rest is how you protect what matters most.

So take walks without destination. Laugh without agenda. Sit in silence until you feel your heartbeat slow to the rhythm of gratitude. Watch the sky change colors and remember that even the sun rests before it rises again.

You are not designed to burn out; you are designed to shine consistently. Rest doesn't make you less devoted—it makes you durable. Because when your soul is restored, your purpose burns brighter.

Preparing for the Unseen

Life will always bring challenges you cannot predict. Giants will evolve, and new ones will rise. But your preparation matters.

- Awareness keeps you grounded.
- Integrity keeps you aligned.
- Courage keeps you moving forward.
- Contribution keeps your life meaningful.

When you live with these principles, you are equipped to handle whatever comes, not reactively, but proactively. You become a force of light, a person who shapes reality rather than being shaped by it.

Daily Practices for Purposeful Living

Purpose is not a destination you arrive at—it's a discipline you practice. You do not live aligned and courageous lives by accident; you live them by design. The same way a soldier polishes his armor daily, or an athlete trains between seasons, the soul must stay conditioned. Each day is both training and testimony.

These practices keep your purpose alive and your spirit sharp.

1. **Morning Reflection: Set Your Intention**

   Begin the day in stillness before the world begins to speak. Ask: "What truth must I live today? What giants might I face, and how can I meet them with courage and grace?"

   Morning reflection anchors your heart before chaos tries to claim it.

2. **Intentional Action: Live on Purpose**

   Choose at least one deliberate act each day that mirrors your values—an act that teaches, heals, forgives, or uplifts.

   Purpose grows when it's practiced, not pondered.

3. **Evening Examination: Harvest the Day**

   Before rest, look back and ask: "Where did I act from fear? Where did I act from faith?"

   Honor victories, own mistakes, and harvest wisdom.

   Reflection turns experience into growth.

4. **Journaling: Record the Journey**

   The giants that seem unbeatable often shrink on paper.

Journaling clarifies thought, calms emotion, and reveals patterns. It's not a diary—it's dialogue with your evolving self.

5. **Connection: Walk with Others**

   No warrior fights alone. Surround yourself with those who reflect your values, challenge your limits, and celebrate your victories. The right community multiplies courage.

6. **Gratitude: Keep Your Heart Soft**

   Gratitude keeps pride and bitterness from taking root. Even on the hardest days, find one thing to thank God for. Gratitude doesn't erase pain, it reframes it, reminding you that you're still growing, still chosen, still here.

7. **Stillness: Return to Center**

   Carve out quiet moments where no demands exist—just breath and awareness. Stillness is not laziness; it is alignment in motion. In silence, you hear what noise tries to drown: the voice of peace, direction, and God.

When practiced consistently, these habits become more than routine—they become rhythm. And rhythm keeps you in motion long after motivation fades.

These daily disciplines don't make you perfect; they make you prepared. Prepared to love deeper. Prepared to lead wisely. Prepared to keep walking no matter how many times the path changes.

Reflection Questions

1. Which daily practices keep me aligned with my purpose?
2. How can I make courage and integrity habitual, not optional?

3. Who benefits from my growth, and how can I amplify that impact?
4. What giants might re-emerge, and how will I face them with grace?
5. How can I transform challenges into lessons for myself and others?

Closing: The Path Forward

The journey beyond this book is your life—the living, breathing testimony of everything you've overcome and everything you are still becoming. Each sunrise is a new invitation to face your giants, thaw frozen hearts, speak truth in love, and walk with purpose. The world won't always applaud your effort, but Heaven notices every act of courage, every moment you choose grace over pride, love over indifference, and faith over fear.

Life will always unfold in cycles of fire and renewal—seasons where you are stretched, refined, and called higher. But you are no longer wandering without direction. You have the armor of integrity, the sword of courage, and the stillness of wisdom to guide your every step. You are not at the mercy of the storm anymore; you are the one who learned to walk through it with peace in your stride.

Remember: Legacy is not something that begins when you are gone—it begins every time you show up with intention. It's written in how you listen, how you forgive, how you love, and how you choose to keep moving when quitting would be easier. It's found in the small moments that no one sees—when you hold your tongue instead of lashing out, when you pray instead of panic, and when you keep your word even when no one is watching. Those moments become the quiet seeds of eternity.

You began this journey walking through fire—uncertain, weary, but willing. You crossed rivers of doubt, faced monsters that hid within, and discovered that your scars were never signs of defeat—they are signatures of transformation. Now you stand in light, not because life suddenly became simple, but because you learned how to carry the fire forward. You've learned that strength is not the absence of struggle but the decision to rise every time you fall.

The story doesn't end here. It continues in every breath you take, every bridge you build, every soul you lift by being your authentic self. It continues in the peace you create in your home, the courage you model for your children, and the compassion you extend to those who have forgotten their worth. It continues in the unseen places where your faith still whispers, "I am not done yet."

You are the bridge between what was and what's possible—the living proof that healing is real, redemption is near, and purpose is worth the pain it took to find it.

So live fully. Contribute boldly. Love relentlessly. Let the journey beyond be your masterpiece—a life painted with grace, truth, and courage. Let it be the evidence of what happens when someone dares to disappear from distraction, confront their giants, and rise into the fullness of who they were always meant to be.

This isn't just the path forward—it's the call to continue walking as light in a world that still needs it.

Final Prayer: The Journey Beyond

Heavenly Father,
Thank You for the fires that refined me,
for the storms that revealed my strength,
and for the giants that taught me to trust You more.

You walked beside me through the shadows,
through fear, doubt, and silence,
and You never let go.
You turned pain into purpose,
brokenness into beauty,
and wandering into wisdom.

As I step beyond these pages,
help me to live with awareness and gratitude.
Teach me to see every challenge
as a sacred opportunity to grow, to give,
and to glorify You.

Give me courage to face what still hides within,
humility to keep learning,
and grace to love others as You have loved me.
Let my life be a beacon—not of perfection,
but of perseverance and faith.

When the giants rise again,
remind me that I do not fight alone.
When doubt whispers,
speak louder with Your truth.
And when my heart grows weary,
breathe Your Spirit of renewal into my soul.

May my words heal,
my actions inspire,
and my legacy honor You.
Let my journey be more than survival; let it be testimony.

And today, Lord...
I thank You.
Because I am no longer my biggest stranger.
I know who I am,
I know whose I am,
and I know why I am here.
In Your strength I began,
in Your grace I continue,
and in Your purpose I will finish strong.
Amen.

Chapter 33

Unwritten

This next chapter is yours.

This is where you step beyond the pages and into your own awakening.

Chapter 33 isn't written because you are meant to write it—with ink, action, or both. This is your invitation to begin your journey out of the dark wood—to start your life, renew your mind, and walk boldly into the light of purpose.

The giants have been named, the chains have been broken, and the path has been revealed. But now the question remains: Will you take the challenge of stepping out of the dark wood or will you stay?

Only you can answer that.

Your story continues here. Your redemption begins here. Your legacy is waiting to be lived.

Write it well.

www.ingramcontent.com/pod-product-compliance
Ingram Content Group UK Ltd.
Pitfield, Milton Keynes, MK11 3LW, UK
UKHW021710190726
13853UKWH00001B/483